Etruscan
Red-Figured Vase-Painting
at Caere

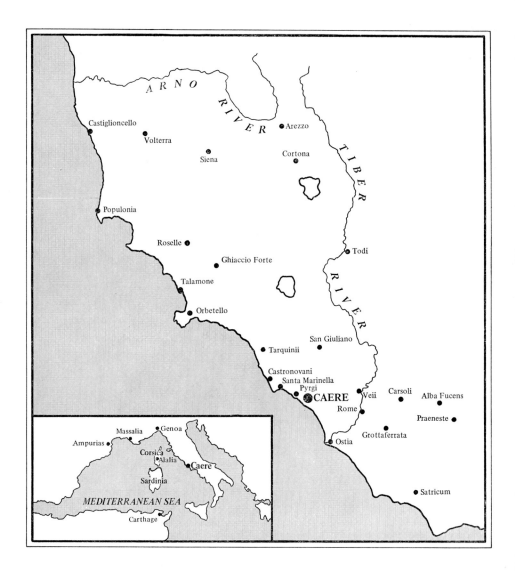

Etruscan
Red-Figured Vase-Painting
at Caere

MARIO A. DEL CHIARO

UNIVERSITY OF CALIFORNIA PRESS
BERKELEY · LOS ANGELES · LONDON

University of California Press
Berkeley and Los Angeles, California

University of California Press, Ltd.
London, England

Copyright © 1974 by
The Regents of the University of California

ISBN: 0–520–02578–4

Library of Congress Catalog Card Number: 73–85785

Printed in the United States of America

To Christina and our children, Kari, Marco, and Paola

Contents

Preface

THIS STUDY, devoted to Caeretan red-figured vase-painting of the fourth century B.C., is the direct outgrowth of a very specialized investigation of a class of Etruscan plates of relatively unimportant shape belonging to the Genucilia Group. Although these plates at first did not seem to merit detailed examination, they eventually disclosed an important ceramic "environment." Soon vases of different shapes and more imposing character, also decorated by Caeretan vase-painters, were examined. The large number of such vases has augmented the original and apparently limited class of Genucilia plates to such a degree that we now recognize a fairly important and prolific red-figured fabric produced at Caere, an Etruscan city of major significance whose pottery must be fully considered in any future discussion of Etruscan art and civilization.

By exposing a Caeretan artistic "environment," made possible by the discovery of a red-figure style, a stylistic analysis can be made to include the engraved scenes on some Etruscan bronze mirrors that may reveal Caere to be the possible center of manufacture. Recognition of a Caeretan red-figured fabric by comparison with better known Faliscan red-figured pottery has already helped to establish a contemporary ceramic industry at ancient Tarquinii—all of which may clarify the artistic and commercial connections between various well-known Etruscan centers. Furthermore, on the evidence of the exceptionally strong influence detected from South Italian vase-painting, particularly Campanian and Apulian, some new avenues of research are now open which should lead to a better understanding of the exact relationships between Etruscan and South Italian. Such detailed investigations in the future will contribute enormously to our knowledge of the political, commercial, and cultural history of Italy and the Mediterranean during the whole of the fourth century B.C.

Although the present study has attempted to bring together as complete a collection of Caeretan red-figure as possible, an unknown number of examples must doubtless exist in various collections which have been inaccessible or have simply escaped my attention. Nevertheless, with their eventual appearance, they should easily fall within the general scheme of the stylistically outlined groups set forth in this publication.

MDC

POST-SCRIPT

The following publications have appeared since the manuscript of this work went to press and could not therefore be included in the bibliography:

> Scavi di Pyrgi in *Notizie degli Scavi di Antichità* 1970, Supplemento II (1973), see pp. 468ff.
>
> J. and L. Jehasse, *La Nécropole Prèromaine d'Aléria (Gallia)*, Supplement XXV (1973).
>
> *Roma Medio Repubblicana*, Catalogue of Exhibition in Rome, May–June, 1973.
>
> *Corpus Vasorum Antiquorum*, France, Fasc. 24, Musée de Limoges and Musée de Vannes by Odette Touchefeu-Meynier.

For the study of Caeretan red-figured vase-painting, the volume of Aléria is by far the most important. Unfortunately, owing to the tentative inventory numbers which accompanied the photographs early received for the Aléria vases incorporated in my catalogue, a concordance must await a future supplemental article. Likewise, the information the Aléria publication now makes available regarding *tomb groups* (see p. 130 in this publication) does not seemingly alter my text nor conclusions, but it will require a detailed study that would unnecessarily delay the timetable of the present work. This is especially expedient since my attention for the following summer months must be devoted to direction of the excavations at the Etruscan site of *Ghiaccio Forte* (Province of Grosseto, Italy) where, it should be noted here, Caeretan Genucilia plates (one with head and two with star) have come to light during the Summer Campaign of 1973 and should thereby list *Ghiaccio Forte* as a new site for the *Distribution* of Caeretan red-figure (see Chapter IV in this publication).

The other volumes contain a number of Genucilia plates of standard head and star type: see especially *Roma Medio Repubblicana*, pls. XXIV, XLIX, and LIX; note in particular the plate no. 46 (pl. XV) on which are incised the letters of the Latin alphabet, and this led to a suggestion that Rome might be a possible center of manufacture.

MDC

June 1974

Acknowledgments

DURING the compilation of this study, I have endeavored to examine all of the specimens here assigned as "Caeretan Red-Figured Vases," and the greater number of other examples attributed to Caeretan vase-painters. This task could never have been accomplished without the kind cooperation of numerous directors, curators, and staffs of the many museums which may, or may not have, possessed vases considered during the course of the present investigation. I must express my deep gratitude to the following museum personnel for their kindness and patience during my visits and throughout my correspondence in search of data and photographs: Austria, Rudolf Noll (Kunsthistorisches Museum, Vienna); Belgium, Jean Ch. Balty and Violette Verhoogen (Musées Royaux d'Art et d'Histoire, Brussels); Czechoslovakia, Jan Bouzek and Jiri Frel (Karlova Universita, Prague), the latter now with the J. Paul Getty Museum in Malibu, California; France, Pierre Devambez (Musée du Louvre, Paris), Jean and Laurence Jehasse (University of Lyons and directors of the Aléria excavations), Odette Touchefeu-Meynier (University of Nantes); Germany, Adolf Greifenhagen (Staatliche Museen, Berlin), Wolfgang Schiering (Martin von Wagner Museum, Würzburg); Italy, Frank E. Brown (American Academy in Rome), Carlo Pietrangeli and Signora Petroni (Palazzo dei Conservatori, Rome), Giacomo Caputo and Guglielmo Maetzke (Soprintendenza alle Antichità d'Etruria, Florence), Mario Moretti (Soprintendenza alle Antichità dell'Etruria Meridionale, Rome), Professor Marchese (Museo Nazionale, Tarquinia), Francesco Roncalli (Museo Gregoriano Etrusco, Vatican), Enrico Fiumi (Museo Guarnacci, Volterra); Spain, Fernández de Aviles (Museo Arqueológico, Madrid), Eduardo Rippoll (Museo Arqueológico, Barcelona); Switzerland, Robert Hess (Hotel Jura, Basel); United States, Dietrich von Bothmer (Metropolitan Museum of Art, New York), and Frank Norick (Robert H. Lowie Museum of Anthropology, University of California, Berkeley).

I owe special thanks to two professors of my student years, D. A. Amyx and the late H. R. W. Smith of the University of California at Berkeley, whose training and guidance over the years have prepared me for the work at hand. Likewise, a certain debt of gratitude must be paid Sir John Beazley for his invaluable publication, *Etruscan Vase-Painting*, without which the present publication may not have been possible. A full measure of my esteem and gratitude must go to Professor A. D. Trendall whose publications in South Italian red-figure have proved of inestimable value to my studies, and for his kind patience, cogent criticism and advice offered during periodic encounters at home and abroad. The President and Regents of the University of California deserve a word of thanks for the Senior Faculty Fellowship awarded me during the academic year, 1967–68 which allowed time from teaching duties at the University of California, Santa Barbara, in order to complete the bulk of the text to the final manuscript.

MDC

Abbreviations

AJA: *American Journal of Archaeology.*

AntCl: *L'Antiquité Classique.*

ArchCl: *Archeologia Classica.*

ArchEspArq: *Archivo Español de Arqueológia.*

Beazley, *EVP*: J. D. Beazley, *Etruscan Vase-Painting* (Oxford, 1947).

Beazley, *Annuario*: J. D. Beazley, "Etruscan Red-Figure in Rome and Florence," *Annuario della Scuola Italiana di Atene* XXIV–XXVI (1946–49), pp. 141–145.

Beazley, *Fest.AR*: J. D. Beazley, "Gleanings in Etruscan Red-Figure," *Festschrift Andreas Rumpf* (Köln, 1950), pp. 10–13.

BullComm: *Bullettino della Commissione Archeologica Communale di Roma.*

Caeretan Figured Group: M. Del Chiaro, "The Caeretan Figured Group," *American Journal of Archaeology* 70 (1966), pp. 31–36.

Cambitoglou-Trendall, *APS*: A. Cambitoglou and A. D. Trendall, *Apulian Red-Figured Vase-Painters of the Plain Style* (Archaeological Institute of America, 1961).

CVA: *Corpus Vasorum Antiquorum.*

Genucilia Group: M. Del Chiaro, *The Genucilia Group: A Class of Etruscan Red-Figured Plates*, University of California Publications in Classical Archaeology (1957), vol. 3, no. 4, pp. 243–372.

Gerhard-Körte, *ES*: E. Gerhard and G. Körte, *Etruskische Spiegel*, vols. 1–5 (Berlin, 1843–1897).

Giglioli: G. Giglioli, *L'Arte etrusca* (Milano, 1935).

Langlotz: E. Langlotz, *Martin von Wagner—Museum der Universität Würzburg: Griechische Vasen* (Munich, 1932).

MAAR: *Memoirs of the American Academy in Rome.*

MélRome: *Mélanges d'archéologie et d'histoire de l'École francaise de Rome.*

Mingazzini: P. Mingazzini, *Catalogo dei Vasi della Collezione Augusto Castellani* II (Rome, 1971).

Minto: A. Minto, *Populonia* (Florence, 1934).

MonAnt: *Monumenti Antichi.*

NSc: *Notizie degli Scavi di Antichità.*

Robinson and Harcum, *Catalogue*: D. M. Robinson and C. G. Harcum, *A Catalogue of the Greek Vases in the Royal Ontario Museum of Archaeology* (Toronto, 1930).

RömMitt: *Mitteilungen des deutschen archäologischen Instituts: Römische Abteilung.*

Roscher: W. Roscher, ed., *Ausführliches Lexikon der griechischen und römischen Mythologie* (Leipzig, 1884–   ).

Pauly-Wissowa: A. Pauly and G. Wissowa, *Real Encyclopädie der klassischen Altertumswissenschäft* (Stuttgart, 1893–   ).

StEtr: *Studi Etruschi*.

Studi L. Banti: M. Del Chiaro, "Caeretan Red-Figured Pottery," *Studi in onore di Luisa Banti* (Rome, 1965), pp. 135–138.

Torcop Group: M. Del Chiaro, "Etruscan Oinochoai of the Torcop Group." *Studi Etruschi* XXVIII (1960), pp. 137–164.

Trendall, *PP*: A. D. Trendall, *Paestan Pottery* (British School at Rome, 1936).

Trendall, *VIE*: A. D. Trendall, *Vasi antichi dipinti del Vaticano-Vasi italioti ed etruschi a figure rosse* (Vatican, 1953).

Trendall, *LCS*: A. D. Trendall, *The Red-Figured Vases of Lucania, Campania, and Sicily* (Oxford, 1967).

Introduction

IN A NUMBER of earlier studies of Etruscan vase-painting—beginning with that of the Genucilia Group,[1] followed by an investigation of the oinochoai of the Torcop Group,[2] and then by a series of short papers devoted to various specific shapes: hydriae,[3] kylikes,[4] epichyseses,[5] and a few others of uncommon form[6]—it has been possible for me to call attention to the existence of a prolific Etruscan red-figured fabric produced during the second half of the fourth century B.C. at Caere, a city to which no red-figured vase-painting had previously been attributed. These earlier investigations, which were mainly confined to vases decorated with female heads painted in profile, soon revealed a more diversified and impressive quantity of vases bearing figured scenes which could be attributed to Caeretan vase-painters.

Many vases that had been grouped and treated within the more general framework of Etruscan red-figure and unassigned to any definite center of manufacture—data so necessary to a clear picture of the political, commercial, and cultural relationships between cities within and beyond Etruria—can now be assigned to Caeretan potters and vase-painters. Sir John Beazley's *Etruscan Vase-Painting* and a later article by him in the *Annuario della Scuola Archeologica di Atene* have proved indispensable to my study of Caeretan fourth-century pottery, for many vases that I have assigned to Caere were already grouped or classified by Beazley, but were as yet unattributed to any specific center of production.

The initial and vital clue to the recognition of the more important and more monumental area of Caeretan red-figure was gained from an investigation of the Torcop Group. This is a series of oinochoai of the popular Etruscan

1. *Genucilia Group.*
2. *Torcop Group.*
3. M. Del Chiaro, "Caeretan vs. Faliscan: Two Etruscan Red-Figured Hydriae," *AJA* 65 (1961), pp. 56–57.
4. M. Del Chiaro, "Caeretan vs. Faliscan: Some Etruscan Red-Figured Kylikes," *MAAR* XXVII (1962), pp. 203–208.
5. M. Del Chiaro, "Caeretan Epichyseis," *ArchCl* XII (1960), pp. 51–56.
6. M. Del Chiaro, "A Caeretan Red-Figured Cista," *ArchCl* XIV (1962), p. 78f; "A Caeretan Red-Figured Mug," *StEtr* XXX (1963), pp. 317–319.

Shape VII; the bodies of the vases are decorated with two confronted female heads in profile and the necks with a single female head of the same character (Pl. 70). Of these oinochoai, two specimens (replicas of one another: see the Villa Giulia Torcop Painter and Pl. 14) presented a decisive change from the normal theme of Torcop decoration. On the neck of the two oinochoai is found the usual profile head; on the body, however, in place of the expected set of confronted female heads, there is painted a *figured scene* which, although it may seem unimportant as far as subject is concerned, is of supreme importance for the stylistic evidence that it offers. The general style of painting noted in the figures depicted on the bodies of these two vases of indisputable Caeretan production, provides a key for examining Caeretan red-figured vases with subjects other than profile heads.

All the photographs referred to as *figures* are in the center of the book; those referred to as *plates* are at the end.

I

⊒⊒⊒

Caeretan Red-figured Vases

IN GENERAL, Caeretan red-figured vases are decorated with subjects which do not appear to contain any significant narrative theme, for the scenes simply treat women, seated or standing, approached by other women, satyrs, erotes and youths, all of whom normally bear gifts in the form of wreaths or beads. By "seated" reference is made to the figures, mainly women, who sit on a large rock with their bodies to the right or left and with their heads frequently turned to look in the opposite direction. The irregularly-shaped rocks, consistent in configuration to the painter's style, are, with rare exceptions, painted white and sometimes embellished with dotted-rosettes or vegetal forms.

Whether seated or standing, the figures normally hold objects which form the standard repertory depicted on Caeretan red-figured vases: mirror, fan, small vase, situla, beads (necklace or bracelet), wreath, cista, tray, tambourine, cushion, thyrsos, and the like. Owing to the fugitive nature of the white paint used to depict these objects, the figures often seem to gesture aimlessly. For example, the satyrs or erotes with raised or lowered "empty" hands originally held a beaded necklace or wreath (compare Pl. 22 and Pl. 25). Standing women generally stride across the picture-field and, in some cases, pass before an altar laden with fruit and skewered meats.

The presence of altars on a number of vases imparts a conspicuous religious aura to these products of Caeretan vase-painters. Likewise, the great frequency of *Dionysiac themes,* made evident through the appearance of satyrs and maenads, augment the religio-funerary context of the figured scenes and suggest some relationship between the Cult of Dionysos and the Dead in Etruria.[1] Themes of

1. See Beazley, *EVP*, p. 152.

3

potentially greater interest exist (see Pls. 40–43), but these are relatively few in number and do not vastly change the general character of the Caeretan vases with figured scenes.

The flesh color of the women is always executed in white, although some examples (e.g., Pl. 18) may not seem to support such practice because of the nearly complete disappearance of the original paint. Unlike the female heads which provide the main theme for earlier known Caeretan red-figure—the Genucilia and Torcop Groups—the women on vases with figured scenes (the sole exception are those represented by the Brooklyn Caeretan Painter) do not wear head cover (sakkos or sphendone), but are occasionally adorned with wreath or diadem. The hair is normally combed back from the forehead, gathered and tied with a fillet at the back of the head, and allowed to fall freely, sometimes in a loose "pony-tail." This hair-styling is often exhibited by erotes or youths, who would be easily mistaken for women were it not for the obvious signs of their sex. Where the sex is not directly discernible, white paint is used for flesh color when the figures are intended to be women.

Satyrs are the most commonly portrayed male companions of the women. They may be beardless ("young satyrs"), or bearded ("old satyrs"), the latter often represented as somewhat obese. It would seem natural to regard the women associated with the satyrs as *maenads*. However, they do not always carry a *thyrsos*—the Dionysiac attribute par excellence—and, since the tambourine is not exclusive to maenads, I shall identify women as *maenads* only on the evidence of *thyrsoi*, although those with tambourines could be maenads as well as dancers and the like.

Next to satyrs, *erotes* most frequently appear with women on Caeretan red-figured vases. Although it is tempting to associate women close to *Eros* in the figured scenes as *Turan* (Greek Aphrodite), unfortunately there is no adequate attribute or detail to justify such an identification. In view of the Etruscan context of Caeretan red-figured vases, I no longer believe it wise to designate the winged females as *Nikai*, which I have done in the past,[2] but now prefer to call them *Lasas*—important Etruscan beings and divinities in their own right.[3] In Etruscan art, *Lasas* frequently display a special feminine charm and grace—lightly clad, bejeweled, well-shod with soft slippers, and bearing objects appropriate to female taste: alabastron, ribbon, sash, and the like. When associated

---

2. *Caeretan Figured Group*, p. 31.
3. See *Lasa* in *Pauly-Wissowa* XII, 1, c. 882f (Fiesel); in *Roscher* (1965 ed.), c. 1902f (Deecke); and in *Enciclopedia dell'Arte Antica* IV, p. 488f (de Marinis). See also R. Herbig, *Götter und Dämonen der Etrusker* (Mainz, 1965), pp. 25ff.

with *Turan*, the goddess of feminine charm, the duties of a *Lasa* would not differ greatly from that performed by *Eros*. At the same time, however, *Lasas* are normally found in scenes of purely funerary character—on sarcophagi, urns, tomb-paintings—which, in such a context, shows that their duties were restricted not only to the living but were also extended to the dead.

The figured scenes of the group, regardless of the particular shape of the vases, are not crowded. Oinochoai, Shape VII, one of the most common vase-shapes used by Caeretan painters, generally show one or two figures at the neck, and sometimes three. On the body, however, four figures are represented on some of the earliest vases, but are soon reduced to the more common three. On the other hand, vases of monumental proportions—stamnoi and a calyx-krater—reveal decorations with one to three figures. There is a conspicuous use of "stock figures" throughout the entire group—striding and seated women, approaching satyrs, erotes and youths, a male standing with one leg raised and a foot resting on a high stone, etc.—which are sometimes ingeniously varied and call attention to red-figured fabrics produced elsewhere, particularly in South Italy. This important relationship will be discussed in detail later in this study (Chapter V).

In the field, that is, the background to the figured scenes, a fondness for "filler" ornaments is clearly demonstrated. The presence of *mesomphalic phialae* and dotted-rosettes, the most common filler motifs, clearly illustrates the close ties between the different groups of Caeretan red-figure thus far recognized, e.g., oinochoai of the Torcop Group (see Chapter II). In addition, there are wreaths, ribbons, sashes, smaller and varied dotted-rosettes, and a number of vegetal / floral forms, all of which are rendered in added white paint. The profusion of these details varies from painter to painter. On the whole, white paint is generously used throughout Caeretan red-figured vases on the figures, the objects they carry, details within the field, and for embellishment of subsidiary decorations.

During the course of my study and analysis of Caeretan red-figured vases, I have arbitrarily made the distinction "Workshop" (Dotted-hem Workshop and Crescent-hem Workshop) to divide vases assigned to the "Caeretan Figured Group"[4] according to the characteristic treatment of the lower edge, that is, the *hem*, of the garments worn by the women depicted in the figured scenes. However, since the designation "Workshop" may create or, in one instance has already created, the impression of two ateliers,[5] I now prefer to regard the two main divisions as "Groups" rather than "Workshops," within each of which

4. *Caeretan Figured Group.*
5. P. Mingazzini, *Catalogo dei Vasi della Collezione Augusto Castellani* II (Rome, 1971), p. 192.

may be distinguished a number of individual painters. Hence, it is through the many elements shared in common rather than by the differences that the vases of the two groups of the "Caeretan Figured Group"—now simply, "Caeretan Red-Figured Vases"—argue more emphatically for a single atelier instead of two physically distinct workshops.

For each of the two chief groups, I have endeavored to distinguish and identify a few individual painters whose works characterize the vases with figured scenes. In addition to the special treatment of the hems, there are several other features of the female garments which may aid recognition and attribution of Caeretan red-figured vases. All of the painters of the Dotted-hem Group show a *fleur de lis* at each shoulder of the garment (e.g., Pl. 5), probably the "bow" of the tied straps or strings for the front and back portions of the garment. Within the Crescent-hem Group, only one artist—the Castellani Caeretan Painter—shows the fleur de lis (e.g., Pl. 40), but its appearance is restricted to a small number of the many vases attributed to his hand.

It is convenient to refer to the sleeveless female garment normally worn by women of the group as a *peplos*, although technically it is not the classic Greek dress generally known by that name. The second feature of note associated with the garment is the *broad band* which runs down the front from neckline to hem. The majority of painters of the Dotted-hem Group render the broad band with two parallel lines to which some artists add a central white line (see Pl. 12 and Pl. 22). However, the painters of the Crescent-hem Group generally paint the white line or stripe directly over a broader black band (e.g., Pl. 53). As will be demonstrated in a later discussion of other red-figured fabrics (Chapter V), the broad band is not unique to Caeretan red-figured vases.

Of special significance is the employment of the relief-line which, on vases of the Dotted-hem Group, tends to disappear from use after it is relegated from the main to the subsidiary decoration. On the other hand, vases of the Crescent-hem Group do not reveal relief-lines in the major or minor areas of decoration. Detection of this change or transition in technique during an investigation of the Genucilia Group[6] will prove of inestimable value when determining a chronology for Caeretan red-figure as a whole (see Chapter VI).

THE DOTTED-HEM GROUP

The characteristic feature which sets off vases of the Dotted-hem Group from other examples of Caeretan red-figured vases is found in the row of dots that

6. *Genucilia Group*, p. 310f.

enhance the hem or lower border of the female garments. Below this row of dots, the actual terminating edge of the garment is usually defined by a continuous, sometimes heavy line or series of short lines.

In complete reversal to the procedure followed in my tentative study of Caeretan red-figured vases—the "Caeretan Figured Group"—I now prefer to consider the Dotted-hem Group (then "Workshop") *before* the Crescent-hem Group. This turnabout is prompted by my present belief that the first products of the Dotted-hem Group represent some of the earliest Caeretan red-figured vases; the style of drawing may also provide a strong link between these specimens and red-figured vases of slightly earlier date produced elsewhere in Etruria (see Chapter V).

At least seven individual artists have been distinguished in the Dotted-hem Group, some of whom utilize the relief-line, and others who are prepared to discard the technique by curiously transferring its use from the main to the subsidiary decoration—primarily in the decorative bands containing tongue- or egg-pattern.

THE VILLA GIULIA CAERETAN PAINTER

The work of the Villa Giulia Caeretan Painter, the most industrious artist of the Dotted-hem Group, serves well to introduce the painters who choose to decorate the hems of the female garments with a row of dots rather than crescents. His drawing is neat and fairly precise, with profuse use of the relief-line in the figured representations as well as in the subsidiary decoration as noted in the tongue- and egg-patterns which are frequently found on his vases. The tendency to abandon the relief-line technique by this painter of the Dotted-hem Group can be readily observed between vase no. 1 (Pl. 1) and no. 15 (Pl. 12).

Of the fifteen vases thus far attributed to the Villa Giulia Caeretan Painter, thirteen are oinochoai, Shape VII. On the bodies of these oinochoai, a change can be traced from more complex compositions of four figures to examples with three and even two figures. A stamnos in Philadelphia, no. 15 (Pls. 12–13) shows only one figure at each side. To judge from the presence of relief-lines in the figured scenes, a clue which I take to indicate an earlier phase of drawing, the more "populated" oinochoai represent his earliest productions of that vase-shape. Likewise, the oinochoe in the Louvre, vase no. 1 (Pl. 1), may be regarded as one of his earliest vases owing to the abundant use of relief-lines and the absence of dots at the hem, thereby an extremely significant work to associate with vases which are not Caeretan in origin (see Chapter V).

The fleur de lis is carefully rendered at the outset, but tends to become larger and clumsy in his later and more hastily decorated vases. As a rule, the

Villa Giulia Caeretan Painter indicates the broad band on the female garments by parallel lines only. Characteristically, this broad band follows an oblique course from the waist to left foot of the women who move across the picture field, as commonly shown on the neck of his oinochoai (e.g., Pls. 5 and 8).

In order to avoid constant repetition throughout the list of vases to follow, it should be noted that, unless otherwise indicated, "oinochoe" will refer to Shape VII (beaked jug), the almost standard oinochoe employed by Caeretan red-figured vase-painters. Furthermore, attention is called to the high probability that "Caere" is the correct provenience for vases of the Castellani (Villa Giulia, Rome) and Campana (Louvre, Paris and various provincial museums in France) Collections, on the evidence of the extensive land-holdings of these two early collectors in the environs of Cerveteri (ancient Caere).

Oinochoai

The initial four oinochoai listed below are placed together because the scenes depicted on their bodies are composed of four figures clearly Dionysiac in character: maenads, satyrs, erotes, women, and youths. To judge by the seated youth with a *thyrsos* in his right hand, who must be intended as young *Fufluns* (Greek *Dionysos*) on the Louvre vase, no. 1 (Pl. 1), the seated and naked youths on the Castellani oinochoai, nos. 2 and 3 (see Pl. 2), may also represent *Fufluns*—although in these instances they do not carry *thyrsoi*. For the Aléria vase, no. 4 (Pl. 4), such an identification may also have been plausible for the standing youth, naked but for *chlamys,* if he held *thyrsos* rather than spear. It should be noted that a second deity, *Turms* (Greek *Hermes*) appears on the neck of Louvre K 445, while *Fufluns* is represented on the body (Pl. 1).

1. Paris, Louvre K 445 (Pl. 1)
   Formerly Campana Collection
   Provenience, probably Caere
   Height, 3 cms.
   NECK: at the right and facing left, *Turms* wearing petasos, chlamys, and laced boots. A *caduceus* is held in the left hand. His right leg is raised, foot resting on high rock. Facing him, a woman is seated with her right arm resting on the rock, the left upraised with tambourine in hand.
   BODY: at the far left, a woman is seated to the left and turning round toward Eros who approaches with an object (bowl?) in his upraised left hand. Behind *Eros* and gazing toward him, sits a naked youth with *thyrsos* who may very well be *Fufluns.* Directly in front of the seated god at the far right, stands a woman with her right foot raised and

resting on a large stone. A large rectangular box (cista) is balanced on her raised right hand.

F. Villard, *Les Vases Grecs* (Paris, 1956, pl. XXXI, fig. 5; *AJA* 70 (1966), p. 34, no. 2 and pl. 13, fig. 12.

The two following vases in the Castellani Collection are replicas of one another. Although one of the two oinochoai is not illustrated here because of the heavy repainting, it reveals an adequate amount of the original drawing to disclose that it is a product of the same artist.

2–3. Rome, Villa Giulia 50604 and 50608 (Pl. 2)
   Castellani Collection
   Provenience, probably Caere

   NECK: at the left, a woman runs to the left while looking round. With her upraised left hand she balances a cista, in her right hand, a tambourine. Following close behind at the right is an old satyr with *thyrsos* held in lowered left hand.
   BODY: four figures comprise the composition: two women, a seated youth (*Fufluns?*), and *Eros*. At the far left, a woman stands facing to the right with cista in upraised left hand. Facing her and seated on a mantle which cushions a rock not indicated, is a naked youth (*Fufluns?*). Directly behind him, *Eros* approaches with left arm down, right arm upraised. At the far right, a woman is seated to the right but looking back.

   Mingazzini, no. 752 and pl. cciv, figs. 1–4; no. 753.

Attention should be called in the above three oinochoai, nos. 1–3, to the mantle and "rock" upon which sit *Fufluns* and the nude youths who may very well be the god without *thyrsos*. No rock is indicated beneath the mantle which has been draped as a cushion for the exposed buttocks of the deity! This very same configuration of rock and drapery, as well as the "heraldic" folds of the mantle, will appear at the necks of the Würzburg oinochoai, nos. 12 and 13.

The following oinochoe, no. 4 (Pls. 3–4), with the interesting provenience of Aléria (ancient *Alalia*) on the island of Corsica, is somewhat fragmentary with portions missing. Nevertheless, it deserves publication for the highly ornate character of the subsidiary decoration at the shoulder of the vase. In addition to the carefully executed tongue-pattern normally placed on the shoulder of the vase at the join of neck to body, an egg-pattern is painted directly below, between the tongue-pattern and the main picture field. The large rocks, upon which the women sit and the old satyr rests his foot, are painted white and carry *dotted-rosettes* in black. This latter detail, unlike the more vegetal forms preferred by the Villa Giulia Caeretan Painter, is common in the work of his colleague, the Sambon Caeretan Painter (see Pl. 25).

4. Aléria, Musée Archéologique 1075a (Pls. 3–4)
Provenience, Alalia
Height, 36.4 cms.

NECK: at the right, a woman is seated to the right but turns round toward an old satyr who stands facing her with left leg raised and foot resting on a high stone. In her left hand, the woman balances a tambourine.
BODY: three female figures and only one male figure comprise the four-figured scene. At the far left a *Lasa*, wearing peplos with *apoptygma* (heavy overfold at waist), approaches the group. In front of the *Lasa*, a woman with mantle wrapped round and over a lighter garment is seated to the left but turns round to look at a youth, naked but for *chlamys*, who holds a spear with his right hand. Behind him sits another woman whose body faces to the right but her head turned toward the youth.

5. Paris, Louvre Cp 1121
Formerly Campana Collection
Provenience, probably Caere
Preserved height, 32 cms. Portion of the mouth is missing.

NECK: maenad, with *thyrsos* in lowered right hand, moves swiftly to the left while looking round. Her left hand is upraised and holds an object partially missing (perhaps a bowl like that carried by the woman directly below on the body). In the field below her left arm, a *mesomphalic phiale*.
BODY: at the far left, a woman is seated to the left but turns round towards a young satyr who seems to be holding something up to her nose in order that she might scent it. Behind the satyr, a woman walks slowly to the left with bowl in upraised left hand. She gazes back toward *Eros* who holds a *situla* in his lowered left hand while he extends the right toward the woman.

AJA 70 (1966), p. 34, no. 1 and pl. 13, fig. 11.

This last oinochoe, no. 5 above, introduces a common theme for the neck area of oinochoai by the Villa Giulia Caeretan Painter and his colleagues, that is, a single female figure, often a maenad striding to the right or left. At the neck of the following four oinochoai, the Villa Giulia Caeretan Painter shows just such a female figure, chiefly a maenad who is generally associated with one or more *mesomphalic phialae* in the field. As placed on the Louvre vase, Cp 1121, such a phiale is found in the vacant area of the field below the left forearm. A characteristic configuration for the rendering of the lower edge of the garment on these striding women is the arch over each foot, the flat, horizontal line between the feet, and bulging folds at the calf of the trailing leg. For the oinochoai, nos. 6, 7, and 8, the number of figures on the body of the vase have been reduced to three and, on the oinochoe no. 9, there is a further reduction to two figures. Consistent with the subjects previously discussed, the scenes include satyrs, erotes, and women—some of whom are maenads.

6. Vienna, Kunsthistorisches Museum IV.4009 (Pl. 7)
   Height, 16.5 cms.

   NECK: a woman strides rapidly to the left while looking round. Her right hand is lowered with beaded bracelet or the like in hand. The trailing arm is upraised and balances an ornate cista or basket with contents. *Mesomphalic phiale* below left arm.
   BODY: at the center, a woman is seated to the right but looking to the left toward a woman who stands facing her. The latter figure has her left leg raised, foot resting on a rock (with dotted-rosette) and seems to hold a mirror in her left hand and tambourine at her right side. To the right, an old satyr approaches slowly with beribboned *thyrsos* in his lowered right hand.

Very often, the Villa Giulia Caeretan Painter does not indicate convincingly the *thyrsos* as being grasped by the individual who carries it, for the "holding" hand is merely placed close and somewhat in front of the shaft of the *thyrsos* (see Pls. 7 and 13).

7. Aléria, Musée Archéologique 696a (Pls. 5–6).
   Provenience, Alalia
   Height, 35 cms.

   NECK: a maenad moves swiftly to the left while looking back. *Thyrsos* in right hand and some object now unidentifiable owing to the missing and repaired portion at the left hand. *Mesomphalic phiale* in the field below left forearm.
   BODY: at the center, a woman is seated to the left and turning round. She wears mantle with broad border wrapped round the legs. A satyr stands facing her to each side; young satyr at the right, old satyr at the left. The young satyr holds *thyrsos*.

In the rendering of the garment for the maenad on the neck of the following oinochoe, a deviation from the norm is clearly visible; a "new look" or "off-the-shoulder" fashion is given to the garment worn by the woman.

8. Florence, Museo Archeologico 4086 (Pl. 8).

> NECK: maenad striding rapidly to the left with head turned back. A *thyrsos* is held in the lowered right hand, tambourine in the upraised left. *Mesomphalic phiale* in the field below left forearm.
> BODY: *Eros* seated at the center, body to right but head turned to the left. At each side stands a woman; that at the right has her right leg raised with foot resting on a stone, while she offers a bowl to *Eros* with her right hand.

The Aléria oinochoe, no. 9 below, has but two figures on its body. At the neck of the vase, the woman conforms in dress to that normally found on vases by this painter. The decorative band below the picture field on the body of the vase carries a series of chevrons facing to the left which, together with an oinochoe in Würzburg, no. 13 below, departs from the usual segmented meander pattern interrupted by "boxes" with checkered-cross, diagonal-cross, or some variant.

9. Aléria, Musée Archéologique 724b (Pl. 9).
Provenience, Alalia

> NECK: a woman strides to the left with head turned back. Her right arm is lowered, the left upraised and supporting a fully laden offering-tray. A large well-preserved *mesomphalic phiale* in the field below tray.
> BODY: a *Lasa* is seated at the right facing *Eros* who approaches from the left with beaded necklace.

An oinochoe in Madrid, no. 10 below (Pl. 10), replaces the single female on the neck with a young satyr who is posed in very much the same manner. Of particular interest, the Madrid vase presents a rare instance in the work of the Villa Giulia Caeretan Painter since the dotted-hem does not appear anywhere on the vase. Nevertheless, the style of drawing is undeniably his. Women and, at times, *erotes* carrying large rectangular "chests" or, better, *cistae* seem to be a favorite theme of the Villa Giulia Caeretan Painter who has represented them on three of his oinochoai (nos. 1, 2, and 6) thus far discussed, as well as the Würzburg vase (no. 13) not yet treated. A new element is encountered in the field on the neck of the Madrid vase above the right forearm of the satyr, namely, a pendant cluster of grapes.

10. Madrid, Museo Arqueológico 11483 (Pl. 10)
    Height, 27 cms.

    NECK: a young satyr, wearing a white animal pelt as mantle, moves swiftly to the left while looking back. In his right hand, he probably holds *thyrsos*, while his upraised left supports a tambourine.

    BODY: at the left, a woman is seated facing to the right. With her left hand she raises one end of her mantle. *Eros* stands in front of the seated woman with his right leg raised and foot resting on a stone. His body is bent forward as he offers a gift (chest) with his right hand.

    ArchEspArq XXXIX (1966), p. 90f. and figs. 3–4.

Calyx-krater

A large calyx-krater in the Louvre, no. 11 below (Pl. 11), in addition to the stamnos, no. 15 to be discussed, clearly illustrates that the Villa Giulia Caeretan Painter did not restrict his efforts to oinochoai alone. Although his drawing does not lend itself well to vases of such large proportions, he nevertheless maintains the monumentality generally expected for kraters. As would seem natural, the figures depicted on both sides of the calyx-krater are consistent with those thus far encountered in his work: maenads, a satyr and *Eros*. Side A seems superior in drawing to side B, but this may be credited to the strong signs of repainting on the latter. Whereas the dots of the hem are missing but possibly present in its original state on the female garment at side B, they are conspicuously present at the lower edge of the seated woman's mantle as well as the hem of her garment. Particularly well-rendered are the wings of *Eros* which are so conceived as to impart the character of completed flight and "touchdown." With the exception of the standard laurel pattern for the decorative zone above the picture field on calyx- and bell-kraters, the three decorative motifs below the picture field (chevrons, egg- and tongue-patterns) have been previously noted on the oinochoai of the Villa Giulia Caeretan Painter. On the calyx-krater, however, he juxtaposes the motifs in parallel registers.

11. Paris, Louvre K 403 (Pl. 11).
    Height, 33.5 cms.; diam. or rim, 28.5 cms.

    A: *Eros*, alighting from the left, offers a long, beaded necklace to a woman seated on a rock at the right. She could be a maenad if the staff were identifiable as a *thyrsos*. Unfortunately, its tip is interrupted by the laurel pattern. A quartered ball in the field between figures.

B: an old satyr at the right pursues a maenad who moves swiftly to left while looking back and fending off the advances of the satyr. Each holds a *thyrsos*. The satyr wears a white animal pelt as mantle. In the field are discs and a dotted sash.

As will occasionally occur during independent studies of special groups of red-figured vase-painting, certain products of an already identified painter may eventually reveal themselves to represent an earlier or later stage in the career of the same artist identified separately under different circumstances. This has been the case with my recognition of the "Villa Giulia Caeretan Painter" and Beazley's "Painter of Würzburg 817" (*EVP*, p. 168). Since my initial and tentative list of the Villa Giulia Caeretan Painter was proposed, additional examples have been attributed to him during progressive study of the Caeretan red-figured vases; a number of specimens already brought together by Beazley for the *Painter of Würzburg 817* has been associated with the former painter through the general style of drawing and some specific details. Although the two painters can now be equated, I believe that the vases of Beazley's artist represent a late phase of the Villa Giulia Caeretan Painter.

THE PAINTER OF WÜRZBURG 817

(THE VILLA GIULIA CAERETAN PAINTER)

Oinochoai

The following three oinochoai are known to me solely from very small and inadequate illustrations which, unfortunately, I have been unable to replace with more suitable photographs owing to the disappearance of the vases for various reasons.[7] The two Würzburg vases, nos. 12 and 13 below, show the use of mantle as cushion with "heraldic" folds and unindicated rock noted for vases nos. 1 and 2 (Pls. 1 and 2) by the Villa Giulia Caeretan Painter. The Würzburg vases exhibit the same general overall style noticeable for the oinochoe from Populonia, no. 14 below, on which the young satyr with white animal pelt as mantle strongly recalls his counterpart on the Madrid vase, no. 10 above (Pl. 10). The substitution of a wave pattern for the meander or key pattern in the decorative band below the picture field on the Würzburg vase no. 13 provides the

7. I am informed by Dr. Wolfgang Schiering that the Würzburg vases 816 and 817 (here vases nos. 12 and 13) were lost during World War II. I have been unable to locate the present whereabouts of the oinochoe discovered at Populonia and published in *NSc* 1934, p. 45, and fig. 69 (here vase no. 14).

second instance of change (see vase no. 9 above, Pl. 9) from his more usual decorative motif at this portion of the oinochoai.

12. Würzburg, University
    Martin von Wagner Museum, 816
    Height, 24 cms.

    NECK: *Eros* seated on mantle which acts as cushion to rock not indicated. In his upraised left hand he holds a chest. Nearby is an altar painted white.
    BODY: at each side a tall column painted in white, stands a young satyr with *thyrsos* at the left, woman with tambourine in raised left hand at the right. Both figures face inwards toward the column.

    Beazley, *EVP*, p. 168; *Langlotz*, p. 145 and pl. 236.

13. Würzburg, University
    Martin von Wagner Museum, 817
    Height, 22 cms.

    NECK: *Eros* seated to the right and turning head to the left. His mantle is used as a cushion for a rock not indicated. *Mesomphalic phialae* in the field at upper right and left.
    BODY: at the left a woman, naked to the waist and draped with a mantle at the legs, faces left but turns head round toward a young satyr, with beribboned *thyrsos*, who moves slowly away to the right. A small altar or marker in the field near the satyr's left leg.

    Beazley, *EVP*, p. 168; *Langlotz*, p. 145f, and pl. 236 (incorrectly identified as "schale").

14. Oinochoe, Shape VII
    Provenience, Populonia

    NECK: woman seated on a rock with body to the right, her head facing to the left toward her upraised right hand which holds a beaded necklace. *Mesomphalic phiale* in the field below the right elbow.
    BODY: of three figures, I can only describe the two visible in the reproduction. A woman facing to the right stands at the center with her head turned to the left toward a young satyr who wears white animal pelt as mantle.

    NSc 1934, p. 45 and fig. 69; *Minto*, pl. LXI, no. 6; Beazley, *EVP*, p. 168.

Stamnos

Like the calyx-krater, no. 11 above (Pl. 11), the present stamnos offers a refreshing change from the oinochoai, Shape VII preferred by the *Painter of Würzburg 817* or, better, the Villa Giulia Caeretan Painter in his late phase. His *Lasa* is once again encountered at side A, whereas side B shows the reappearance of his well-known young satyr. The stamnos is especially illustrative of the ornate character of subsidiary floral / vegetal decoration used by this painter. The decorative band below the main picture field introduces a new pattern: "L" motifs alternating up-and-down, which seem to be an abbreviated form of the segmented meander or key pattern.

15. Philadelphia, Pennsylvania University
    Museum MS 400 (Pl. 12–13).

> A: *Lasa* walking to the left and looking round. Her wings are represented outstretched to each side of her body. *Mesomphalic phialae* (with the white paint fugitive) in the field.
>
> B: young satyr walking to the right with head turned back. A *thyrsos* is held in his lowered left hand, his right hand upraised and may have originally held beads. *Mesomphalic phiale* between his feet.

Beazley, *EVP*, p. 168; *Genucilia Group*, p. 105, fig. C.

THE VILLA GIULIA TORCOP PAINTER

One of the most significant Caeretan vase-painters is the Villa Giulia Torcop Painter, whose name—including the word "Torcop"—clearly stresses his position within two known groups of Caeretan red-figure. As was pointed out in the Introduction to the present study, two oinochoai which are replicas of one another, nos. 16 (Pl. 14) and 17 below, have provided the *key* to the discovery of a greater and far more important area of fourth-century Caeretan vase-painting than seemed possible during initial studies of late red-figure at Caere.

Although it may be argued that his name will lead to confusion with a previously identified painter of the Dotted-hem Group—the Villa Giulia Caeretan Painter—the incorporation of "Torcop" should prevent such confusion and, at the same time, disclose the interesting relationship between different groups of Caeretan red-figure and the productive scope of its potters and vase-painters. The Villa Giulia Torcop Painter exhibits a particularly fine style of drawing which gains increased sharpness because of the profuse use of relief-lines clearly visible in the illustration of one of his oinochoai (Pl. 14). In his application of added white, the Villa Giulia Torcop Painter demonstrates commendable care.

All of his vases decorated with figured scenes are oinochoai, Shape VII, of which one is a "miniature" (no. 19 below) and does not exhibit the talent expected of him.

Oinochoai

The two oinochoai listed below are not only replicas of one another, but are found in the same collection with identical inventory number. There is no need here to give but the briefest description of the female profile heads on the neck of the oinochoai, for they receive detailed treatment and analysis in my investigation of the *Torcop Group* (Chapter II). Like the Villa Giulia Caeretan Painter, the Villa Giulia Torcop Painter renders the broad band of the garment without central white stripe.

16. Rome, Villa Giulia 30 (Pl. 14)
    Provenience, Caere
    Height, 19.5 cms.

    NECK: female head wearing full-sakkos and facing to the left.
    BODY: at the left, a woman seated on a white rock and facing to right. Her right arm braces the body, the upraised left hand supports tambourine. Large, floppy fleur de lis at each shoulder. A young satyr approaches from the right with gift of long, beaded necklace between outstretched arms, the left high, the right low.

    Torcop Group, p. 142, no. 8 and pl. X, fig. 3; *Studi L. Banti*, p. 139, no. 1 and pl. XXXIII.

17. Rome, Villa Giulia 30
    Provenience, Caere
    Height, 19.5 cms.

    NECK: replica of no. 16.
    BODY: replica of no. 16.

    AJA 70 (1966), p. 34, no. 1 and pl. 13, fig. 13.

Vase no. 18 below, another oinochoe but very fragmentary, remains unrestored and no longer possesses the high neck and beaked mouth. I must apologize for the improvised character of the photograph and elastic band present in the reproductions of this exceptional vase (Pls. 15–16), but it was necessary to hold together the several large fragments that comprise the unmended body of the oinochoe. Irrespective of the poor state of preservation of the vase, its extremely fine drawing and crisp, precise use of relief-lines, particularly evident in the tongue-pattern on the shoulder of the vase, should not be overlooked. Like the early vases of the Villa Giulia Caeretan Painter, this specimen by the Villa Giulia Torcop Painter shows a more complex composition comprised of four figures.

18. Cerveteri, Magazzino (Pls. 15–16)
   Provenience, Caere
   Preserved height, 20.5 cms.

   NECK: missing
   BODY: four figures are grouped in pairs. At the left, a woman seated to the left and looking round at a young satyr who stands behind her. The woman's left arm supports her body, her right is upraised. The young satyr holds his left arm down to the side, his right hand upraised with a beaded necklace within its grasp. His fillet, painted in white with two upright strokes above the forehead, is identical to that on vases nos. 16 and 17. Two long beaded necklaces run in "bandolier" fashion across his torso. At the right, a woman walks slowly to the left while looking round toward a young satyr who stands behind with a *thyrsos* in his upraised right hand. In his lowered left hand, he holds a beaded necklace. Like his colleague, the young satyr wears fillet and bandolier of beads.

A fourth vase attributable to the Villa Giulia Torcop Painter is a "miniature" when compared to the usual oinochoai by his hand. It may very well be that the much reduced scale of the vase shape accounts for the noticeable worsening of his style.

19. Tarquinia, Museo Nazionale 1930
   Provenience, Tarquinii
   Height, 14 cms.

   NECK: female head in profile to the left wearing full-sakkos.
   BODY: maenad moving swiftly to the left with *thyrsos* held diagonally across the body between left and right hands. *Mesomphalic phiale* in the field below left elbow.

The subsidiary decoration in the bands near the mouth and at the shoulder of the vase differs from that known for the three preceding vases of the Villa Giulia Torcop Painter. At the neck, there are two rows of parallel dots, whereas the shoulder decoration is composed of a series of vertical strokes which provide a hasty substitute for the tongue-pattern. Vase no. 18 shows a meander pattern which is very much simplified on oinochoai nos. 16 and 17. These last two vases are decorated at the shoulder and neck by an egg-pattern with white embellishment. The far superior but unfortunately very fragmentary oinochoe no.

18 carries one of the most precisely rendered tongue-patterns to be found throughout Caeretan red-figure.

THE BROOKLYN CAERETAN PAINTER

The representations of a female profile head on the neck and single figure on the body of an oinochoe, as noted on the last vase discussed for the Villa Giulia Torcop Painter (vase no. 19), leads directly to the consideration of an oinochoe, also of miniature proportion with similar configuration of the main decoration. This small oinochoe, now in the Brooklyn Museum which gives its name to the Brooklyn Caeretan Painter, suggests his position in the early phase of Caeretan Red-Figured Vases, particularly by his use of relief-lines to indicate the folds of the drapery. The presence of both relief-lines and lines executed in diluted glaze-paint is particularly apparent in the textural contrast between the inner folds of the garments, the parallel lines of their broad bands—without central white stripe—and the terminating lower edges. The dotted-hem is visible for the two seated women on the body of oinochoe no. 21 (Pl. 17), and omitted altogether on vase no. 22 (Pl. 18).

Oinochoai

20. Brooklyn, Museum 27.730
    Height, 15.5 cms.

    NECK: female head in profile to left wearing full-sakkos.
    BODY: *Lasa*, with wings outstretched to each side of her body, moving to the right. Her left hand is upraised, the right is lowered and holds a beaded necklace. *Mesomphalic phiale* in the field at the lower left.

    AJA 70 (1966), p. 34, no. 1 and pl. 14, fig. 18.

    The style of the profile head and the unusual rendering of the full-sakkos at the neck of the small oinochoe, vase no. 20 above, when compared to those found on the previously unattributed and unique terracotta *cista* in the Castellani Collection (Villa Giulia 50576, Pl. 88),[8] and the Genucilia Group plate in Parma (Museo Nazionale di Antichità C. 108, Fig. 7), clearly reveal the three products to be by the same hand.

21. Paris, Louvre K 470 (Pl. 17)
    Formerly Campana Collection
    Provenience, probably Caere
    Height, 32 cms.

8. M. Del Chiaro, "A Caeretan Red-Figured Cista," *ArchCl* XIV (1962), p. 78f.

NECK: a woman seated to the right with bowl or tray in upraised left hand.

BODY: at the center, a woman walks slowly to the left with bowl or tray supported in upraised right hand. To each side, and looking towards her, is a woman seated to the left. The woman at the right seems to hold a mirror in her raised right hand; the woman at left reaches with her left hand for the contents of the bowl offered by the central woman.

The flattish sakkos with opening at the top which permits protrusion of the hair somewhat piriform in shape, together with the general "nervous" character of the drawing, reveal the oinochoe listed below to be the work of the Brooklyn Caeretan Painter. Although the egg-pattern with relief-lines in the decorative bands at the mouth and shoulder of the vase parallels that known for the Louvre specimen, no. 21 above, the painter introduces a new double-registered, decorative motif below the picture field, namely, a wave pattern with a narrower band of evenly-spaced dots above (Pl. 18). The wave motif in itself is not an innovation on vases of the Dotted-hem Group, for it has been encountered on an oinochoe by the Villa Giulia Caeretan Painter (see the *Painter of Würzburg 817*, vase no. 12).

22. Würzburg, University (Pl. 18)
    Martin von Wagner Museum 814
    Height, 31.5 cms.

    NECK: figure (male or female?) seated to the left with head turned round, perhaps frontally but difficult to determine owing to the present condition of the painting. A large alabastron is held high in the right hand. *Mesomphalic phialae* in the field behind the figure.

    BODY: two women are seated at the left and right, facing inwards toward an altar. The woman at right holds a stylus in her upraised right hand, and an indiscernible object in her left. The *mesomphalic phialae* in the field have been elaborated by diagonal lines.

    Beazley, *EVP*, p. 168; *Langlotz*, p. 145 and pl. 236.

Since the object held in the upraised right hand of the woman seated at the right on the body of this last vase (no. 22) can be rightfully regarded as a *stylus*, then the indiscernible object in her left hand must be a *diptych*. Such an identification would not solely explain the rectangular form in the field behind her left shoulder, which may also represent a diptych, but would provide added interest for the vase because it marks the only instance for the representation of this ancient writing paraphernalia (stylus and diptych) known to me in Caeretan red-figure or, for that matter, in Etruscan vase-painting.

THE CAMPANA CAERETAN PAINTER

Although I have been tempted to regard the seven vases listed below, all oinochoai from Caere, to be products of two artists, close analysis has disclosed a proximity in style and detail that argues strongly in favor of a single Caeretan vase-painter who seems to display an earlier (nos. 23–25) and later (nos. 26–29) phase in his style of drawing. It is interesting to note that in the early vases the central white stripe on the broad bands running down the center of the garments is omitted—as has been the case with vases of the Dotted-hem Group thus far discussed. In the *later* specimens, however, the Campana Caeretan Painter introduces the central white stripe which becomes characteristic of the Crescent-hem Group. In addition, the oinochoe, no. 25, and *all* of his later specimens reveal a special fondness for white paint which embellishes the general details and "filler" in the picture field. In particular, the vegetal / floral weed-like motif (see Pls. 20 and 22) heralds the work of the Castellani Caeretan Painter of the Crescent-hem Group (see Pl. 44).

Changes are noticeable on the earlier and later oinochoai in the difference between the decorative bands at the mouth, the shoulder, and below the picture field. Vases nos. 23–25, with the exception of the mouth which is missing on no. 24, show an egg-pattern at the mouth and shoulder, but on no. 25 it is more "tongue" than "egg." Below the picture field there are poorly executed chevrons or "Z"s for nos. 23 and 24, whereas no. 25 has the more elaborate and painstaking meander pattern with crossed-box. The later oinochoai, nos. 26–29 show no decorative band at mouth, an egg-pattern at the shoulder for no. 26 only, and chevrons (to the left) at the shoulder and below the picture field for all vases except no. 29 where it is omitted below the picture field.

It may be especially significant to note that the vases believed to be representative of the early stage in the work of the Campana Caeretan Painter show relief-lines (nos. 23–25), whereas none of the later examples (nos. 26–29) disclose their use even in the subsidiary areas.

Oinochoai

23. Paris, Louvre Cp 1183
    Formerly Campana Collection
    Provenience, probably Caere
    Height, 31.5 cms.

NECK: a woman seated to left with tambourine balanced in her out-stretched right hand.

BODY: a woman seated at the right and facing to the left toward *Eros* who offers a long, beaded necklace. His left leg is raised with foot resting on a small stone.

At the neck of the following oinochoe, an entirely new element is introduced for Caeretan vases with figured scenes, namely, a *bird* in full flight with a sash firmly clutched in its claw. The bird, perhaps an eagle to judge by its curved beak, is painted entirely in added white with details rendered in diluted glaze-paint.

24. Paris, Louvre K 439 (Pl. 19)
    Formerly Campana Collection
    Provenience, probably Caere
    Preserved height, 32 cms. The tip of the mouth is missing.

    NECK: bird in flight to the left with sash clutched in its claws. *Mesomphalic phialae* in the field.
    BODY: *Lasa* seated at the left, facing to the right and holding a tambourine in her upraised left hand. A young satyr stands before the *Lasa* with his right foot raised and resting on a small stone. With his outstretched hands he offers a long, beaded necklace.

25. Paris, Louvre K 450
    Formerly Campana Collection
    Provenience, probably Caere
    Height, 37 cms.

    NECK: *Eros* approaches from the left with long, beaded necklace which he offers a woman seated at the right.
    BODY: at the far left and right, a woman is seated to the left. Each looks toward the center where a young satyr offers a long, beaded necklace to the woman at right. Profuse use of white detailing diadems and "filler" ornament, including a dotted-rosette, within the field.

Vase no. 26 below is delightful for its scene of music and dancing. Two women—one playing the double-flute, the other castanets—sway, twist, and twirl. Movement is suggested by the billowing character given to the lower edge of the garments, particularly for the woman with castanets.

26. Paris, Louvre K 469 (Pl. 20)
    Formerly Campana Collection
    Provenience, probably Caere
    Height, 29 cms.

NECK: a woman standing and facing to the right with large *aryballos* suspended from her lowered left hand; a mirror is held in the upraised right hand.

BODY: at the left, a woman faces to the right and plays a double-flute. At the right, another woman, also facing to the right, looks back and downwards as she plays castanets. They are obviously performers who gyrate while playing their instruments.

AJA 70 (1966), p. 34, no. 1 and pl. 14, fig. 16.

27. Paris, Louvre K 441 (Pl. 21)
    Formerly Campana Collection
    Provenience, probably Caere
    Height, 28.5 cms.

NECK: maenad standing and facing to the left with *thyrsos* in upraised hand and beaded bracelet in the lowered left.

BODY: a *Lasa* with fan in upraised left hand is seated at the left and faces to the right. A woman at the right walks slowly away with fully laden tray or bowl balanced on her right hand, a sash or wreath in the lowered left. A dotted-rosette appears in the field between the figures below the right arm of the standing woman.

The broad flattish bowl, basket or tray, laden with fruit and skewered meat, as suggested by the round and piriform objects, and columns of dotted lines topped by "v"-shaped finials, is represented once on the above vase, no. 27, and twice on no. 29 below. Although the characteristic details for this or any other vases of the Dotted-hem Group are conspicuously present in the hems of the women's garments, I call special attention to the hem of the maenad's garment at the neck of this vase, no. 27 (Pl. 21): the *crescents*—with lower edging in white—are rendered directly below the usual row of dots. This rare appearance of crescents—the identifying feature for vases of the Crescent hem Group—on a vase of the Dotted-hem Group offers important evidence for the interrelationship of the two groups and the hypothesis that they may comprise a single "Workshop."

The following oinochoe is striking for the manner in which *Eros* is represented on the body of the vase in that curious half-seated, half-leaning pose so frequently encountered in the engraving of Etruscan bronze mirrors.[9] On this same vase, the somewhat oversized fleur de lis is more clearly visible than on other vases by the Campana Caeretan Painter, and sets the stage for the type normally used by the Florence Caeretan Painter discussed next.

9. M. Del Chiaro, "Two Etruscan Mirrors in San Francisco," *AJA* (1955), pp. 277ff.

28. Rome, Villa Giulia (Pl. 22)
    Provenience, Caere
    Height, 27 cms.

NECK: a woman seated to the left with right arm raised and long sash in hand.
BODY: at the right, a woman sits to the right but looks round toward *Eros* who offers a long, beaded necklace. The object held in the woman's left hand is a tambourine. A well-preserved *mesomphalic phiale* in the field below the right leg of Eros.

On the above oinochoe, no. 28, the white rock upon which the female figures sit obtains an anvil-like shape owing to the sharp point created by the women's drapery which conceals the normal form of the stone. The rocks on this vase and no. 25, and the drawing of the fingers of the hands which rest upon the stone, are remarkably similar. On other vases by the Campana Caeretan Painter, these hands are not always so well preserved.

29. Cerveteri, Magazzino
    Provenience, Caere
    Height, 28 cms.

NECK: a woman seated to the left with right arm upraised and supporting a large, ornate tray or basket with fruit and skewered tidbits. *Mesomphalic phiale* at the right knee.
BODY: at the right, a woman is seated to the left and gazes toward an approaching *Eros* with long, beaded necklace. The woman balances a fully laden bowl with her upraised hand.

THE FLORENCE CAERETAN PAINTER

Four oinochoai are unquestionably by the hand of a single painter of the Dotted-hem Group who receives his name from the example in Florence, no. 30 below. A distinctive feature of his seated women, who appear at least once on each of his vases, is their usually large, extra long and clumsy arm that rests on one knee or, in one case (no. 32), is upraised. The folds of the drapery at the inside leg nearest the rock fall vertically rather than in radiating fashion, as is more common in the works of the preceding painters (e.g., Pls. 14 and 21).

The relief-line is not employed by the Florence Caeretan Painter on any of his vases with the possible exception of no. 30. A hastily executed egg-pattern provides the only motif in the decorative bands found only at the shoulders of his oinochoai, for the artist omits decorative bands altogether at the mouth and below the picture field. Of major importance is the inclusion of a hanging *wreath* in the field between the two figures on vases nos. 31 (Pl. 23) and 33. This feature, together with the *mesomphalic phiale* in the field of no. 32 (Pl. 24), calls special attention to oinochoai of the Torcop Group on which the form of the hanging wreath is similar to that used by the Brussels Torcop Painter (compare Pl. 72 with Pl. 23).[10] Hence, there is once again good evidence for connections between the various Caeretan red-figured "Groups," a relationship that will be taken up later in this study (Chapter III).

Oinochoai

On the neck of the first two vases, nos. 30 and 31, the maenad is identical in pose and details.

30. Florence, Museo Archeologico 4119
    Height, 36.5 cms.
    NECK: a maenad moves to right with head turned back. The right arm trails to the side, the left upraised with *thyrsos* in hand.
    BODY: at the left, a woman is seated and facing to the right with her right arm resting on the left leg. Before her stands *Eros* with right leg raised and foot resting on a stone. He offers the woman a ribbon or fillet.

31. Rome, Palazzo dei Conservatori 26 (Pl. 23)
    Height, 33 cms.
    NECK: replica of vase no. 30 above.
    BODY: the woman at the left repeats her counterpart on vase no. 30 above. A young satyr slowly approaches from the right with left hand upraised, the right extended towards the woman, possibly with ribbon or fillet as gift. In the field between the seated woman and satyr hangs a heavy wreath.

32. Tarquinia, Museo Nazionale 5436 (Pl. 24)
    Provenience, Tarquinii
    Preserved height, 33 cms. Upper portion of the neck is missing.
    NECK: a woman seated to the left with right arm raised.
    BODY: at the right, a woman is seated to the left with long and clumsy right arm (perhaps repainted) upraised. A young satyr approaches from the left with long, beaded necklace.

33. Paris, Louvre K 463
    Formerly Campana Collection
    Provenience, probably Caere
    Height, 32 cms.
    NECK: Lasa moving to left with both arms lowered and long sash held between each hand.

10. Torcop Group, p. 150f.

BODY: at the left, a seated woman as on nos. 30 and 31 above. Before her, with right leg raised and foot on stone, stands *Eros* who offers a long, beaded necklace. A wreath hangs in the field between the figures.

AJA 70 (1966), p. 34, no. 1 and pl. 14, fig. 17.

THE SAMBON CAERETAN PAINTER

The name of this interesting painter of the Dotted-hem Group is derived from two oinochoai which were once in the Sambon Collection in Paris and are known to me only from photographs acquired at the German Archaeological Institute, Rome, Photographic Archives (negatives, nos. 60.427 and 60.428). Consequently, my description of them is limited to the sides visible in the photographs. Refreshingly, the Sambon Caeretan Painter has decorated three stamnoi in addition to oinochoai.

Although his style is not of the highest aesthetic order, it is unquestionably bold and sure. His very distinctive style offers a number of details which facilitate attribution to his hand: long, slipper-like feet in white carefully outlined in black; two short parallel strokes which mark a break—doubtlessly indicating overfold —in the broad band down the center of the female garments; and the fleur de lis, two "v"-shaped projections in white clearly outlined in black. The placement of the feet of the striding women is consistent throughout his vases, the advancing foot in profile and the trailing foot shown in strict frontal, foreshortened view.

The Sambon Caeretan Painter displays a special interest in winged figures, *Lasas* and *Erotes*; the wings follow normal practice for Caeretan Red-Figured Vases and are painted entirely white. This artist adds two rows of evenly-spaced dots along the contours of the wing near its upper and deeply curved edge and directly above the sweeping feathers. A fondness for a *situla* or bucket is apparent from his three stamnoi, nos. 38–40. In all three cases, the situla is born by women in their lowered right hand (see Pls. 26 and 28). *Mesomphalic phialae* are placed in the field on both oinochoai and stamnoi. On vases nos. 34–36 (e.g., Pl. 25), the decorative band—composed of bold, sweeping egg-pattern—is used only at the shoulder. Oinochoe no. 37, however, shows the egg-pattern at the mouth and shoulder, and a decorative band with chevrons facing to the left is painted below the picture field. The dotted-rosettes painted in black on the white rock at the neck of oinochoe no. 35 recall similar treatment by the Villa Giulia Caeretan Painter (see Pl. 3).

34. Formerly Paris, Sambon Collection
    German Archaeological Institute, Rome,
    Photographic Archives, negative no. 60.427.

NECK: *Lasa* moving to the right with arm trailing and left upraised with object in hand.

BODY: visible in the central and left portion of the vase, a woman at far left moves to the right toward a central *Eros* who faces her with left arm up, right down. *Mesomphalic phialae* in the field.

Studi L. Banti, p. 137, no. 2 and pl. XXXIV, c.

35. Formerly Paris, Sambon Collection (Pl. 25)
    German Archaeological Institute, Rome,
    Photographic Archives, negative no. 60.428.

    NECK: a woman seated to the left but with head turned round to the right. Her left arm is fully extended and balances a large tray or basket. Dotted-rosettes painted in black on the white rock; *mesomphalic phiale* in the field below left forearm.

    BODY: visible in the central and right portion of the vase is a woman at the far right striding to the left toward an *Eros* who stands with his back to her. His pose and gesture is the same as that of his counterpart on vase no. 34 above.

36. Rome, Palazzo dei Conservatori 22
    Height, 34 cms.

    NECK: replica of no. 35 above.
    BODY: replica of no. 35 above.
    Between the outstretched hands of *Eros*, a long beaded necklace is clearly visible.

The following oinochoe has been heavily repainted, yet the personal style of the Sambon Caeretan Painter shows through. An old satyr stands with right leg raised and foot resting on a carefully placed square resembling a "foot-stool." This curious, almost "portable" footrest will be noted on two unattributed oinochoai of the Dotted-hem Group (see Pls. 35 and 37).

37. Rome, Palazzo dei Conservatori 90
    Height, 30 cms.

    NECK: a woman seated to the left but turning round. Her left arm is lowered, the right upraised with tambourine in hand. *Mesomphalic phiale* in the field to the right.

    BODY: at the center stands an old satyr with right leg raised and foot resting on a block. To each side and facing him stands a woman with mirror in upraised hand.

Stamnoi

Although the three stamnoi listed below are basically the same in shape and stand on a ring base, the handles on no. 40 differ from nos. 38 and 39. On nos. 38

and 39, the horizontal handles curve up sharply and terminate where they join the body in a manner strongly suggestive of human hands with outspread fingers.[11] The curvature of the handles on no. 40 are simple and relatively gentle; a series of upright lines only hint at the tongue pattern which is more carefully rendered on stamnoi nos. 38 and 39. In addition to the tongue-pattern, a hastily drawn upright egg-pattern appears around the neck of stamnos no. 39.

38. Rome, Villa Giulia (Pls. 26–27)
   Provenience, Caere
   Height, 32 cms.

   A: *Eros* at the left moves to the right with right arm upraised and left extended, and bears a long beaded necklace between his hands. From the right, a woman advances with *situla* in lowered right hand, tambourine (?) in upraised left.
   B: *Lasa* moving from right to left with long ribbon or sash in trailing left hand. *Mesomphalic phiale* in the field below her right elbow.

   Studi L. Banti, p. 137, no. 3 and pl. XXXV.

39. Rome, Villa Giulia
   Provenience, Caere
   Height, 31 cms.

   A: replica of no. 38 above but with deep bowl instead of tambourine (?).
   B: replica of no. 38 above but with deep bowl in upraised right hand.

   AJA 70 (1966), p. 34, no. 1 and pl. 14, figs. 14–15.

The following stamnos differs from the two listed above specifically in its shape and in its proportions of width to height; the marked swell to the bodies, noted for vases nos. 38 and 39, is absent. The vase is supported by a heavy ring base, and the body curves gently into a relatively broad, flat shoulder. The added white paint is remarkably well preserved throughout. Extreme haste in the decorative zone at shoulder and rim is evident from the vertical strokes which suggest the more usual tongue-pattern.

40. Rome, Villa Giulia (Pls. 28–29)
   Provenience, Caere
   Height, 17.5 cms.

   A: a woman moves to the left with *situla* or bucket in lowered right hand, large deep bowl in upraised left.

11. The strong suggestion of "human hand" in the join of handle and body of the vase may be a survival of handle-types known specifically for bronze vessels on which the handle terminates in the form of human hands, e.g., *StEtr* X (1936), pl. IX, fig. 1.

B: a woman moves to the left with mirror in upraised right hand, tambourine in upraised left. Large exceedingly well preserved *mesomphalic phiale* in the field below and left elbow.

THE VOLTERRA CAERETAN PAINTER

An artist whom I have originally named the "Caeretan Stamnos Painter" on the strength of the predominance of stamnoi to oinochoai assigned to him in my preliminary study of Caeretan red-figured vases with figured scenes [12] should, I now believe, be better named the Volterra Caeretan Painter. This change in identification is prompted by the discovery of additional oinochoai (Shape VII) attributable to his hand, three of which are in the Museo Guarnacci at Volterra, nos. 41, 43, and 44 below. Furthermore, this painter was earlier regarded as a member of the Crescent-hem "Workshop" (now Group), but recently encountered oinochoai in Volterra disclose that he is best assigned to the Dotted-hem Group.

The Volterra Caeretan Painter may or may not include the expected row of dots to the hem of the female garments. Regardless of their presence, however, the actual termination of the garment is rendered by a series of short strokes which in some cases (e.g., Pl. 30) takes on a *crescent* aspect, but this is not decisive enough to justify placing him within the Crescent-hem Group. This apparent ambiguity, which led me to place his vases midway—"transitional"— between products of the Dotted-hem and Crescent-hem Groups,[13] reasserts the strong possibility of a single Workshop for the two Groups.

Oinochoai

Sir John Beazley has assigned oinochoe no. 41 to his "Orbetello Group" which, as I have attempted to demonstrate, is in fact comprised of vases that belong to two different Etruscan red-figured fabrics.[14] Although a *bird* has previously appeared on the neck of an oinochoe of the Dotted-hem Group— vase no. 24 by the Campana Caeretan Painter (Pl. 19)—another species of bird, a *swan*, is novel as the sole decoration on the neck of a Caeretan red-figured oinochoe (Shape VII)—vase no. 43 by the Volterra Caeretan Painter. A far more interesting innovation is the appearance of a *griffin*, originally painted entirely in white on the neck of vase no. 42 (Pl. 30).

12. *Caeretan Figured Group*, p. 34.
13. M. Del Chiaro, "The 'Orbetello Group,' Two Etruscan Red-Figured Fabrics," *StEtr* XXXVIII (1970), pp. 91–102; see p. 94f in particular.
14. *Ibid.*

Decorative bands, when used by this artist, may carry egg-patterns—as found on the shoulders of all the oinochoai and rims of the stamnoi—chevrons, or, as a totally new motif, a large dot alternating with two short vertical strokes —as near the mouth of the Volterra vase no. 43. Decorative details of considerably greater importance, however, are the *wreaths* and *mesomphalic phialae* employed as "fillers" in the field. The association of a wreath—specifically, a *hanging* wreath—directly above a *mesomphalic phiale* (which I termed "patera" in *Torcop Group*), provides an additional link between Caeretan red-figured vases with figured scenes and oinochoai of the Torcop Group (e.g., Pls. 69–70). In all probability, the Volterra Caeretan Painter, like his colleague the Florence Caeretan Painter (e.g., Pl. 23), may have also decorated Torcop Group oinochoai.

41. Volterra, Museo Guarnacci
    Provenience Volterra
    Height, 35 cms.

    NECK: a woman moves swiftly to the right while looking back. Fan-like object held in left hand. The right side of the vase not visible in the Alinari Photo (no. 34715) at my disposal.
    BODY: visible at right side only: a nude, rather effeminate youth with hair in long pony-tail, runs to left with egg-shaped cushion or tambourine in his extended right hand. In the field, wreath and *mesomphalic phiale*.

    Beazley, *EVP*, p. 147; *StEtr* XXXVIII (1970), p. 92, no. 1 and pl. VII, a.

42. Milano, Formerly market (Pl. 30)
    Height, 30.4 cms.

    NECK: griffin facing to left. Originally painted entirely white. *Mesomphalic phiale* between forelegs and hindlegs.
    BODY: visible at right side only: a maenad with crudely painted *thyrsos* (?) in left hand moves swiftly to the left while looking back. Two sets of hanging wreath and *mesomphalic phiale* in the field.

    A. Stenico, *Finarte* 5 (Auction Catalogue, March, 1963), no. 130, pl. 68; *StEtr* XXXVIII (1970), p. 93, no. 4 and pl. VII, d.

43. Volterra, Museo Guarnacci
    Provenience, Volterra
    Height, 35 cms.

    NECK: swan standing to the right with outstretched wings and long neck craned upwards.

BODY: at the center is a simple altar approached from the right by *Eros* with arms extended.
A woman moves away from him at the left but looks back. In her up-raised left hand she balances a rectangular chest.

StEtr XXXVIII (1970), p. 93, no. 3 and pl. VII, c.

44. Volterra, Museo Guarnacci
    Provenience, Volterra
    Height, 37.5 cms.

    NECK: *Eros*, very much like the youth on the body of vase no. 1 above, moves to the left.
    BODY: at the left, a woman is seated to the right with tray-like object in upraised left hand. From the right *Eros* approaches. He is a replica of his counterpart on the neck of the vase.

    StEtr XXXVIII (1970), p. 93, no. 2 and pl. VII, b.

I know the Würzburg oinochoe, no. 45 below, only from a small illustration in *Langlotz*, for it was lost during World War II. Although its details are rather obscured, the recognizable style of the Volterra Caeretan Painter is not entirely obliterated. One of his characteristic features may be seen in the shape of the rock upon which the women sit; the rock is more block-like than thus far noted in the works of preceding painters. He also includes a diadem on his vases which is clearly visible at the forehead of the seated woman on the neck of standard oinochoai.

45. Würzburg, University,
    Martin von Wagner Museum 815
    Height, 33.7 cms.

    NECK: a woman seated to the right with fully laden tray in upraised left hand.
    BODY: barely discernible women at the far left and right to each side of *Eros* who wears beaded necklace and stands facing to the left.

    Beazley, *EVP*, p. 168; *Langlotz*, p. 145 and pl. 236.

46. Aléria, Musée Archéologique 616 c (Pl. 31)
    Provenience, Alalia
    Height, 34 cms.

    NECK: a woman seated to the left with small (egg-shaped) cushion or tambourine in upraised right hand.
    BODY: at the left, a woman moves rapidly to the left while looking back and balancing a tray or chest in upraised left hand. At the right, a youth or satyr (portions of vase missing) stands facing to the left

with right leg raised and foot resting on low stone. His left hand is raised with index finger crooked as if in gesture of speech (see also, vase no. 43 above).

47. Cerveteri, Magazzino (Fig. 1a)

NECK: fragment: woman seated to left. The decorative band at the shoulder contains an ivy pattern in silhouette with leaves alternating to each side of a sinuous stem. Dots have been used for embellishment.

Stamnoi

The stamnoi listed below are identical in shape and basically carry the same subsidiary decoration: egg-pattern at the rim, tongue-pattern on the shoulder, and meander below the picture field. The two stamnoi in the Villa Giulia, nos. 48 and 49, exhibit a relatively unusual rendering of the fan-palmette most frequently found below the handles. Here, the tall central leaf possesses a diamond-shaped tip and the curious core is flatly arched and enhanced with a row of dots. The seated woman on side A of stamnos no. 48 holds the egg-like cushion or tambourine characteristic of the Volterra Caeretan Painter's other vases, whereas the female figure at the opposite side of the vase closely parallels the maenad and woman represented on oinochoai nos. 42 and 46 (Pls. 30–31).

48. Rome, Villa Giulia
    Provenience, Caere
    Height, 33 cms.

    A: at the left, a woman is seated to the right with small egg-like cushion or tambourine in upraised left hand. From the right, *Eros* approaches slowly with long, beaded necklace as gift.
    B: female figure moving rapidly to the left while looking back. *Mesomphalic phialae* in the field to each side.

    Beazley, *Annuario*, p. 145; *MonAnt* XLII (1954) c. 932, no. 32; *AJA* 70 (1966), p. 34, no. 1 and pl. 12, figs. 9–10.

49. Rome, Villa Giulia (Pls. 32–33)
    Provenience, Caere
    Height, 34.6 cms.

    A: at the left, a woman is seated to the right with mirror in upraised left hand. A nude woman approaches from the right with fully laden tray in right hand and necklace with *bullae* in the lowered left hand.
    B: replica of side A.

    Beazley, *Annuario*, p. 145; *MonAnt* XLII (1954), c. 932, no. 31 and figs. 219A and B.

A fragmentary stamnos now stored in the Magazzino at Cerveteri (Pl. 34), but once in the Villa Giulia, closely resembles the work of the Volterra Caeretan Painter. However, there is something finer in the quality of the drawing that suggests this fragment is not by his hand. If it is, it must be one of his very early pieces. The slightly curved short lines to the hem of the garment do, nonetheless, recall a similar treatment on oinochoe no. 42, formerly on the Milano market (Pl. 30). At present, I am not familiar with any vases attributable to the painter of this fragmentary stamnos which would serve to link the style more strongly with that of the Volterra Caeretan Painter.

The meticulous rendering of the chevrons which point to the right in the decorative band below the picture field presents a totally different character than thus far encountered in this common motif of the Dotted-hem Group. On the shoulder, however, a significant motif which associates this stamnos with the Volterra Caeretan Painter may be found in the pointed ivy leaves which alternate to each side of a sinuous stem, like that already noted on the neck fragment of an oinochoe (Shape VII) also in the Magazzino at Cerveteri, no. 47 above (Fig 1).

50. Cerveteri, Magazzino (Pl. 34)
    Fragmentary Stamnos
    Provenience, Caere
    Preserved height, 30 cms.
    The neck is missing.

    A: a woman (*Hecate ?*) moves slowly to the right past an altar on which are four skewers. Her arms are extended out to each side with a long torch in each hand. Carefully painted *mesomphalic phialae* in the field at lower left and top right.
    B: woman like that at side A with no altar, yet a finely drawn *mesomphalic phiale*.

    MonAnt XLII (1954), c. 721, fig. 162A.

The woman represented at each side of this interesting but highly fragmentary stamnos may, by reason of the beribboned *torch* carried in each hand, be *Hecate* and would thereby offer another departure from the more usual themes depicted on Caeretan red-figured vases with figured scenes.

MISCELLANEOUS

This section contains a number of vases which are indisputably products of the Dotted-hem Group but, by reason of their style, are not attributable to the hand of any of the painters treated in the preceding pages. In some cases, however, it is possible at least to relate the vases to one or another of the artists thus far recognized in the Group.

Oinochoai

Although the following two oinochoai closely resemble the work of the Villa Giulia Caeretan Painter, their drawing differs sufficiently to argue against attribution to a single artist. Vase no. 51 (Pl. 35) gains a special importance from the presence of the "dot-stripe" border to the broad band of the maenad represented on the neck. This feature draws attention to South Italian red-figure, particularly Paestan, and will be discussed in more detail in Chapter V because of its obvious relationship to Caeretan fourth-century vase-painting. On this same vase two details are paralleled in the works of several other painters of the Dotted-hem Group whose general styles, however, are markedly different: (1) the block "footrest," already associated with an old satyr on the body of an oinochoe in the Palazzo dei Conservatori by the Sambon Caeretan Painter (vase no. 37); and (2) the wave motif in the decorative band below the picture field as seen on the Würzburg oinochoe by the Brooklyn Caeretan Painter (Pl. 18).

Oinochoe no. 52 (Pl. 36) discloses three new and interesting features: (1) the rocks upon which the women sit are not painted white in the customary fashion, but are simply outlined in white with added decoration in black comprised of dots, small x's, and a flowering plant which can be imagined as growing near the rock; (2) a series of flat "S" motifs placed diagonally in the decorative band below the picture field; (3) a double or single column with ornate capital of *Aeolic* type.[15] This column is placed between the two seated women on the body of the vase, and is rendered partly in added white, and partly reserved with the volute outlined.

51. Rome, Villa Giulia (Pl. 35)
    Provenience, Caere
    Height, 27 cms.

    NECK: maenad moving swiftly to the right while looking back. A *thyrsos* in her lowered left hand; the left arm trails behind. *Mesomphalic phiale* in the field at left below the hand; a quartered ball (?) above.
    BODY: at the center, a woman stands facing to the left with left arm held high and mirror in hand. The far left shows a seated woman to

15. The distinctive variation of the *Aeolic* capital in Etruria has been fully discussed and illustrated by A. Ciasca, *Il Capitello detto Eolico in Etruria* (Florence, 1962).

the left but looking to the right. At far right, an old satyr stands facing to the left with right leg raised and foot placed on curious block-like footrest.

Mesomphalic phialae in the field between figures and floral motifs.

52. Rome, Villa Giulia (Pl. 36)
    Provenience, Caere
    Height, 28 cms.

    NECK: a woman seated to the right with left arm extended and hand balancing a cista.
    BODY: at left and right, to each side of an ornate column, a woman is seated with her back to the column but head turned round to gaze toward her colleague. Each has one arm lowered, the other upraised. The upraised hand of the left-hand woman holds tambourine, that of the right-hand woman a distaff (?).

The following oinochoe in the Villa Giulia, vase no. 53 below (Pl. 32), is reproduced here to illustrate both the degeneration and ineptness of drawing sometimes found on examples of the Dotted-hem Group. An interesting allusion to the "Spotted Rock Group" of Campanian red-figure, as denoted on the neck of the vase by the treatment of the rock upon which the young satyr sits, will concern us later in this study (Chapter V).

53. Rome, Villa Giulia (Pl. 37)
    Provenience, Caere

    NECK: a young satyr sits on a rock facing to the right. He wears a mantle which flows out to the left in a curious manner, and is embellished with parallel rows of black and white dots. In his upraised left hand he holds a mirror, in his lowered right he grasps a beaded bracelet. The rock, reserved and outlined in white, carries black and white "dots."
    BODY: an old satyr, with his left leg raised and foot resting on the strange, blocklike footrest, stands facing to the right. In his extended right hand he holds a *thyrsos*. In front of the old satyr, a woman is seated to the right but looks back at him. A tambourine is held in her upraised left hand. Behind the head of the satyr, there is an unusually rendered hanging *wreath*.

Two additional vases of the Dotted-hem Group, for which I rely solely on incomplete notes made during my initial studies of Etruscan vase-painting, are placed here for the sake of completeness. The oinochoai are replicas of each other, and differ only in the gestures of the young satyrs represented in their figured scenes.

54. Rome, Villa Giulia 50603
    Castellani Collection
    Provenience, probably Caere
    Height, 23 cms. Very poor condition

    NECK: a woman seated to the left with right hand upraised.
    BODY: at the left, a woman is seated to the right with mirror held in upraised right hand. A young satyr stands before her with hands extended in her direction and right knee bent.

    Mingazzini, no. 759.

55. Rome, Villa Giulia 50609
    Castellani Collection
    Provenience, probably Caere
    Height, 23 cms.

    NECK: replica of no. 54 above.
    BODY: replica of no. 54 above with the exception of *thyrsos* in the right hand of the young satyr, and the position of his left arm which hangs down.

    Mingazzini, no. 758 and pl. CCVII, figs. 1–2.

Stamnoi

There is something in the drawing of the old satyr at side A of a stamnos discovered at Caere (no. 56 below) that is strongly reminiscent of the old satyr on the body of oinochoe no. 51 above (Pl. 35). The stamnos and this latter oinochoe may well be by the same hand.

56. Rome, Villa Giulia
    Provenience, Caere
    Height, 34.5 cms.

    A: an old satyr moves to the right with right arm upraised and cushion (?) in his extended left hand. *Mesomphalic Phiale* in the field between his legs.
    B: a naked "maenad" with mantle.

    MonAnt XLII (1954), c. 720, fig. 161A.

Another stamnos, no. 57 below, was also noted during my early studies in Etruscan red-figure. Although I possess no photographs, it is strongly associated with the work of the Florence Caeretan Painter.

57. Rome, Villa Giulia 50669
    Castellani Collection
    Provenience, probably Caere
    Height, 25 cms.

A: *Lasa* moving to the right while looking round. Her left arm is lowered with hand resting on a large round object very likely a shield. The upraised right hand holds a long sash or ribbon.

B: replica of side A.

Mingazzini, no. 748 and pls. CXCIX, fig. 3, CC, fig. 1.

The pattern in the decorative band below the picture field on this last stamnos, no. 57 above, is unusual for Caeretan red-figured vases: a series of touching or abutting triangles which alternate up-and-down rendered with carefully placed parallel lines.

Skyphos

A new shape for the Dotted-hem Group and Caeretan red-figured vases with figured scenes is provided by the following *skyphos* which employs the distinctive dotted-hem on the garment of the maenad depicted at one of its sides. The much damaged representation of the maenad reveals a style of drawing similar to the Villa Giulia Painter during his later phase when he had already abandoned relief-lines. In addition, the young satyr on the opposite side of the skyphos is strongly reminiscent of the satyr on one of the oinochoai discovered at Aléria (vase no. 7 and Pl. 6).

58. Cerveteri, Magazzino 49800 (Pls. 38–39)
    Provenience, Caere
    Height, 23.5 cms.; diam. of rim, 23 cms.

    A: a maenad moves to the right with *thyrsos* in left hand. *Mesomphalic phialae* in the field.

    B: a young satyr faces to the right with left leg slightly raised. In his outstretched hands he holds a tambourine. *Mesomphalic phialae* in the field; crudely rendered *halteres* (?) at the top left.

THE CRESCENT-HEM GROUP

As the name "Crescent-hem Group" implies, the distinguishing feature of the vases assigned to this second arbitrary grouping of Caeretan Red-Figured Vases is found in the small crescent-shaped brushstrokes used to define the lower edge (the *hem*) of the garment at the feet of the women who appear in the figured scenes. These crescents, which denote the folds of the garment, are indicated by the Castellani Caeretan Painter with an outer line in black and an adjoining inner line in white. These are generally represented in groups of four or five, thereby imparting a somewhat agitated look to the folds. As noted earlier, this feature was heralded in one rare instance in the Dotted-hem Group in the work of the Campana Caeretan Painter (vase no. 27 and Pl. 21) and, to a certain degree, on vases by the Volterra Caeretan Painter (e.g., Pl. 30). The artists of the Crescent-hem Group who follow the Castellani Caeretan Painter diminish the number of crescents and also abandon added white paint for embellishment.

Likewise, the fleur de lis, one of the characteristic features of the Caeretan red-figured vases with figured scenes, is already omitted on some vases by the Castellani Caeretan Painter, and missing altogether on vases by subsequent painters of the Group. Whereas the artists of the Dotted-hem Group prefer to indicate the vertical broad band of the garment by parallel lines only, the painters of the Crescent-hem Group first paint a broad black stripe over which a narrower line is then applied in white. None of the three major vase-painters thus far distinguished for the Crescent-hem Group uses the relief line in the main *or* subsidiary decoration, an important feature of technique to be discussed later (Chapter V).

Since, as stated earlier, I feel that the vases of the Dotted-hem and Crescent-hem Groups may actually be products of a single Workshop, the consecutive system of numbering given the Caeretan Red-Figured Vases of the Dotted-hem Group will be continued uninterrupted into the Crescent-hem Group.

THE CASTELLANI CAERETAN PAINTER

By far the most talented and prolific vase-painter of the Crescent-hem Group, having decorated nearly two dozen vases—oinochoai, stamnoi, and a kylix—the Castellani Caeretan Painter clearly demonstrates some of the more careful and detailed aspects of Caeretan Red-Figured Vases. As mentioned in the brief introduction to the Crescent-hem Group, relief-lines have been abandoned altogether, but the lines employed by this artist are so exceptionally fine in his better vases that they could very well be taken for relief-lines in the illustrations.

The striding woman or maenad depicted on the neck of his oinochoai is always shown striding by an altar which is generally laden with offerings—fruits, including pomegranates, and skewered meats. Of special interest are his altars which reveal a conscientious effort at perspective, for the short side is painted in a color contrasting the white frontal portion. In the majority of cases, his satyrs, erotes, etc., carry a beaded necklace as a gift, which is not often visible due to the fugitive nature of the added white paint used to depict the individual beads. There is, nevertheless, a profuse use of white for such details as ribbons, sashes, and vegetal forms in the field, a feature to be shared by the American Academy Caeretan Painter who will be discussed next. The choice of motifs within the decorative bands, when present, conforms to the usual variety—tongue- and egg-patterns, chevrons, or more hastily rendered "c" motifs—as well as a new type composed of alternating meander and crossed-box with dot or dots in each quadrant.

Oinochoai

For the sake of convenience, the oinochoai to follow are listed according to the number and type of figures represented at the neck. The oinochoe most appropriate to be designated the work of the Castellani Caeretan Painter—both because of its size, one of the few very large Caeretan Red-Figured Vases known to me, and the fine quality of its painting—is his name-piece in the Castellani Collection of the Villa Giulia, vase no. 59 below (Pl. 40).

The subject represented on the body of this monumental oinochoe marks one of the rare departures from the usual subject matter on Caeretan red-figured vases with figured scenes. Unmistakenly drawn from Greek mythology, the scene illustrates the Musical Contest between *Aplu* (Greek *Apollo*) and *Marsyas*, a subject well known to Etruscan, Greek, and South Italian vase-painting.[16] Marsyas, who wears an animal pelt painted in white over his shoulder and knotted at his neck, holds one reed of the *aulos* in each hand. A winged female, who in the present context cannot be identified as a *Lasa* but as a *Nike*, bears a wreath in both hands with which she crowns Aplu, the victor of the contest. The lyre of the victorious god is carefully rendered in white, the curved frame terminating in swan-heads, and his *plectrum* upraised as if completing the upward sweep of his final chord. Another noteworthy detail on the neck of the vase, where the reflection in the mirror held by the seated woman (*Turan ?*) is amusingly shown in profile, recalls similar representations on Etruscan mirrors and in South Italian red-figure where it is not uncommon.[17]

16. For the *Contest between Apollo and Marsyas* in vase-painting, see Beazley, *EVP*, pp. 74ff; C. Clairmont, "Studies in Greek Mythology and Vase-Painting," *Yale Classical Studies* XV (1957), pp. 161–178; and K. Schauenburg, "Marsyas," *RömMitt* 65 (1958), pp. 42–46, and "Der besorgte Marsyas," *RömMitt* 79 (1972), pp. 317ff. See also A. D. Trendall, "The Felton Painter," *In Honour of Daryl Lindsay*, pp. 45–46.

17. On Etruscan mirrors, see Gerhard-Körte, *ES* V, pl. 96 and G. Richter, *Greek, Etruscan and Roman Bronzes in the Metropolitan Museum* (New York, 1915), p. 275, no. 799. Although not uncommon on Italiote red-figured vases which show a woman holding a hand mirror, the profile reflection is not always discernible in the illustrations provided in various publications. An excellent example may be seen on the reverse of the calyx-krater by the Dolon Painter in the Cabinet les Médailles (no. 422; Trendall, *LCS*, no. 532); cf. also Boston Museum of Fine Arts, no. 00:348 (*Greek Gods and Heroes*, fig.

WITH SATYR AND SEATED WOMAN AT NECK

59. Rome, Villa Giulia 50668 (Pl. 40)
Castellani Collection
Provenience, probably Caere
Height, 43 cms.

NECK: at the right, a woman is seated and facing to the left with mirror in upraised right hand. Her reflection on the polished surface of the mirror is shown in profile. An old satyr approaches slowly from the left with beaded necklace in his right hand, his left touching the woman's thigh.

BODY: *Aplu* is seated to the right at the center of the scene. His raised right hand holds *plectrum*, the right grasps his lyre. *Marsyas*, as a young satyr, appears at the right facing the god and holds a reed of his flutes (*auloi*) in each hand and wears animal skin tied round his neck. At the far left, a Nike steps forward to crown Aplu with victor's wreath. Carefully rendered petalled flower between the legs of Aplu and Marsyas.

Mingazzini, no. 749 and pls. CCI, figs. 1–3; CCII, figs. 1–3.

The following oinochoe carries the most ornate decorative band to be found on any of the vases by the Castellani Caeretan Painter. Below the picture field, the artist has carefully rendered an alternating meander motif and box with diagonal-cross and dots placed in a triangular pattern within each quarter. Instead of a simple egg-pattern, this vase shows egg-and-dart at the mouth and shoulder.

60. Paris, Louvre K 460
Formerly Campana Collection
Provenience, probably Caere
Height, 48.5 cms.

NECK: at the right, a woman is seated facing to the left with right hand upraised. An old satyr approaches from the left and places his left hand gently on the woman's thigh in much the same manner as his counterpart on vase no. 59 above.

BODY: scene composed of four figures; at the far left, a woman seated to the left turns round to face *Eros* who bears an extended wreath in both hands. Behind him a woman moves to left past an altar where a nude youth stands with *phiale* in his lowered right hand. A mantle

---

15), where a profile reflection occurs in a contest with Marsyas. Normally, the reflection and the "bronze" of the hand mirror are distinguished by the contrast of added white paint and the reserved portion of the disc; see *CVA* Lecce, Museo Provinciale Castromediano 2, pl. 57, fig. 1 and pl. 60, figs. 1 and 3.

painted in white is draped over his left shoulder, round his waist, and up over the left forearm.

The satyr on vase no. 61 below (Pl. 41), like his colleagues on the neck of the preceding vases, gently places his left hand on the right thigh of the seated woman. It is droll to note the rather Gaelic profile that the Castellani Caeretan Painter has given this young satyr. In the decorative band on the shoulder of the oinochoe, a novel motif appears: a series of carefully rendered and evenly-spaced vertical tear-shaped forms left completely reserved. But most important is the subject depicted on the body of the vase, for it too introduces an entirely new theme on Caeretan Red-Figured Vases, namely a chariot drawn by four stags. The charioteer may be identified as *Artumes* (Greek *Artemis*) who appears in a similar context on a vase by the American Academy Caeretan Painter (see Pl. 52),[18] and brings to mind parallels in South Italian red-figure reserved for later discussion (Chapter V).

61. Paris, Louvre K 433 (Pl. 41)
   Formerly Campana Collection
   Provenience, probably Caere
   Height, 42 cms.

   NECK: replica of no. 60 above with exception of a young rather than old satyr.
   BODY: a chariot drawn swiftly to the right by four stags while a small hare, rendered in white, keeps pace beneath the sharp hooves of the animals. The stags are alternately white and spotted. The charioteer is a woman, possibly *Artumes,* who delicately holds reins in upraised left hand, goad in right. The reins and goad are faintly visible.

The four oinochoai to follow, like the three examples listed above, show a satyr in the brief scene on the neck. However, here they are not associated with seated women but appear alone or, in the case of vase no. 62 (Pl. 42), accompanied by two naked youths who aid his drunken steps. This last oinochoe contains two items of special interest: the inclusion of an elaborate incense-burner carried by a youth at the far right on the body of the vase, and the manner of dress for

18. An engraved bronze mirror from Orvieto shows *Artumes,* with her name inscribed, riding "side-saddle" on one of two stags; see Gerhard-Körte, *ES* V, pl. 10. Another mirror in the Villa Giulia, inv. no. 15697, includes a stag amongst four animals which draw a chariot, i.e., stag, griffin, lion and leopard. The four human figures incorporated within the scene are Fortuna, Victoria, Minerva and possibly Jason ("Hiaco"): see "Ulisse," "Tetrologia . . . etruscologia," *StEtr* VI (1932), pp. 555ff and pl. XXXIV, fig. 1. Attention should be called also to a South Italian red-figured vase in the Hermitage with *stag-biga* driven by "Dionysos" and "Ariadne," *ibid.*, pl. XXXV, fig. 3.

carried by a youth and the women between them which differs markedly from that normally encountered on Caeretan red-figured vases.

62. Paris, Louvre Cp 1152 (Pl. 42)
    Formerly Campana Collection
    Provenience, probably Caere
    Preserved height, 42.5 cms.
    Tip of mouth missing.

    NECK: a drunken, obese satyr is supported by two naked youths as they stagger to the left. The old satyr has placed his arms around the shoulders of the youths who entwine their arms behind his back.
    BODY: like vase no. 60 above, the scene is composed of four figures: a mixed couple at the left look to the right toward a woman in *peplos* with extra long *apoptygma* who approaches with wreath or necklace in upraised right hand, and pitcher in lowered left. Behind her a youth who arrives with an elaborate incense-burner (painted entirely in white) grasped in his right hand.

The two vases in Florence, nos. 63 and 64 below, are near replicas of each other in the painted scenes: on the neck, obese satyr with beribboned *thyrsos* in right hand and pointed amphora cradled in his left arm;[19] on the body, a young satyr with gifts standing in front of a seated woman.

63. Florence, Museo Archeologico 4089
    Height, 32 cms.

    NECK: an old obese satyr moves to the left while looking back. A *thyrsos* is held in the right hand, pointed amphora cradled in the left arm. *Mesomphalic phiale* in the field at right.
    BODY: a young satyr at the left stands to the right with left leg raised and foot on low block-like footrest. A beaded necklace dangles from his right hand; a *thyrsos*, faintly visible, is at his left hand. A woman at the right is seated facing him, and holds wreath in her upraised right hand.

    Studi L. Banti, p. 136, no. 2 and pl. XXXIV, b.

64. Florence, Museo Archeologico 4076
    Height, 31 cms.

    NECK: replica of no. 63 above.
    BODY: a seated woman holds mirror or fan in upraised right hand; her left arm cradles a *thyrsos*. A young satyr approaches from the left with wreath in right hand and necklace formed of six *bullae* in his lowered left hand.

    Beazley, *Annuario*, p. 143.

19. For an extremely hairy satyr with amphora see Gerhard-Körte, *ES* V, pl. 42.

The neck of the vase, no. 65 below (Pl. 43), shows a young satyr riding a goat, while no. 66 carries a most common neck decoration, a female figure striding across the picture field. The subjects on the body of the two vases are near replicas: quadriga and charioteer represented frontally, but with chassis of the chariot curiously placed *in front* of the horses (perhaps due to the inability of the Castellani Caeretan Painter to render correctly so difficult a foreshortened composition). Only the protomai of the horses are represented: a pair to each side with the pole-horses facing inward and the trace-horses outward. Within the chassis of the chariot, the female charioteer stands in strict frontal view with both hands upraised to each side. The reins are faintly preserved on no. 65, but not on no. 66 where the charioteer's hands are placed against the heads of the pole-horses in a somewhat "chucking" fashion. Rather than *Artumes*, who drives a stag-quadriga on vase no. 61 above (Pl. 41), this female driver may be *Eos*, the dawn-goddess in her Etruscan aspect. She is shown here with the more "horse-powered" *quadriga*—perhaps borrowed from her superior, *Helios*—rather than her usual vehicle, the *biga.* The chassis of the chariot is decorated with upright rays punctuated by dots and is better preserved on vase no. 65 and no. 66 where it is a more simplified version without dots. The horses were originally painted in white, most of which has disappeared on the latter oinochoe.

65. Paris, Louvre Cp 1201 (Pl. 43)
    Formerly Campana Collection
    Provenience, probably Caere
    Preserved height, 37 cms. Tip of the mouth is missing.

    NECK: a satyr rides a spirited goat to the right. A mantle trails behind from the neck. *Mesomphalic phialae* below the goat which is painted entirely white.
    BODY: frontal quadriga with chassis decorated with rays. Charioteer (*Eos?*) depicted frontally with both arms upraised, reins in hand.

WITH FEMALE STRIDING TO LEFT AT NECK

66. Paris, Louvre K 435
    Formerly Campana Collection
    Provenience, probably Caere
    Preserved height, 40.5 cms. Large portion of the mouth is missing.

    NECK: a woman, preserved only from shoulders down, moves to the left past an altar. Her right arm is upraised, the left trails down behind. *Mesomphalic phiale* at the left.
    BODY: replica of no. 65 above but larger in scale with less space between the charioteer and heads of the pole-horses which she seems to chuck.

AJA 70 (1966), p. 33, no. 4 and pl. 11, fig. 4.

67. Paris, Louvre K (451 (Pl. 44)
Formerly Campana Collection
Provenience, probably Caere
Height, 30 cms.

NECK: a maenad strides swiftly past an altar to the left with *thyrsos* in upraised right hand and *situla* in trailing lowered left. The unusual squat proportions of the maenad may be due to the restricted space created by the thick horizontal fillet near the mouth.
BODY: at the far left, a woman seated to the left but turning round to accept a long, beaded necklace offered by a young satyr who stands facing her with right foot resting on low stone. At the far right, a woman approaches with a *kottabos-stand.*

WITH FEMALE STRIDING TO THE RIGHT AT NECK

68. Rome, Villa Giulia
Provenience, Caere
Height, 33 cms.

NECK: a maenad strides to the left past an altar with *thyrsos* in her lowered and trailing right hand; tambourine in upraised left.
BODY: a nude youth at center faces to the left with long extended wreath between upraised left and lowered right hands. To the left, a woman seated to left turns round, a beaded bracelet in her right hand. At far right, a woman is seated to the left with fan in upraised right hand.

Studi L. Banti, p. 136, no. 1 and pl. XXXIV, a; *AJA* 70 (1966), p. 33, no. 1 and pl. 11, fig. 1.

69. Cerveteri, Magazzino (Pl. 45)
Provenience, Caere
Height, 40 cms.

NECK: a maenad moves swiftly to the right past an altar. A *thyrsos* is cradled in her right arm, wreath in upraised left hand. Petalled flower at the left.
BODY: at the left, a woman seated to the left while looking round. A tambourine in her upraised right hand. Approaching from the right, an *Eros* with extended arms, right down and left up, and long, beaded necklace between his hands.

MonAnt XLII (1954), c. 778, fig. 173.

A good example of hasty and slovenly painting which presents difficulty in attribution is illustrated by the representation on the neck of vase no. 70 below. If it were not for the analogies that are possible for the figures on the body with those on no. 69 above (Pl. 45), the vase could easily have been considered a poor imitation of the work of the Castellani Caeretan Painter. However, the oinochoe is his. The rectangularly shaped cushion held by the seated woman on the neck recalls that depicted on vase no. 74; and the woman with tambourine on the body of the Cerveteri specimen, vase no. 69 (Pl. 45), is nearly identical. With minor variation and addition of *alabastron*, the figure of *Eros* on the Tarquinia vase closely resembles his counterpart on the latter vase.

70. Tarquinia, Museo Nazionale 1002
    Provenience, Tarquinii
    Height, 37 cms.

    NECK: a woman seated to the left with unusually large pillow held in upraised right hand.
    BODY: a woman seated at the left is a replica of her counterpart on no. 69 above. *Eros*, who approaches from the right, holds an *alabastron* (painted in white) in his left hand, his right hand held high.

71. Florence, Museo Archeologico 4135 (Pl. 46)
    Height, 40 cms.

    NECK: a woman strides to the right past an altar. A *phiale* is held in the lowered right hand, a fully laden tray or basket in the extended left. *Mesomphalic phiale* at left.
    BODY: at the center, a woman is seated to right with long-stemmed *unguentarium* in her upraised left hand. In front of her stands a young satyr with gift of long, beaded necklace. To the far left and behind the seated woman, *Eros* with beribboned *thyrsos* stands facing to the right.

    Beazley, *Annuario* p. 144 where "4195" should be corrected to "4135."

72. Cerveteri, Magazzino (Fig. 2)
    Preserved height of neck only, ca. 17 cms.

    NECK: a maenad striding to the right past an altar with *thyrsos* in lowered right hand and tambourine in raised left.

WITH STRIDING MALE FIGURE ON THE NECK

73. Florence, Museo Archeologico 4134
    Height, 39 cms.

    NECK: *Eros* moving to the right past altar. His arms are down to the sides. In the right hand he holds *phiale*, in the left a *situla* or basket.
    BODY: at the center, a woman is seated to the left and holds an object in her upraised right hand which may have originally been a mirror or *unguentarium* (as on vase no. 71 above). A young satyr approaches from the left with right hand high, left low. At the far right behind the seated woman, a nude youth with mantle over his left shoulder,

round his waist, and up over the left forearm recalls his counterpart on vase no. 60 above.

WITH SEATED WOMAN ON THE NECK

The women seated in solitude on the necks of the oinochoai listed below are very similar to their sisters on vases nos. 59–61, with the exception of the objects held in their upraised right hands.

74. Paris, Louvre K 456
    Formerly Campana Collection
    Provenience, probably Caere
    Height, 32 cms.

    NECK: a woman seated to the left with large cushion supported by up-raised right hand.
    BODY: a woman seated to the left between a young satyr (at the right) and *Eros* (at the left) who offers a large wreath with both hands.

    AJA 70 (1966), p. 33, no. 3 and pl. 11, fig. 3.

75. Paris, Louvre K 449
    Formerly Campana Collection
    Provenience, probably Caere
    Height, 40 cms.

    NECK: replica of no. 74 above. Petalled flower at the left.
    BODY: a young satyr stands at the center with right foot resting on a low block-like footrest. His left arm up, right held down. Before him sits a woman facing left, but turning round to accept a beaded neck-lace no longer preserved. At the far right behind the satyr, a woman moves away with *phiale* in upraised right hand, *situla* or basket in low-ered left hand. *Mesomphalic phiale* in the field at left.

    AJA 70 (1966), p. 33, no. 2 and pl. 11, fig. 2.

The two following examples are mere fragments: no. 76 (Fig. 3), frag-mentary neck only; no. 77, fragment of neck and portion of body. It is indeed a pity that so little remains of the latter oinochoe, for its drawing—with care-fully rendered egg-and-dart pattern at the shoulder—ranks among the finer works of the Castellani Caeretan Painter.

76. Cerveteri, Magazzino (Fig. 3)
    Provenience, Caere
    Preserved height of neck only, 15 cms.

    NECK: a woman seated to the left with fully laden tray balanced in upraised right hand. Petalled flower in the field to the right.

77. Cerveteri, Magazzino
    Provenience, Caere
    Preserved height, ca. 25 cms.

    NECK: a woman seated to the left with upraised right hand. Petalled
    flower at the right.
    BODY: extant: young satyr standing to the right, and a maenad with
    thyrsos moving to the right at the far right.

Stamnoi

The Castellani Caeretan Painter employs the two basic stamnos-types already encountered in the Dotted-hem Group, that is, on high foot or on flat
ring base. In addition, the join of handle to body of the Louvre stamnos, no. 81
below, brings to mind the "hand-like" character noted on the stamnoi of the
Sambon Caeretan Painter (nos. 38–39; e.g., Pl. 26).

78. Rome, Villa Giulia (Pls. 47–48)
    Provenience, Caere
    Height, 32 cms.

    A: at the left, a maenad moving to the right with *thyrsos* in lowered
       right hand, and upraised left hand grasping a large wreath also
       held by the right hand of an obese old satyr with wineskin slung
       over his left shoulder.
    B: old satyr at left, moving to the left, with *thyrsos* in right hand and
       small calyx-krater balanced on the palm of his left hand. At the
       right, a woman approaches the old satyr with right hand upraised
       and left hand at a missing portion of the stamnos.

The obese old satyr at side A of this last vase (Pl. 47) doubtless belongs
to the same family as the old satyrs on the necks of oinochoai, nos. 62 (Pl.
42), 63, and 64 above.

79. Tarquinia, Museo Nazionale RC 4797 (Pl. 49)
    Provenience, Tarquinii
    Height, 37.5 cms.

    A: at the right, a woman moves toward a young satyr at left to accept
       from him a beaded necklace which he offers with his right hand.
    B: replica of side A.

The following stamnos bears such an interesting and novel theme for a
product of Caeretan red-figured vase-painters—an Etruscan *Skylla*—that I was
prompted to publish the vase in a separate and special study once the unique vase

came to my attention.[20] On the shoulder of the stamnos, the Castellani Caeretan Painter has chosen a wave pattern which, thus far, is unique but most appropriate for the dreaded monster of the sea.

80. Paris, Louvre K 416 (Pl. 50)
    Formerly Campana Collection
    Provenience, probably Caere
    Height, 28.2 cms.

   A: the sea-monster *Skylla* moving to the right with wreath in up-raised left hand and her attribute, a *rudder* brandished as a weapon in her upraised right hand. She is nude to the waist where the fish tail begins with leafy growth from which springs the protomai of three fierce and awesome dogs.
   B: replica of side A but heavily encrusted.

   ArchCl XXI (1969), p. 210 and pl. LXVI.

The voracious character of the dog-protomai with their inherent frightful bark, springing forth from the leafy girdle at Skylla's waist, adds to the fierce aspect of the sea-monster, and cannot fail but summon up the apt descriptions of Skylla in Vergil (*Aeneid* III, 426ff) and Ovid (*Metamorphoses* XIII, 730ff). The combination of *fish* and *dog* in the representation of Skylla has interesting overtones in *"pesce cane,"* the Italian for "shark," which is a predatory sea crea-ture still feared by fishermen.

81. Paris, Louvre K 420
    Formerly Campana Collection
    Provenience, probably Caere
    Preserved height, 31 cms. Ring base portion of the vase is missing.

   A: a maenad, with *thyrsos* in her trailing and lowered left hand, strides to the left.
   B: replica of side A, but shows a beaded bracelet in the upraised right hand.

   AJA 70 (1966), p. 33, no. 5 and pl. 11, fig. 5.

82–83. Cerveteri, Magazzino (Fig. 4)
    Fragments of two stamnoi

   Kylix

The cup listed below, vase no. 84 (Pl. 51), is unquestionably by the hand of the Castellani Caeretan Painter and marks one of only two speciments of this

20. M. Del Chiaro, "Skylla on a Caeretan Red-Figured Vase," *ArchCl* XXI (1969), pp. 210–215.

shape known to me for Caeretan red-figured vases with figured scenes. The second kylix is treated as "miscellaneous" because I am not certain whether it is by his hand or by the painter to follow. The decorative band which sets off the medallion on the "Preyss" kylix duplicates one found below the picture field on stamnos no. 78 above (Pls. 47–48). I know nothing about the exterior or dimensions of this kylix from either the description or the illustration.

84. Formerly Munich, Adolf Preyss Collection (Pl. 51)
German Archaeological Institute, Rome,
Photographic Archives, negative no. 60.432.

I: maenad striding to the right past an altar; her bent left arm balances a pillow, the lowered right holds a beribboned *thyrsos*. Setting off the medallion is a decorative band with alternating meander and crossed-box with a single dot in each quadrant; white dots are found in the center of some meanders and crossed-boxes.

Beazley, *EVP*, p. 167 and pl. XXXVIII, fig. 1; *Studi L. Banti*, p. 137, no. 5; *AJA* 70 (1966), p. 34, no. 9.

THE AMERICAN ACADEMY CAERETAN PAINTER

A second painter in the Crescent-hem Group, the American Academy Caeretan Painter, though not as prolific as the Castellani Caeretan Painter, is closely related in style; eleven oinochoai and a single stamnos are attributable to his hand. In general, the subjects represented on his vases closely follow those already distinguished for the Castellani Caeretan Painter, including the unusual stag-drawn chariot, with variation, on the Villa Giulia vase no. 85 below (Pl. 52).

The striding women of the American Academy Caeretan Painter do not move past an altar as do the women of the Castellani Caeretan Painter. In general, his figures are more animated and he has a conspicuous fondness for long ribbons and sashes. A characteristic difference between these two painters is noticeable in the rendering of the folds on the garments at the breasts of the women. The Castellani Caeretan Painter acknowledges the existence of breasts by the configuration of the folds, whereas the American Academy Caeretan Painter makes no effort to suggest the breasts but renders the folds in bold, downward parallel strokes.

Of primary significance, the fleur de lis is omitted from the garments of his women with one or two exceptions, and the crescents on the hems become exaggerated arches over the feet, with only a few smaller crescents indicated between them. In sharp contrast to the white rocks preferred by the Castellani Caeretan Painter, the present artist paints a far less anvil-shaped variety. On the whole, the work of the American Academy Caeretan Painter is more hasty and less exact in its detail.

For his decorative bands at the mouth, shoulder, and below the picture field of oinochoai, the American Academy Caeretan Painter draws on a variety of known motifs. Tongue- or egg-pattern is generally used for the shoulder, whereas the mouth area receives either no decorative band, or one with an egg-pattern or simple series of dots. Below the picture field, including his stamnos in the Palazzo dei Conservatori, vase no. 96 below, the decorative band may carry dots, chevrons facing either left or right, or a reserved band which may contain one or two horizontal lines.

Oinochoai

The listing of oinochoai according to the number and type of figures represented at the neck, as followed for the Castellani Caeretan Painter, will prove equally convenient for oinochoai by the American Academy Caeretan Painter.

WITH FEMALE STRIDING TO LEFT OR RIGHT

The subject of the body of vase no. 85 below (Pl. 52) recalls an oinochoe by the Castellani Caeretan Painter (Pl. 41), which also shows a stag-drawn chariot, but with a *quadriga* rather than *biga* as depicted here by the American Academy Caeretan Painter. The stags are especially well drawn and painted entirely white with some details, indicated by diluted glaze-paint, still preserved. The antlers of the stags on the oinochoe by the American Academy Caeretan Painter are more delicate and ornate—almost floral in character—as compared to those painted by the Castellani Caeretan Painter. As noted for the stag-chariot vase by the latter painter (no. 61), *Artumes* might be identified as the charioteer on the stag-chariot vase by the American Academy Caeretan Painter. It is interesting to find a strong suggestion of landscape-setting in the continuous rocky terrain in the background. If the chariot were conceived as racing across the skies—as those customarily driven by gods and goddesses—it would then seem highly probable that the painter intended to show a distant mountainous topography.

85. Rome, Villa Giulia (Pl. 52)
    Provenience, Caere
    Height, 31.5 cms.

    NECK: a woman moving swiftly to the left while looking back. In her lowered right hand she holds a sash, the right arm trails behind. *Mesomphalic phialae* in the field at right.

BODY: *Artumes* driving a stag-drawn *biga* to the left across rocky landscape. *Mesomphalic phialae* in the field.

86. Populonia, Antiquario
    Provenience, Populonia
    Height, 32 cms.

    NECK: a woman striding to the left while looking back. In her upraised left hand she holds tambourine. A *mesomphalic phiale* below left forearm.
    BODY: a young satyr, standing to the left with right foot raised and resting on a stone, offers beaded necklace to a woman seated at the left. Behind the satyr, a woman moves away swiftly while looking back. Her upraised right hand holds a beaded bracelet.

    NSc 1957, p. 39, fig. 62, right.

87. Aléria, Musée Archéologique 946a (Pls. 53–54)
    Provenience, Alalia
    Height, 42 cms.

    NECK: a woman striding rapidly to the left while looking back. In each hand, the left upraised and the right lowered, she carries a long sash. *Mesomphalic phiale* at the right.
    BODY: at the center, *Eros* faces to the left with sash in lowered right hand. His wings are outstretched to each side. To the right and left, a woman is seated with her back to the satyr, but turning round to look toward him. *Mesomphalic phiale* in the field between *Eros* and woman at right.

88. Vatican, Museo Gregoriano Etrusco Z 126
    Height, 33 cms.

    NECK: a woman striding to the right with right hand upraised, left lowered. *Mesomphalic phiale* at left.
    BODY: a young satyr at the center moving to the left with *thyrsos* in his lowered right hand. At far left, a woman seated to left but turning round to offer bowl or tray to the satyr. At the far right, a woman moves away as on vase no. 86 above.

    Beazley, *Annuario*, p. 144 where given as "X 21"; Trendall, *VIE* pl. LXV, h.

89. Florence, Museo Archeologico 81915 (Pl. 55)

    NECK: a woman striding rapidly to the right while looking back. In her upraised right hand she holds long sash.
    BODY: *Eros* at the center and facing to the right with right hand up, left down. To each side, a woman is seated with her back to him but turning round to gaze at him. Each woman has one arm upraised.

NSc 1905, p. 58 in fig. 5; *Minto*, pl. LX in fig. 3; possibly Beazley, *Annuario*, p. 145, no. "4119."

Vase no. 90 below shows signs of repainting on the eyes and contours of the horses, as well as on the facial features of the figures.

WITH SEATED WOMAN TO LEFT OR RIGHT

90. Paris, Louvre K 437
Formerly Campana Collection
Provenience, probably Caere
Height, 34.5 cms.

NECK: a woman seated to left with tambourine held in upraised right hand.
BODY: two unharnessed horses moving to the left. At the far left, a naked youth races up to hinder and soothe (by petting and chucking) the lefthand horse. At the right a *Lasa* (?), but here perhaps *Nike*, stands facing the spirited horses.

91. Vatican, Museo Gregoriano Etrusco Z 124
Preserved height, 32 cms. Much of the front portion of the neck is missing.

NECK: only the lower third of the woman seated to the left is extant.
BODY: *Eros*, with outstretched wings to each side of his body, moves slowly to the right. To each side and facing him, is a woman with one arm upraised.

Beazley, *Annuario*, p. 144 where given "X 23"; Trendall, *VIE*, pl. LXV, g.

92. Populonia, Antiquario
Provenience, Populonia
Height, 32 cms.

NECK: a woman seated to the right with large, fully laden tray balanced in her upraised left hand.
BODY: at the center, a young satyr with *thyrsos* in his left hand and unidentifiable "gift" dangling from his right hand. To the far left, a woman moves swiftly to the left with long sash between her lowered hands. At the right, a woman runs toward the satyr. *Mesomphalic phiale* between head of the right-hand woman and tip of *thyrsos*.

NSc 1957, p. 39, fig. 62, left.

93. Cerveteri, Magazzino
Provenience, Caere
Preserved height, 35 cms. Much of the front portion of the neck is missing.

NECK: only half of the woman seated to the right is extant.
BODY: a young satyr at the center moves slowly to the left with *thyrsos* in his left hand held diagonally across his body. To each side and seated away from him, a woman turns to gaze at him. The arms of the left-hand woman are down, whereas her colleague shows upraised left hand.

With Satyr and Seated Woman

94. Rome, American Academy 1839 (Pl. 56)
    Height, 38.5 cms.

    NECK: at the right, a woman is seated to the left with arm extended toward a young satyr who approaches slowly from the left.
    BODY: composed of four figures; at the far left, a woman is seated to the left but turns round to gaze and reach toward a young satyr who moves slowly in her direction. At the right, another woman is seated to the right, but turns to look at the young satyr just mentioned while ignoring a second young satyr who stands before her with right leg raised and foot resting on a high stone.

Oinochoe no. 95 below is most fragmented, the neck totally missing and the base restored.

95. Aléria, Musée Archéologique 763b
    Provenience, Alalia

    NECK: missing
    BODY: at the left, a woman is seated to the right with her left hand upraised. From the right, *Eros* approaches with left arm extended and right lowered.

Stamnos

At least one stamnos known to me is a product of the American Academy Caeretan Painter. It stands on a foot, its handles placed very near the shoulder.

96. Rome, Palazzo dei Conservatori 130
    Height, 31 cms.

    A: at the left, a woman is seated to the left but looking round toward a young satyr who moves off to the right. The right hand for each figure is upraised. A *mesomphalic phiale* in the field between them.
    B: badly worn surface which shows a woman striding to the right while looking back.

THE PAINTER OF BRUSSELS R 273

This Caeretan painter received his name from Sir John Beazley after an oinochoe (Shape VII) in Brussels, vase no. 97 below. Together with a replica in the same collection (vase no. 98 below, Pls. 57–58), Beazley associated three other oinochoai in a preliminary grouping (*EVP*, p. 167f.) which was later augmented by five more specimens (*Annuario*, p. 144f.). Of these vases attributed to the Painter of Brussels R 273 by Sir John, I have retained the original two oinochoai and reassigned the others throughout Caeretan Red-Figured Vases.

On the replicas in Brussels and the oinochoe at Viterbo, no. 100 below, the Painter of Brussels R 273 employs the usual subjects of Caeretan red-figured vases with figured scenes—maenads, satyrs, women and youths. On the Louvre and Rome specimens, however, he represents deities which, with one exception, have not previously been encountered (Turms on vase no. 1 by the Villa Giulia Caeretan Painter, Pl. 1); new to the repertory of Caeretan Red-Figured Vases are *Menrva* (Greek *Athena*) and *Hercle* (Greek *Herakles*).

In his choice of decorative bands, this painter of the Crescent-hem Group shows novelty, best seen in the "bracketed" dot motif below the picture field on the Brussels vases. On the other hand, the up-and-down "L" motif, although rare, is employed on a vase by the Villa Giulia Caeretan Painter (*Painter of Würzburg 817*, see Pl. 12). Likewise, the elaborate alternating meander and crossed-box visible on the Rome oinochoe, vase no. 101 (Pl. 60), was also used by the Castellani Caeretan Painter for a stamnos (Pl. 47) and a kylix (Pl. 51).

An additional decorative feature of unique character is on the mound-shaped rock of the Louvre oinochoe (no. 99 below) upon which a woman is seated: a net pattern created by cross-hatching is rendered in finely painted dark lines on the original white paint. The fleur de lis, already abandoned on a majority of vases by the American Academy Caeretan Painter, is entirely omitted by the Painter of Brussels R 273. All the vases by his hand known to me are oinochoai, Shape VII.

Oinochoai

The following two vases, including his name-piece, are replicas and carry, as mentioned above, a motif in the decorative band below the picture field which is new to Caeretan Red-Figured Vases: a series of large "bracketed" dots.

97. Brussels, Musées Royaux d'Art et d'Histoire R 273
    Height, 28 cms.

    NECK: a young satyr walking slowly to the left with *thyrsos* in low-
    ered left hand.
    BODY: at the left, a maenad has moved past an altar. In her upraised
    right hand, a *thyrsos*; a tambourine in the left. At the right, an effemi-
    nate youth with both hands held low and close together, moves to the
    right, but turns his head to the left toward the maenad.

    Beazley, *EVP*, p. 167; *CVA* fasc. 2, IV Be pl. 1, 10.

98. Brussels, Musées Royaux d'Art et d'Histoire R 274 (Pls. 57–58)
    Height, 28.5 cms.

    NECK: replica of no. 97 above.
    BODY: replica of no. 97 above.

    Beazley, *EVP*, 167; *CVA* fasc. 2, IV Be pl. 1, 8.

The bodies on oinochoai nos. 99 and 100 (Pl. 59) below share a common
theme: seated woman and satyr, "young" on the former, "old" on the latter.
The satyr's pose, with right leg raised and foot on a low, block-like "footrest,"
is not new, but the figure receives a somewhat more animated character than
hitherto encountered on vases discussed in this study. This may be due to the
more pronounced forward crouch of the satyr and the gesture of the hands
which display a beaded necklace, clearly preserved on vase no. 99 but "fugitive"
on no. 100.

Vase no. 99 is of particular interest for the representation of the god,
Turms, who holds a long staff-like *caduceus* and is naked except for high boots—
painted in white—long mantle, and *petasos* slung at the back of his neck.

99. Paris, Louvre Cp 1176
    Formerly Campana Collection
    Provenience, probably Caere
    Height, 29 cms.

    NECK: *Turms* standing to the left with *caduceus* held in his upraised
    right hand, beaded bracelet in his lowered left. He is naked except
    for high boots, mantle, and petasos which is hanging at the back of
    his neck.
    BODY: at the left, a woman seated to the left but looking back. Both
    hands are upraised, *thyrsos* in right, mirror in left. At the right, an old
    satyr stands with right foot on low stone, his hands extended to offer
    gift of beaded necklace. In the field between woman and satyr is an
    ornate dotted-rosette.

AJA 70 (1966), p. 34, no. 1 and pl. 12, fig. 8.

100. Viterbo, Museo Civico 336/33 (Pl. 59)
   Anselmi-Rossi Danielli Collection
   Height, 27.5 cms.

> NECK: a woman standing to the left with elaborate fan in upraised
> right hand. She is dressed in *chiton* and *himation* with right arm
> akimbo under the himation.
> BODY: at the left, a woman seated to the left but turning round with
> fan in upraised left hand. A young satyr stands at the right with his
> right leg raised and foot on low stone. Both of his hands are extended
> as if to offer beaded necklace no longer visible. The decorative hori-
> zontal band below the picture field is unusual.

The following vase in Rome, no. 101 (Pl. 60), deserves special investigation and publication because of the unusual character of its composition and
subject.[21] The conscientious effort to space the figures on the body of the oinochoe,
and the strong allusion to the sculptural prototypes Pheidian and Polykleitan
in the representations of *Menrva* and *Hercle*, have given this vase added
importance.

101. Rome, Palazzo dei Conservatori 115 (Pl. 60)
   Height, 35 cms.

> NECK: a youth stands with body to the right but head turned to left.
> He is naked except for a mantle which runs knee-high across the front
> of his body. His right hand is upraised, the left near his left hip.
> BODY: *Hercle* wearing lion skin and resting his club on the right shoul-
> der, left hand down to his side. To the left, *Menrva* stands majestically
> with both arms lowered; her left hand rests on the shield against the
> left leg, the right hand holds a faintly visible spear positioned di-
> agonally across her body. To the right, a woman (*Hebe?*) stands
> facing the two deities. She holds a mirror in her upraised left hand,
> the right hangs down.

> *BullCom* 1911, pp. 69ff.; Beazley, *EVP*, p. 173; *AntCl* XXXIX
> (1970), pl. 1.

MISCELLANEOUS

The vases listed below, oinochoai of the familiar shape VII and a single kylix,
clearly belong to the Crescent-hem Group by the characteristic treatment of
the female garment—with the exception of the kylix which shows satyr only.
Because the style of their drawing does not fit precisely with the work of the

---

21. M. Del Chiaro, "A Caeretan Red-Figured Vase by the Painter of Brussels R 273," *AntCl*
   XXXIX (1970), pp. 41–45.

previously distinguished painters, the vases must be considered somewhat apart, but nevertheless associated with some works of the preceding artists of the Crescent-hem Group.

Vases nos. 102 and 103 are not too far from the work of the Castellani Caeretan Painter, whereas the oinochoe no. 105 and the kylix no. 106 show something of both the Castellani and the American Academy Caeretan Painters.

Oinochoai

Oinochoe no. 102, with some signs of repainting, reveals the more careful nature of the Castellani Caeretan Painter, best seen in his rendering of the altar at the neck and various details and general aspects of composition on the body. The five-figured composition is unique and marks the largest number of individuals depicted on the body of a vase attributable to Caeretan Red-Figured Vases. Admittedly, there is a greater vigor and animation to the figures than known for the Castellani Caeretan Painter, but the unusual scale of the figures may have been necessary in order to include so many into one scene. Irrespective of these qualities, the vase recalls the Louvre oinochoe, no. 62 (Pl. 42) by the Castellani Caeretan Painter. Distinctively new to Caeretan red-figured vases with figured scenes are the heraldically arranged goats which stand on their hind legs to each side of the striding maenad at the neck of the vase.

102. Rome, Palazzo dei Conservatori 273
Preserved height, 40 cms. Top portion of the mouth is missing.

NECK: at the center, a maenad moves to the left past an altar with *thyrsos* in lowered left hand and tambourine in raised right. To each side, with their backs to the central figure, two goats stand on their hind legs.
BODY: composed of five figures; at the center, a woman moves to the right carrying *phiale* (?) and *situla*. To her right are a young satyr, with animal-pelt mantle and thyrsos, and woman seated on a stone seat or altar. At the far left, an old satyr, with right leg raised and foot on low stone, faces a woman who is seated on a stone "bench."

Vase no. 103 below exhibits the rather short and squat proportions to the figures already encountered on the Louvre oinochoe, no. 67 (Pl. 44) by the Castellani Caeretan Painter.

103. Florence, Museo Archeologico 4029
Height, 32 cms.

NECK: woman seated to the left with right hand upraised.
BODY: a maenad with *thyrsos* in right hand and tambourine in left moves toward an altar which is placed at the center of the scene.

From the right, a young satyr approaches with *phiale* in his right hand, *thyrsos* in his left.

The oinochoe in Tarquinia, no. 104 below, is difficult to attribute to either the Castellani or American Academy Caeretan Painters and therefore may stand somewhere between. On the neck, a lethargic figure carries a long sash in the manner of women by the American Academy Caeretan Painter.

104. Tarquinia, Museo Nazionale 904
    Provenience, Tarquinii
    Height, 29 cms.

NECK: a woman walks listlessly to left with long sash between up-raised right hand and lowered left.
BODY: at the right, a woman seated to the right with upraised left hand holding a beaded bracelet. Before her, *Eros* moves away with wings outstretched to each side of his body.
CVA fasc. 1, IV B, pl. 2, fig. 2.

Although the following oinochoe in Madrid, no. 105 below, shows something of the character noted for the last vase, it is conspicuously different.

105. Madrid, Museo Arqueológico 11480
    Height, 36 cms.

NECK: maenad striding to the left past an altar with *thyrsos* in low-ered left hand, cushion or tambourine in upraised right.
BODY: at the right, a maenad moves past altar to her right. In lowered left hand she carries *thyrsos*, the right is raised. At the left, a young satyr stands with left leg raised and foot on low stone. He offers beaded necklace with outstretched hands.

ArchEspArq XXXIX (1966), p. 91, fig. 2.

Kylix

The cup no. 106 below (Pl. 61), and that by the Castellani Caeretan Painter (Pl. 51), are the only examples of kylikes thus far known for Caeretan red-figured vases with figured scenes. The following vase is not as well preserved as the kylix discussed earlier, for the handles are missing and only half of its bowl is preserved. Fortunately, however, at least three-quarters of its medallion remains. In this case, there are no crescents to serve as clues for attribution to the Crescent-hem Group. Nevertheless, there are qualities of both the Castellani and American Academy Caeretan Painters in the drawing and, for the former, the petalled flower so frequently encountered on his vases.

106. Rome, Palazzo dei Conservatori 547 (Pl. 61)
Height, 9 cms.; diam., 22.5 cms.

I: an old satyr, semi-crouched so that the contours of his back follow
that of the medallion, faces to the left. Petalled flower in the field
below his extended left hand. Sash or mantle in the field at top right,
rocks at lower right. The medallion is set off by a simple, narrow
reserved band.

UNIDENTIFIED GROUP

To this section will be assigned vases which are very closely related in style
to those of the two preceding Groups. Attribution is primarily based on the
presence of the broad vertical band on the female garment, and not by the rendering of the hem, for none of the vases displays dots or crescents. Even though
oinochoe no. 107 (Pl. 62) by the Frontal Satyr Caeretan Painter shows a dotted
hem, I do not believe it properly forms part of the Dotted-hem Group because
the dots appear at the edge of the *mantle* rather than the *peplos*. Furthermore,
the style of drawing on any of the following oinochoai does not suggest a direct
similarity with the preceding vases. Since three vases (nos. 107–109) show the
style of a single hand, I have not hesitated to individualize the artist whom I
have named the Frontal Satyr Caeretan Painter.

THE FRONTAL SATYR CAERETAN PAINTER

Three oinochoai, of which two are the familiar Shape VII and the third a
standard trefoil type, are decorated by an artist named after the strange satyr
who is depicted in an unusual frontal pose on the Louvre vases. This wild,
droopy-eared creature with double-flute brings to mind an Etruscan bronze mirror engraved with a woman—not a satyr—playing a double-flute in a crudely
rendered frontal pose which is particularly uncommon in late Etruscan art.[22]
The surface of the Louvre vase no. 108 is badly worn and encrusted, but nevertheless reveals the god *Aplu* (Greek *Apollo*) with his lyre. Hence, it is safe
to assume that the satyr is *Marsyas* and that once again the celebrated Musical
Contest between *Aplu* and *Marsyas* has been chosen as the chief decoration for
Caeretan red-figured vases with figured scenes (cf. oinochoe no. 59 by the Castellani Caeretan Painter, Pl. 40). On the evidence of this last vase, the musical
satyr on the Louvre vase no. 107 may very well be *Marsyas*.

22. Gerhard-Körte, *ES* V, pl. 48.

Oinochoai

The rendering of the hem for the woman who dances vigorously, to judge by the billowing nature of the lower portion of her garment, is unusual for its decoration: long, bold, dart-like forms or rays recall a more subtle appearance on an oinochoe by the Villa Giulia Caeretan Painter of the Dotted-hem Group (Pl. 3).

107. Paris, Louvre K 447 (Pl. 62)
     Formerly Campana Collection
     Provenience, probably Caere
     Height, 31.5 cms.

     NECK: woman dancing and twirling to the right with arms out to the sides and long branch in right hand.
     BODY: at the left, frontal satyr playing double-flute. A couple at the right shows a young satyr standing to the right with left foot raised and facing a woman who is seated to the left. Over her *peplos* and lower part of the body, she wears *himation* with dotted hem. In the upraised hands of this latter young satyr and women are faint traces of branches or some floral / vegetal forms.

108. Paris, Louvre K 467
     Formerly Campana Collection
     Provenience, probably Caere
     Height, 31 cms.

     NECK: at the left, a satyr (*Marsyas?*) playing double-flute, who is rendered frontally as the satyr on the body of vase no. 107 above. A maenad moves off to the right with *thyrsos* in her right hand.
     BODY: at the center, *Aplu* with lyre flanked by two naked youths, possibly satyrs.

Trefoil Oinochoe

The trefoil oinochoe, no. 109 below (Pl. 63) is the first such specimen encountered for Caeretan red-figured vases with figured scenes, but known for another Caeretan production, that of the Torcop Group (Pl. 82) to be discussed in Chapter II.

109. Florence, Museo Archeologico 81909 (Pl. 63)
     Provenience, Populonia

     At the center, *Eros* faces to the right with his left leg raised and foot resting on a high stone. Facing him at the right is a woman seated to left with right hand upraised. Behind him, a woman is seated to the left but turns round to gaze in his direction. *Mesomphalic phiale* in the field between *Eros* and woman at left. Broad decorative band above the picture field with tongue-pattern embellished with white lines.

NSc 1905, p. 58, fig. 5; *Minto*, pl. LX, fig. 3.

MISCELLANEOUS

The following vases stand conspicuously apart from the foregoing examples and, particularly in the case of no. 110 below, reveal a marked degeneration and barbarization in the work of the Caeretan red-figured painters.

Oinochoe

110. Rome, Museo di Villa Giulia
Provenience, Caere
Height, 21.2 cms.

NECK: a maenad walking slowly to the left past a high altar. A *thyrsos* is cradled in her left arm, the right hand upraised.
BODY: at the right, a woman is seated to the left. An altar appears between her and a young satyr who approaches from the left with beaded necklace between outstretched hands. Sashes, painted in white, hang in the field.

MonAnt XLII (1954) c. 928, fig. 218.

The bracketed dots in the horizontal decorative band seem to resemble subsidiary decoration by the Painter of Brussels R 273 (see vase no. 100, Pl. 59).

Stamnos

I am somewhat uneasy about the attribution of the following stamnos, vase no. 111 below, to Caeretan red-figured vases. However, on the evidence of the hands of the satyr, which recall those of the satyr on a stamnos from the same tomb at Caere and placed within the Dotted-hem Group (miscellaneous, vase no. 56), the stamnos may well be a product of one of its painters.

111. Rome, Villa Giulia
Provenience, Caere
Height, 31 cms.

A: an old satyr about to caress a nymph who is more willing to accept the advances of the satyr than does her counterpart at Side B.
B: similar scene of old satyr and nymph who, in this instance, attempts to ward off the satyr's advances.

MonAnt XLII (1954), c. 722, fig. 163A.

SUMMARY

Although not intended as absolute, the arrangement and sequence of discussion for Caeretan Red-Figured Vases was presented in the preceding sections according to what I believe is the general course of development within the respective Groups. Evidence for contemporaneous or overlapping production is provided by the Campana and Volterra Caeretan Painters of the Dotted-hem Group, whose vases reveal an awareness and interrelationship with the Crescent-hem Group through the *crescents* suggested at the hem on their vases (see Pl. 21 and Pl. 30), and the general fondness for white detailing in the field for the Volterra Caeretan Painter, as seen in the floral / vegetal forms. The choice of vase-shapes, the general configuration and similarity of subjects, and the types of "filler" in the field—all commonly shared by the Dotted- and Crescent-hem Groups—clearly disclose the strongly interknit character of the Caeretan red-figured vases with figured scenes. Hence it seems reasonable to assume that the vases assigned to the Dotted-hem, Crescent-hem, and "Unidentified" Groups forms an integral part of a single Caeretan Workshop.

Of the two chief Groups, the Dotted-hem Group is by far the more prolific in number of artists and products, accounting for more than half, fifty eight, of the one hundred odd vases attributed to the Caeretan Workshop. At least forty-eight examples are thus far known for the Crescent-hem Group, and the remaining vases are within the "Unidentified" Group. In range of time, I believe the activity of these Caeretan Groups, or better, "Workshop," does not exceed one generation of artists, and that the vases were produced within a relatively short space of time. The noticeable contrasts and differences in the quality of drawing are more likely due to the relative skill of the vase-painters than to their "chronological" position.

The preferred vase-shape for Caeretan Red-Figured Vases is unquestionably the oinochoe (Shape VII), followed by the stamnos with high foot or ring base. A detail of special significance to establish a working chronology for Caeretan red-figured vases with figured scenes and its related Caeretan products is found in the gradual abandonment of the *relief-line technique*. It has been pointed out that relief-lines were already falling into disuse in the Dotted-hem Group as, for example, on vases by the Villa Giulia Caeretan Painter. For the Crescent-hem Group, on the other hand, there is a conspicuous absence of relief-lines altogether. The chronological importance of this change in technique will be discussed in a more appropriate section of this study devoted to chronology (Chapter VI).

II

〓〓〓〓

Vases with Female Heads
in Profile

IN STUDYING Caeretan red-figure vase-painting, my attention was first drawn
to the rather monotonous theme of a female head rendered in profile which,
with the exception of four or five among hundreds of specimens, faced to the
left. As mentioned earlier, the investigation of Genucilia plates led to the recognition of a Caeretan Branch for the Genucilia Group as a whole. Once Caere
was established as the center of production for one branch of the Genucilia
Group, the environmental studies evolving from it helped to broaden knowledge
of the productivity of its ceramic workshops to a point which has led to the
present study. From the information amassed during investigation of the Genucilia Group, there quite naturally followed a detailed study of the oinochoai of
the Torcop Group which, through their association with the Genucilia Group,
suggested Caeretan fabrication. The head covering for the women differs markedly in type between the Genucilia and Torcop Groups. Characteristic for women
on *Caeretan* Genucilia plates is the "half-sakkos," so described by me in the past
but better designated henceforth as a *sphendone.* On vases of the Torcop Group
and assorted shapes associated by similar head covering, I have and—for the
sake of convenience—will continue to use the term "full-sakkos"[1] to designate
a *kerkryphalos* which contains the hair except for a broad strand at the forehead,
a loose tress dangling at the temple, and a dense lock that escapes freely from a
hole at the top or back of the head (see Pls. 78–79).

1. Although *kerkryphalos* would be technically correct, I retain the term "full-sakkos"
   because it has been consistently used throughout my earlier publications.

THE GENUCILIA GROUP

The name applied to the plates of the Genucilia Group,[2] normally stemmed and decorated with a female head in profile ("Head plate," see Pls. 64–66 and Fig. 13b) or a design of geometric character ("Star plate," see Pl. 67), is derived from one example bearing under its foot the dipinto, *P. Genucilia*. Approximately six hundred specimens were studied and listed in my original publication for the group which, from their style of drawing, fell into two main subgroups, a division which the proveniences confirmed.[3] The distribution of the "finds" revealed that plates decorated in one of these styles was centered in *Caere*, the other at *Falerii Veteres*. Accordingly, the plates were assigned respectively to the Caeretan or the Faliscan branch of the group, with the exception of a few plates classed as "Falisco-Caeretan" in recognition of their Faliscan provenience and their Caeretan appearance (Fig. 20).[4] This last classification has taken on a new and not surprising significance in the present study of Caeretan Red-Figured Vases because it offers an interesting analogy to be discussed later in some detail (Chapter V).

The sphendone type most commonly represented by the painters of the group is a "net," simulated by a cross-hatched pattern (see Pls. 64–65) or, more rarely, a cloth with "embroidered" designs based on those found in Caeretan star plates (e.g., Pl. 67).[5] In addition to the sphendone, a *diadem*—the rendering of which was crucially important for the attribution to individual painters and workshops of the group—generally carried two "spikes" (more in the earlier specimens).

The dimensions for the average Caeretan Genucilia plate range between 13 to 15 cms. in diameter and 4 to 6 cms. in height. They stand on a foot— "stemmed"—although a few examples of smaller dimensions are known which are "flat" and rest on a ring base. At their exterior (Fig. A), the plates are simply decorated: the turned-down lip and the rim of the foot are painted black,

FIG. A. Caeretan Genucilia plate. Typical profile.

2. *Genucilia Group.*   4. *Ibid.*, Chapter II.
3. *Ibid.*, Chapter VIII.   5. *Ibid.*, Chapter V.

and a broad black band encircles the underside of the "bowl." The medallion is bordered by a flattish rim which is ornamented with a wave motif; six to seven individual waves are the most common number, but there are more in earlier than in later examples (compare Pl. 64 with Pl. 65).

Since the publication of *Genucilia Group*, many examples of Caeretan Genucilia plates—both head and star variety—have come to light in scattered archaeological excavations which have augmented the number of sites known to have disclosed these very common Caeretan products. These plates have been published or mentioned in various appropriate archaeological journals, chiefly the *Notizie degli Scavi*, and will doubtless continue to appear periodically as excavations are conducted in regions consistent with their distribution (see Maps of Distribution in *Genucilia Group*; see also the *frontispiece* and Table of Proveniences, Chapter IV).

Some of the "new" sites or proveniences of Caeretan Genucilia plates are of special interest: Roselle,[6] Aléria (Alalia),[7] Pyrgi,[8] Santa Marinella,[9] and Alba Fucens.[10] This latter provenience, in addition to Cosa,[11] will be reconsidered in the light of a revised dating of the Genucilia plates which I found necessary since the publication of *Genucilia Group* (cf. *Caeretan Figured Group*, p. 36).

Because of their unusual decoration, two specimens of the group deserve special attention: the first (Fig. 5) was discovered during the summer of 1965 in a "pozzo" within the *Regia* by the American Academy excavation in the Roman Forum;[12] the second plate (Fig. 6) was known to me during the initial

6. *StEtr* XXXIII (1965), fragment of Head plate, p. 165, inv. 1761 and pl. XLIX; fragment, p. 176, inv. 2006 and pl. LII.

7. The current French excavations at Aléria conducted by Professor Jean Jehasse (University of Lyons) have brought to light a considerable quantity of Genucilia Group plates, all of which belong to the Caeretan branch of the group, together with a goodly number of Caeretan red-figured vases with figured scenes (see Index of Collections). I am very grateful to Professor and Madame Jehasse for information and photographs of their Caeretan finds, and the kindness extended me during my visit to Aléria (ancient *Alalia*).

8. See G. Colonna in *NSc* 1959, pp. 231 and 234.

9. A fragment of a Caeretan Genucilia Group Star plate with dotted-chevron discovered in the "Santuario di Punta della Vipera" (Santa Marinella) is exhibited in the Museo Nazionale at Civitavecchia.

10. *AntCl* XXIII (1954), p. 100, fig. 15, 2 and p. 373, figs. 23, 1–3.

11. *MAAR* XXV (1957), p. 74, A4, and pl. I, A4.

12. I wish to thank Professor Frank E. Brown, Director of the American Academy in Rome excavations in the *Regia* (Foro Romano), for calling to my attention the eight Caeretan Genucilia Group plates—including the extremely interesting "Fufluns" specimen—

investigation of the Genucilia Group, but has not been hitherto published.[13]

A stemmed plate with seven waves encircling its flat rim (Fig. 5) carries a subject indeed rare in Etruscan as well as Greek vase-painting. It was discovered in the *Regia* together with seven other Caeretan Genucilia plates—three with heads and four with stars (see the Index of Collections). The theme, as I shall attempt to illustrate, treats an episode from the life of *Dionysos* (Etruscan *Fufluns*) which is best known pictorially through the celebrated sixth century eye-cup in Munich (Staatliche Antikensammlungen, inv. no. 2044) by the Attic black-figure master, *Exekias*. This unusual Caeretan Genucilia plate once again represents the *Sea Voyage of Fufluns*: the god is kidnapped by Tyrrhenian pirates whom he turns into dolphins (Homer's *Hymn* VII).

Rendered in strict silhouette style, "Fufluns and the Pirates" is represented on the *Regia* Caeretan Genucilia plate within the medallion which is surrounded by the usual, but in this "nautical" instance very appropriate, Genucilia Group wave pattern. A prow of a large ship is seen sailing to the left across a sea indicated by four gracefully undulating rows of dots—varying from large on the top row to small on the bottom—which forms the *exergue* of the medallion composition. Characteristic of ancient Mediterranean ships, a large eye is painted on the prow, as well as a snake-like form above the eye, and a birdlike element above the eye to the left of the "snake." Three round shields "hang" near the rail at the right.

Five figures are seen at the railing; the foremost in position and size, and thereby the most important figure of the group, is shown with his right arm extended and "holding" a *dolphin* by its tail. This figure I take to be *Fufluns*. The metamorphosis of the pirates into dolphins is already taking place—but not completed as on the Munich kylix by Exekias—for one of the captors has been transformed into a dolphin in the right hand of *Fufluns*, while the remaining pirates await a similar fate. Just as Exekias followed the Homeric *Hymn to Dionysos*, the Caeretan vase-painter alluded to the grape-vine—an attribute of the god—which sprouted from the ship's mast. On the Regia Genucilia plate, a vegetal form can be seen extending its branches at the upper right, presumably "growing" from the mast which is "off-medallion" to the right.

Curiously, the style of the drawing on the *Regia* Genucilia plate leaves

---

discovered in "Well no. 7, South Pozzo" of the *Regia*. I am especially grateful for his kind permission to publish the "Fufluns" plate in this study.

13. At the time of my *Genucilia Group* researches, the plate was known to me from storage in the Villa Giulia and duly recorded; see *Genucilia Group*, p. 287, no. 7.

much to be desired and, paradoxically, is more appropriate to Italo-geometric vases of the eighth and seventh centuries B.C. than to Etruscan vase-painting of the late fourth century B.C. This stylistic anachronism may be due to the Caeretan vase-painter's cognizance of just such "geometric" vases of "remote" age which could have been unearthed in the environs of Caere during his time. However, it may be argued that a closer parallel, more "chronologically" consistent with the Genucilia plate, is found in the *aes grave* of the Roman Republic, which shows a ship's prow as a device.[14] This analogy presents a problem of dating which is more appropriately considered later in this study (Chronology, Chapter VI).

The second Caeretan Genucilia plate of unusual character is basically a star plate, but with curious additions to three of the four quadrants created by the star pattern (Fig. 6). It was last in the Magazzino at Cerveteri and carried no inventory number. At first glance, the small and crudely painted profile heads found in the quadrants appear fraudulent. Surprisingly, however, close examination reveals the entire decoration of the plate to be authentic.

I do not believe that the profiles, two of which are bearded males and the third a youth or perhaps woman, were actually intended as conscientious caricatures by a skilled painter, but were rendered more in the spirit of a "doodle" by a Caeretan Painter of star plates who may have become a trifle bored by his normal routine.

Although the decoration in the medallion and on the rim of the following stemmed plate (Fig. 7) differs from that on the two previous examples, it should be placed here in view of its characteristic Genucilia Group shape. Instead of the usual wave pattern, the rim of the plate carries an elaborate ivy with dotted-triangle motifs rendered in silhouette. Within the medallion, the sketchy drawing of a bearded satyr head in profile to the left reveals the distinctive style of the Brooklyn Caeretan Painter. He has already been recognized for vases with figured scenes and is also responsible for the terracotta "cista" to be discussed later in this chapter (Pl. 88).

Parma, Museo Nazionale di Antichità C. 108 (Fig. 7)
Height, 5.5 cm.; diam. of rim, 16.2 cms.

CVA fasc. 2, IV B, pl. 10, figs. 1–2, where the plate has been rightly associated by Rossignani with the Castellani terracotta cista by the Brooklyn Caeretan Painter.

14. For pertinent naval types, see S. Paglieri, "Origine e Diffusione della Navi Etrusco-Italiche," *StEtr* XXVIII (1960), pp. 109ff.

The unusual outline treatment of the profile heads on these last two Caeretan Genucilia Group plates (Fig. 6 and Fig. 7) shares something in common with the drawing to be found on Campanian *kemai*, a subject reserved for discussion in Chapter V.

THE TORCOP GROUP

The name "Torcop" was given to the Group by Beazley after examples of oinochoai in Toronto and Copenhagen. These oinochoai (Shape VII) are decorated with female heads in profile on the neck and body: one facing to the left at the neck, and two confronting each other on the body (Pls. 68–72). They are shown wearing a full-sakkos with a small opening at the top which permits a lock of hair to escape freely (Fig. B1). The twenty examples brought together by Beazley[15] have been augmented by more than fifty oinochoai in my special study of the Torcop Group.[16] Since then, the number has increased periodically.[17]

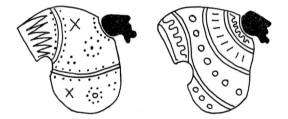

FIG. B. Generalized full-sakkos type. 1. Caeretan. 2. Faliscan.

In the earlier discussion of Caeretan Red-Figured Vases, three oinochoai by the Villa Giulia Torcop Painter (vases no. 16 and Pl. 14, nos. 17 and 19) and vase no. 20 by the Brooklyn Caeretan Painter, which carry the characteristic Torcop Group profile on the neck but figured scene on the body, clearly illustrate the strong link between the Torcop Group and Caeretan red-figured vases with figured scenes. Additional clues for the interrelationships between

---

15. Beazley, *EVP*, p. 168f (eight examples); *Annuario*, pp. 24ff (nine examples); *Fest.AR*, p. 13 (three examples).
16. *Torcop Group.*
17. See *ArchCl* XII (1960), pl. XI, fig. 2; *RömMitt* 67 (1960), pl. 10, fig. 4; *AJA* 65 (1961), pl. 31, fig. 3; *Études et Travaux* IV (1970), p. 7, fig. 4, p. 8, figs. 5–6, p. 9, figs. 7–8, and p. 11, fig. 9; and *AJA* 74 (170), pl. 73, figs. 1–2.

these two Caeretan groups are found in the common "filler" motifs used in the field—hanging wreath and *mesomphalic phialae* ("paterae"); compare vases by the Florence and Volterra Caeretan Painters (Pl. 23 and Pl. 30) with oino-choai by the Brussels Torcop Painter (Pl. 72) and the Populonia Torcop Painter (Pl. 70) who is the most prolific artist of the Torcop Group.

Since publication of *Torcop Group*, four oinochoai (Shape VII) have come to my attention which deviate from the decoration normally found on vases of the Group but which, nevertheless, properly belong to its workshop. Although they have received special treatment in two individual articles,[18] the oinochoai are listed here for the sake of completeness. One example (Fig. 8), because of the unique appearance of *Eita* (Greek *Hades*) in Caeretan red-figure, deserves a brief recapitulation.

The following oinochoe in Limoges carries the expected confronting female profiles on the body. On the neck, however, an upright palmette is substituted for the usual single profile head. The presence of palmette on the neck recalls contemporary Faliscan red-figured oinochoai which, because of their general similarities, were investigated together with vases of the Torcop Group, and classified as the Faliscan "Barbarano Group."[19] Attribution of the Limoges vase to a recognized artist of the Torcop Group is not difficult, for the relaxed and cumbersome style is certainly that of the Pennsylvania Torcop Painter.

1. Limoges, Musée 78.93 (Pl. 73)
   Formerly Campana Collection
   Provenience, probably Caere
   Height, 26 cms.

   CVA, Limoges, pl. 20, 5 and 6; *AJA* 74 (1970), p. 39f. and pl. 73, fig. 2: correct "Populonia" to Pennsylvania Torcop Painter.

The second Torcop Group oinochoe of special interest is in Warsaw; the composition of its decoration conforms to usual Torcop Group practice with the vase somewhat apart.

2. Warsaw, National Museum 140471
   Height, 31.4 cms.

   NECK: female head in profile to the left with hair contained by a hair-net embellished with beading.

18. M. Del Chiaro, "Some Unusual Vases of the Etruscan Torcop Group," *Études et Travaux* IV (1970), pp. 6–12 and "Two Unusual Vases of the Etruscan Torcop Group: One with Head of *Eita* (Hades)," *AJA* 74 (1970), pp. 292–294.
19. In *Torcop Group*, pp. 159ff.

BODY: confronting profile heads of a young satyr and female who wears the usual embroidered full-sakkos. Between the heads, an upright triangle with rows of black and white dots.

Etudes et Travaux IV (1970) p. 6 and p. 7, fig. 4.

On this vase, only faint traces remain of the white paint originally used for the flesh color of the woman. Consequently, such details as mouth, eye, eyebrow, nostril, ear, and jewelry, as well as the characteristic wavy tress of hair near the ear are barely discernible or missing altogether. The head of the young satyr is adorned with diadem or wreath painted in white, its loose or trailing ends daintily tied about his horsey-ear. The juxtaposition of confronting female *and* satyr profiles on the body of oinochoai (Shape VII) is not without precedent in Etruscan red-figure,[20] but such juxtapositioning is new to Caeretan. Like the Limoges oinochoe (Pl. 73), the Warsaw vase can be attributed to the Pennsylvania Torcop Painter.

The third oinochoe of characteristic Torcop Group Shape VII, is particularly intriguing for the bearded head with animal-skin cap represented on the body of the vase.

3. Paris, Louvre K 471 (Fig. 8)
   Formerly Campana Collection
   Provenience, probably, Caere
   Height, 34.5 cms.

   NECK: female head in profile to the left with hair (including bun) completely contained by a hairnet embellished with beading.
   BODY: confronting profiles; at the left, a female with hairnet similar to that at the neck of the vase; at the right, a bearded male wearing animal-skin (wolf) cap.

   Etudes et Travaux IV (1970), p. 8 and fig. 6; *AJA* 74 (1970), p. 292f. and pl. 73, fig. 1.

At first glance, the bearded head with animal-skin cap may be interpreted as that of *Hercle* (Greek *Herakles*), a hero already encountered on a Caeretan red-figured vase with figured scene (see the Painter of Brussels R 273, vase no. 101 and Pl. 60). Close examination and comparison with figures wearing similar animal-skin caps in specific well known Etruscan monuments, has convincingly revealed that the bearded male wears *wolf-skin* rather than the lion-skin cap of *Hercle*. In this case, a better identification for the bearded male is *Eita* (sometimes *Aita*). Of the three excellent Etruscan parallels, in the *Tomba*

20. On a contemporary Faliscan red-figured oinochoe (Shape VII), see *ibid.*, pl. XVI, fig. 12a.

Golini I,[21] on the *Torre San Severo Sarcophagus*[22] at Orvieto, and the *Tomba dell'Orco* at Tarquinia,[23] the last example presents the closest analogy. On this evidence, I believe there can be no question that the bearded head with wolf-skin cap on the Louvre oinochoe is *Eita*, and thereby leads to an interesting conjecture that the female companion, in this instance, may be intended as his consort, *Phersipnai* (Greek *Persephone*). It is encouraging to encounter such a stimulating departure from the usual repertory in some specific groups of Caeretan red-figure, for it instills new life to the otherwise monotonous theme of decoration.

A fourth but fragmentary specimen of Torcop Group workmanship, by reason of its sketchy style of painting, has prompted reconsideration of an oinochoe which did not properly fit into the general scheme of the Torcop Group and was subsequently classified by me as "North Etruscan."[24]

4. Orbetello, Antiquario Comunale 256
Provenience, Orbetello
Preserved height, 10.5 cms.

NECK: missing
BODY: shoulder missing. Confronting profile heads. At the right, head of young man (unbearded) facing female head at the left. She wears a sakkos which contains the hair but for a few loose tresses at the ear and back of the neck. The earring is a simple button with concentric circle and central dot.

Etudes et Travaux IV (1970), p. 11 and fig. 9.

The style of drawing for this Orbetello vase is superior to that generally encountered on vases of the Torcop Group. Surprisingly, for stylistic analogies, one must turn not to Torcop Group Painters but to Caeretan artists who decorated Genucilia plates, for example, the Carthage Genucilia Painter (Pl. 64).[25] Note

21. *Giglioli*, pl. CCXLV.
22. F. De Ruyt, *Charon, Démon Étrusque de la Mort* (Brussels, 1934), no. 103, fig. 41. *Giglioli*, pl. CCCXLVIII, 1; R. Herbig, *Die jüngeren etruskischen Steinsarkophage* (Berlin, 1952), no. 73, pl. 36; L. Banti, *Il Mondo degli Etruschi* (Rome, 1960), pl. 104, bottom. Although the authenticity of the Torre San Severo Sarcophagus has been recently challenged—see D. von Bothmer and J. Noble, "Etruscan Terracotta Warriors," *Papers of the Metropolitan Museum of Art*, no. 11 (1961), p. 8 and M. Gagiano de Azevedo, "L'Autenticità del Sarcofago di Orvieto da Torre San Severo," *RömMitt* 77 (1970), pp. 10–18—the major portion of details, etc., is well founded.
23. *Giglioli*, pl. CCXLVIII, 3; M. Pallottino, *Etruscan Painting* (Geneva, 1952), p. 111; L. Banti, *op. cit.*, pl. 96.
24. *Torcop Group*, p. 156, no. 2.
25. *Genucilia Group*, pp. 255ff and pls. 18f and 19a–b.

in particular, the rendering of the profile eye, the linear character of the nose with its sharp tip, and the crisp yet sensitive treatment of the mouth which is deeply undercut between lower lip and chin. Nonetheless, a conspicuous difference is noticeable in the depiction of the ear.

Knowledge of the Orbetello oinochoe has brought a more proper focus to the following vase in Florence which, in the context of the Torcop Group investigation, was classified with a query as "North Etruscan." This vague attribution was, I must confess, based rather tenuously on stylistic resemblances with vases assigned by Sir John Beazley to "Volterrae" and attributed by him to the "Nun Painter."[26] The Orbetello vase with its sketchy style has called attention to the Florence specimen; these two may be favorably compared for affinities with the general style disclosed by the Warsaw and the Louvre (Fig. 8) Caeretan oinochoai just treated. Two major features to be considered are: the absence of the full-sakkos which normally characterizes oinochoai of the Torcop Group, and the generous use of diluted glaze-paint in the spontaneous drawing of some of the heads.

5. Florence, Museo Archeologico 4043

NECK: bareheaded female profile to left.
BODY: bareheaded female profiles confronting each other with large altar between them. *Mesomphalic phialae* or quartered-balls in the field.

Torcop Group, p. 156, no. 2; *Etudes et Travaux* IV (1970), p. 10 and p. 9, fig. 8.

ASSORTED VASES

In addition to the plates of the Genucilia Group and the oinochoai of the Torcop Group, I have been able to attribute to Caeretan vase-painters of the second half of the fourth century B.C. a goodly number of vases of varying shapes which carry one or more female heads in profile for their decorative theme. As mentioned at the outset of the present study,[27] these Caeretan examples have been published in a series of short papers, each devoted to a specific given shape: kylix, hydria, epichysis, mug, etc. Substantial evidence for attribution to Caeretan vase-painters was provided by the style of the profile and, more emphatically, by the type of head cover worn by the women.

26. Beazley, *EVP*, p. 128 and pl. XXIX, figs. 7–10.
27. See, *Introduction*, n. 3–6.

As noted for the women of the Torcop Group, the normal head cover is the full-sakkos (Fig. B1) which is generally decorated (embroidered) with two bands bordered by a series of dots or dashes, one running from the ear to the back of the sakkos, the other curving upward from above the ear to the top of the head. Additional "embroidery" is found in the dotted-rosettes, dotted-triangles, crosses and the like which are placed within the portions marked off by the bands. At the forehead appears a diadem painted in yellowish-white which I have termed "comb-diadem" because of its tooth-like configuration. At the top of the sakkos, an aperture permits a loose lock of hair to escape freely. For the sake of convenience and completeness, some of the assorted vase shapes treated in earlier studies and a number of newly discovered specimens are brought together in this section.

LARGE PLATES

A large plate with low ring base discovered at Tarquinii discloses an extension of the Caeretan Genucilia Group style to vases other than the small stemmed variety. The already poor drawing has been further barbarized by the incompetent modern repainting which awkwardly places the nostril and the eye too far forward.

1. Tarquinia, Museo Nazionale RC 2839
   Provenience, Tarquinii
   Height, 8 cms.; diam., 31.5 cms.

   Repainting of the eye, eyebrow, mouth and nostril. Very faint traces of the original eye and eyebrow are visible to the right of the repainting.

In a sense, the large Tarquinia specimen can be considered a "super" Genucilia plate because of its consistency in the type of sphendone of common net variety, and the presence of an encircling wave pattern on the flattish rim. This plate and the following two examples reveal a significant feature shared in common, namely, holes at the rim above the head for suspension which were made *before* firing.

The second large plate received attention in the original study of the Genucilia Group, at which time the conspicuous difference between the sakkos type and that utilized by the Caeretan Genucilia painters was pointed out.

2. Vienna, Kunsthistorisches Museum 4035
   Height, 4 cms.; diam., 28.4 cms.

   Genucilia Group, p. 316f. and pl. 28b.

White paint has not been used to indicate the flesh color of the woman on the Vienna plate, but is used for the comb-diadem, the fillet which binds the loose hair at the aperture of the sakkos, and for the elliptical blobs between the individual waves of the rim decoration. There can be no question that the Caeretan artist responsible for the large Vienna plate also decorated Genucilia plates. Previously, an example by the Tarquinia Genucilia Painter has been compared with the Vienna plate (*Genucilia Group*, pl. 28a).

A third specimen (Fig. 9), which has been previously reported by me as a "kylix,"[28] is, I now believe, better regarded as a large plate similar in general shape to the preceding two examples. Although it is a mere fragment of its original size, one of the two holes for suspension is still visible. The fragment, together with a number of Caeretan Genucilia head and star plates, was discovered on the Palatine where they are now located in the *Antiquario*. In her early and excellent study of the archaeological evidence of the Forum environs, Inez Ryberg has called it "Faliscan."[29] However, as I have later attempted to show, it is a product of Caeretan vase-painters.

KYLIKES

Amongst the various shapes of red-figured vases decorated with figured scenes, the *kylix* has been noted on only two occasions (see Pls. 51 and 61). Among Caeretan painters who prefer female heads in profile as the standard decoration, however, the kylix enjoys considerably more popularity. The kylikes here listed all bear a female profile facing to the left in their medallions and can be divided according to the type of head cover. For example, some specimens are directly related to the Genucilia plates, and some more analogous to the Torcop Group—that is, with sphendone or full-sakkos.

With Sphendone

The kylikes, nos. 1 and 2 below, are obviously by two different artists and are clearly the products of Genucilia painters. An earlier classification based on the nature of their decoration,[30] "Caeretan Genucilia Kylikes," will be retained to designate appropriately the particular style of their decoration.

1. Hollywood, Collection Dr. N. Neuerburg (Pl. 75)
   Height, 7.4 cms.; diam., 16.2 cms.
   MAAR XXVII (1962), p. 207 and pl. IV, figs. 14–15.

28. *MAAR* XXVII (1926), p. 206, n. 9.
29. I. S. Ryberg, *An Archaeological Record of Rome* (Philadelphia, 1940), pl. 24, fig. 125b.
30. *MAAR* XXVII (1962), p. 217f.

2. Berkeley, Robert H. Lowie Museum of Anthropology 8/2301 University of California
Height, 8 cms.; diam., 22 cms.

The greater portion of the bowl is missing, yet most of the female head in the medallion is preserved.
The exterior carries a pattern similar to no. 1 above: a wave motif to the left.

Genucilia Group, p. 319f. and pl. 30; *MAAR* XXVII (1962), p. 207 and pl. IV, figs. 12–13.

I have been unable to attribute either of the last two kylikes to any specific Genucilia Group painter; let it suffice to place the two specimens within the overall workshop of the Caeretan Genucilia Group.

With Full-Sakkos

Although the sakkos type on the following two kylikes changes from the sphendone to the full-sakkos, there can be no doubt that they are both the work of a Caeretan Genucilia artist, most probably the Ostia Genucilia Painter.[31] The kylikes, now in the Magazzino at Cerveteri, are quite fragmentary and without inventory number. Their decorations are replicas of each other except for the choice of motif in the decorative band which encircles the medallion: a meander pattern for vase no. 3, and an egg-and-dart pattern for vase no. 4. Neither kylix shows the use of white paint for either flesh color or decorative embellishment.

3–4. Cerveteri, Magazzino
Provenience, Caere

Genucilia Group, p. 320 and pl. 31b; *MAAR* XXVII (1962), p. 204f. and pl. III, fig. 9.

THE CAERETAN KYLIX PAINTER

Because the four kylikes listed below are the work of a Caeretan artist who is known to me exclusively from these four specimens, he shall be named the Caretan Kylix Painter. In these vases alone, it is possible to trace the painter's style from relatively good to excessively poor. As noted for kylikes nos. 3 and 4 above, the Caeretan Kylix Painter makes no use of white paint for the flesh color but, in sharp contrast, does employ white to enhance the decoration of the sakkos and decorative bands for vases nos. 5, 7, and 8, and for the varied "filler" motifs in the field on the latter two specimens.

31. *Genucilia Group*, p. 261 and pl. 19e.

5. Rome, Villa Giulia
   Provenience, Caere
   Height, 9 cms.; diam., 23.4 cms.

   MonAnt XLII (1954), c. 931, no. 35, fig. 220; *MAAR* XXVII
   (1962), p. 203f. and pl. I, fig. 3.

6. Rome, Palazzo dei Conservatori 346 (Fig. 10)
   Height, 8.2 cms.; diam., 21.8 cms.

   MAAR XXVII (1962), p. 203f. and pl. I, figs. 102.

7. Paris, Louvre 1101

   Ibid., p. 208 and pl. V, fig. 16.

8. Paris, Louvre K 499 (1103)

   Ibid., p. 208 and pl. V, fig. 17.

Of the four kylikes by the Caeretan Kylix Painter above, I know the exterior decorations for only nos. 5 and 6. Both carry a black laurel or olive spray which runs from the handle zone toward the center of the vase (see Fig. 10), and thereby differs markedly from the wave pattern preferred by the painters of the Caeretan Genucilia kylikes, nos. 1 and 2 above (see Pl. 75). The cups with a laurel or olive motif around their exterior are interestingly analogous to a kylix represented as hanging on a peg on the left pillar in the *Tomba dei Rilievi* at Cerveteri (Fig. 11), a tomb which has been variously dated between the fourth and third centuries B.C. by different scholars.[32]

There remains one more Caeretan kylix which deserves to be included in the present listing.[33] The rendering of the head is conspicuously and notably different from any of the preceding examples for white paint is used for the flesh color of the female profile. This feature, together with the presence of the full-

32. See *MAAR* XXVII (1962), p. 204.
33. Having become far more familiar with Caeretan red-figured vase-painting since publication of *Genucilia Group*, I wish to withdraw from consideration as "Caeretan," the kylix in Rome (Museo di Villa Giulia, inv. no. 43972) which appeared in *Genucilia Group*, p. 320 and pl. 31a; see also *NSc* 1924, p. 190f and fig. 7, and *Giglioli*, pl. CCLXXVIII, 7. Although special details of the sakkos, hair, etc., suggest Caeretan production, there are certain inconsistencies which I now find difficult to explain. Furthermore, the provenience "Vignanello" in the *Ager Faliscus* is acceptable for a Faliscan vase but would mark a unique appearance for any Caeretan product. If an explanation may be attempted, very tentative and tenuous at that, the Vignanello kylix may provide a rare instance when a Faliscan red-figured painter displayed any interest in or influence from Caeretan vase-painting.

sakkos, brings the Tarquinia kylix into closer relation with the Torcop Group than any of the previously discussed kylikes.

9. Tarquinia, Museo Nazionale 977
   Provenience, Tarquinii
   Height, 7.5 cms.; diam., 17 cms.
   MAAR XXVII (1962), p. 206f. and pl. III, figs. 10–11.

Repainting of the eye and eyebrow prevents attribution of the Tarquinia kylix to any of the recognized painters of the Torcop Group, one of whom is certainly responsible for this cup. Like the Caeretan Genucilia kylikes, nos. 1 and 2 above, the Tarquinia kylix is decorated at its exterior with a wave pattern, and a large dot has been added between each wave.

SKYPHOI

Three skyphoi, one large specimen (Pl. 76) and two slightly less than half that size (kotylai), are assuredly products of the Villa Giulia Torcop Painter.

1. Barcelona, Museo Arqueológico 608 (Pl. 76)
   Provenience, Ampurias
   Height, 26 cms.; diam. of rim, 25.5 cms.
   Mended in antiquity.
   A: confronting female profile with full-sakkos. Between the heads a
      hanging wreath and *mesomphalic phiale.*
   B: the same but greatly restored.
   ArchEspArg XXXIX (1966), pl. p. 93, figs. 5–6; *CVA* 1, pl. 36,
   fig. 2.

The style of drawing on the Barcelona skyphos demonstrates the more hasty and careless character of the Villa Giulia Torcop Painter and is remarkably close to that found on a mug with knotted handle in Paris, oinochoe, Shape VIII B (Pl. 83), which may actually be by this painter.

On the other hand, the two small skyphoi—one discovered at Orbetello (Pl. 77) and the other at Caere—display the more careful nature of the Villa Giulia Torcop Painter. The smaller scale of these skyphoi probably limited the number of profile heads to one at each side, rather than the two confronting heads seen on the larger Barcelona skyphos.

2. Orbetello, Antiquario Comunale 257 (Pl. 77)
   Provenience, Orbetello
   Height, 11 cms.; diam. of rim, 9 cms.

A: female profile with full-sakkos to the left. Back portion of the sakkos restored.

B: the same, but face missing in the restoration.

3. Cerveteri, Museo Nazionale Cerite 6712 (?)
Provenience, Caere
Height, 9.5 cms.; diam. of rim, 9.7 cms.
Fragmentary but restored.

A: female profile with full-sakkos to the left.
B: the same.

Since all of the facial details on these last two cups are missing or obscured, owing to the fugitive nature of the white paint used for the flesh color, we must turn to the long-handled cup in Kassel by the Villa Giulia Torcop Painter (Pls. 78–79) in order to find convincing analogies for attribution. Regardless of the absence of facial details, the Orbetello and Cerveteri skyphoi can be properly assigned to the same hand. Note, for example, the general outline of the profile head itself, as well as the configuration and embroidery of the full-sakkos.

LONG-HANDLED CUPS

Of the three long-handled cups listed below, no. 1 has already been linked to the last mentioned skyphos. On all three examples which stand on a ring base, the handles are placed horizontally with slight upward curve. The characteristic female head in profile, wearing full-sakkos and facing to the left, appears three distinct times on each of these cups: once at either side of the exterior, and once within the deep medallion. All heads are rendered with flesh color in white.

1. Kassel, Hessisches Landesmuseum T545 (Pls. 78–79)

Genucilia Group, p. 317 and pl. 29, a and c; *AJA* 65 (1961), p. 56f. and pl. 32, fig. 5.

2. Basel, Robert Hess Collection
Hotel Jura

AJA 65 (1961), p. 56f., and pl. 32, fig. 6; R. Hess, *Aus einer privater Antikensammlung*, pl. 46.

3. Rome, Villa Giulia
Castellani Collection
Provenience, probably Caere

Comparing the heads on the Kassel cup, no. 1 above, with the profile head on the neck of oinochoe no. 16 (Pl. 14) by the Villa Giulia Torcop Painter, readily illustrates that the two vases are by the same Caeretan artist. This may also be true for the long-handled cups, nos. 2 and 3 listed above, which, unfortunately, do not preserve their decoration as well as the Kassel specimen. Nevertheless, the overall character of the profile strongly suggests a single authorship.

HYDRIAE

When the following hydriae first came to my attention, I knew the Toronto specimen, vase no. 2 below, only from its small reproduction in Robinson and Harcum, *Catalogue.* Since I have acquired a working photograph of the hydria,[34] which has a rather worn surface, it is my conviction that this vase *and* the one in Marseilles, vase no. 1 below, are by the Villa Giulia Torcop Painter.

1. Marseilles, Musée Archéologique Borély 7538 (Pl. 80)
   Height, 13.2 cms.

   AJA 65 (1961), p. 56 and pl. 31, fig. 1.

2. Toronto, Royal Ontario Museum C. 698
   Height, 12.3 cms.

   Robinson and Harcum, *Catalogue*, pl. LXXIX, no. 426; *AJA* 65 (1961), p. 57, note 9.

STAMNOI

Two stamnoi at Cerveteri, replicas in size and decoration except for very slight details, are the work of a single artist who, once again, can be recognized as the Villa Giulia Torcop Painter. A female head in profile to the left and wearing a full-sakkos is represented on each side of the vase, an upright palmette beneath each handle. The stamnoi stands on a ring base rather than on an elevated foot.

1. Cerveteri, Museo Nazionale Cerite 66625 (Pl. 81)
   Provenience, Caere
   Height, 23 cms.

   A: female profile with full-sakkos to the left. In the field to the right, vegetal form, to the left, vegetal form and *mesomphalic phiale*.
   B: the same, but without vegetal form in the field at left.

2. Cerveteri, Museo Nazionale Cerite 66626
   Provenience, Caere
   Height, 23 cms.

34. Recent acquisition of an adequate photograph of the Toronto hydria has prompted me to reverse an earlier opinion expressed in *AJA* 65 (1961), p. 57, n. 9, that the Marseilles and Toronto hydriae were by two different hands. This is no longer the case, for I am convinced that the two vases are by the Villa Giulia Torcop Painter.

A: female profile with full-sakkos to the left. In the field to each side
of the head, a vegetal form.
B: the same.

TREFOIL OINOCHOE

The Villa Giulia Torcop Painter's interest in decorating vases of varying shapes
is again demonstrated by an oinochoe with trefoil mouth discovered at Tarquinii.
On the body of the vase is a quite standard Torcop Group composition of confronting female heads wearing full-sakkos; between the heads, a hanging wreath
and tear-shaped form. On the neck, where a female head in profile would be expected, the Tarquinia oinochoe carries a simple horizontal line bordered by a
row of dots, all of which is executed in added white paint.

> 1. Tarquinia, Museo Nazionale 908 (Pl. 82)
> Museo Nazionale
> Provenience, Tarquinii
> Height, 24.5 cms.
> *ArchEspArq* XXXIX (1966), p. 93, fig. 7.

OINOCHOE (SHAPE VIII B)

As with the skyphoi, long-handled cups, hydriae, and the trefoil oinochoe previously discussed in successive order, the following two vases are also the work
of the prolific and diversified Caeretan artist, the Villa Giulia Torcop Painter
to whom we shall return (Chapter III) when considering the interrelationship
between the different Caeretan red-figured groups thus far treated in this study.

The vase-shape represented by specimens, nos. 1 and 2 below,[35] is technically the oinochoe, Shape VIII B with knotted handle, but more commonly
identified as "mug." Essentially, it is a shape more at home in Apulian red-
figure which, like the *epichysis* to be discussed next illustrates the strong influence of South Italian red-figured pottery on Etruscan during the second half
of the fourth century B.C. (see Chapter V).

> 1. Paris, Louvre K 487 (Pl. 83)
> Formerly Campana Collection
> Provenience, probably Caere
> Height, 14.3 cms.
> *ArchEspArq* XXXIX (1966), p. 93, fig. 8.

As mentioned earlier, the Paris mug reflects the more relaxed style of the
Villa Giulia Torcop Painter exhibited on the skyphos from Ampurias in Barce-

---

35. M. Del Chiaro, "A Caeretan Red-Figured Mug," *StEtr* XXX (1963), pp. 317–319.

lona (Pl. 76). The following mug shows the more usual full-sakkos type and displays a noticeably more ornate motif between the confronting heads. This "filler" is composed of elaborate floral-scrolls flanking an altar upon which a large bird (swan) is perched to the left. The form of the floral-scrolls recalls that depicted by the same painter between the confronted heads on one of his special Torcop Group oinochoai (Pl. 68). An altar between profile heads is not new to Caeretan red-figure and appears on other oinochoai of the Torcop Group.[36]

> 2. Rome, Villa Giulia 50605 (Pls. 84–85)
> Castellani Collection
> Provenience, probably Caere
> Height, 13.5 cms.
>
> *StEtr* XXX (1962), p. 317–319 and pl. XXVII; *Mingazzini*, no. 754 and pl. CCV, figs. 1–3.

EPICHYSEIS

Another vase-shape employed by Caeretan red-figured artists that decisively points to South Italian pottery, particularly Apulian, is the *epichysis*.[37] More commonly, the epichysis consists of a flat, cylindrical body with moulded edges, like that of a pyxis, surmounted by a long neck and high handle resembling the upper part of a lekythos (Fig. 12). A characteristic feature of the vase is the long, beaked spout, generally with eye-like discs at each side of the mouth near the join of mouth and handle.

On the shoulder of each of the three Caeretan epichyseis is found the chief decoration, a floral motif flanking female heads in profile: two confronting profiles with an altar between them on the Siena specimen (Pl. 86), and a single head on the Volterra and Tarquinian epichyseis.

> 1. Siena, Museo Archeológico (Pl. 86)
> Height, 15 cms.
>
> *ArchCl* XII (1960), p. 52 and pl. IX, figs. 1–2.

> 2. Tarquinia, Museo Nazionale 7478
> Provenience, Tarquinii
> Height, 13 cms.
> Much of the nozzle has been incorrectly restored.
>
> *Ibid.*, p. 52 and pl. XI, fig. 1

> 3. Volterra, Museo Guarnacci (Fig. 12)
> Provenience, Volterra
> Height, 16.5 cms.

36. E.g., *Torcop Group*, pl. IX, fig. 6.
37. M. Del Chiaro, "Caeretan Epichyseis," *ArchCl* XII (1960), pp. 51–56.

Ibid., p. 52 and pl. X, figs. 1–2.

Undoubtedly, the Siena and Tarquinia epichyseis, and probably the Volterra, are products of the Villa Giulia Torcop Painter. An altar between confronting female profiles—as seen on the Castellani "mug" in the Villa Giulia (Pl. 84) and on the Siena epichysis—reflects oinochoai of the Torcop Group.

LEKYTHOI

The number of lekythoi attributable to Caeretan red-figure is surprisingly small for a vase type so commonly employed. Only four examples are known to me: one large (vase no. 1) and three small (vases nos. 3–5). As would be expected, they are decorated with the characteristic female head in profile with full-sakkos; there are two confronting profiles on the large Paris lekythos which is probably due to the greater surface available for decoration.

Large Lekythos

The following lekythos bears two confronting female profiles with an altar and pendant palmette in the field between them. It is interesting to note that the artist responsible for this vase—the Pennsylvania Torcop Painter—has attempted to indicate a three-quarter view of the altar reminiscent of the Castellani Caeretan Painter (e.g., Pl. 46).

1. Paris, Louvre
Upper portion of neck and mouth missing.

Small Lekythoi

All three of the lekythoi listed below can be attributed to known artists of the Torcop Group. Nos. 2 and 3 are by the Brussels Torcop Painter,[38] whereas vase no. 4 offers another vase-shape decorated by the Villa Giulia Torcop Painter. Each carries a single vertical handle running from the body to join of neck and mouth. The height ranges from 6 to 9 cms.

2. Tarquinia, Museo Nazionale RC 7929
Provenience, Tarquinii

3. Cerveteri, Magazzino
Provenience, Caere
Height, 9 cms.

4. Cerveteri, Magazzino
Provenience, Caere
Height, 6 cms.

38. *Torcop Group*, p. 150f and pl. XII, fig. 2.

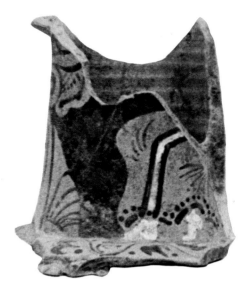

FIG. 1. *Above, left,* Fragment of an oinochoe by the Volterra Caeretan Painter. Cerveteri, Magazzino.

FIG. 2. *Above,* Fragment of an oinochoe by the Castellani Caeretan Painter. Cerveteri, Magazzino.

FIG. 3. *Left,* Fragment of an oinochoe by the Castellani Caeretan Painter. Cerveteri, Magazzino.

FIG. 4. *Below,* Fragments of stamnoi by the Castellani Caeretan Painter. Cerveteri Magazzino.

FIG. 5. *Above,* Caeretan Genucilia plate.
Discovered in the *Regia,* Roman Forum.
Photo: J. Felbermeyer, Rome.

FIG. 6. *Above, right,* Caeretan Genucilia
star plate with outlined heads.
Cerveteri, Magazzino.

FIG. 7. *Below,* Stemmed plate by the
Brooklyn Caeretan Painter. Parma, Museo
Nazionale di Antichità C. 108.

FIG. 8. *Left,* Torcop Group oinochoe by
the Populonia Torcop Painter. Paris,
Louvre K 471. *Photo:* M. Chuzeville, Paris.

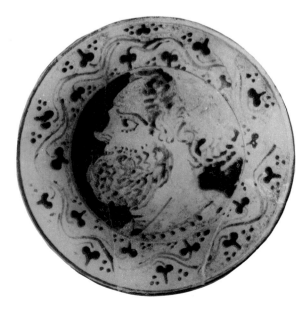

FIG. 9. Fragment of a large Caeretan plate.
Rome, Palatine, *Antiquario.*

FIG. 11. Pillar with hanging kylix.
Cerveteri (Caere) : Tomba dei Rilievi.
Photo: Alinari.

FIG. 10. Kylix by the Caeretan Kylix Painter. Rome, Palazzo dei Conservatori 346.
Side view. *Photo:* Palazzo dei Conservatori.

FIG. 12. Caeretan epichysis. Volterra, Museo Guarnacci. Side view. *Photo:* Museo Guarnacci, Volterra.

FIG. 13. Similarity between Torcop and Genucilia female profiles. *Top,* neck of Torcop Group oinochoe. Rome, Villa Giulia 30. *Bottom,* Caeretan Genucilia plate. Rome, American Academy 326.

FIG. 14. Detail of side A. Stamnos by the Sacrifice Painter. Vatican, Museo Gregoriano Etrusco Z 63. *Photo:* Archivo Fotografico Vaticano.

FIG. 15. Terracotta female torso from Caere. *StEtr* X (1936), pl. XXVI, 4.

FIG. 16. Faliscan oinochoe by
the Full-Sakkos Painter. Basel,
Robert Hess Collection.
Photo: Courtesy owner.

FIG. 17. Faliscan stamnos. New York,
Metropolitan Museum of Art 91.1.441.
Photo: Courtesy Trustees of the
Metropolitan Museum of Art.

FIG. 18. *Left,* Tarquinian oinochoe by the
Painter of Geneva MF 142. Tarquinia,
Museo Nazionale RC 5343. *Photo:*
Valeristi, Tarquinia.

FIG. 19. *Below,* Tarquinian skyphos by the Painter of
Geneva MF 142. Tarquinia, Museo Nazionale 912.
Photo: Valeristi, Tarquinia.

FIG. 20. "Falisco-Caeretan" Genucilia Group Plate by the Berkeley Genucilia Painter. Berkeley, University of California, Robert H. Lowie Museum of Anthropology 8/922. *Photo:* R. H. Lowie Museum of Anthropology.

FIG. 22. Apulian "mug" or oinochoe by the Lampas Painter. Reading, England, Reading Corporation Museum and Art Gallery 22.50.

FIG. 21. Faliscan stamnos. Rome, Villa Giulia. *Left,* side A. *Right,* side B. *Photos:* Soprintendenza Antichità, Rome.

FIG. 23. Silver coin of Terina, late fifth century B.C.

FIG. 24. Detail of side A. Calyx-krater of the Campanizing Group. Bonn, Akademisches Kunstmuseum 83. *Photo:* Archivo Fotografico Vaticano.

Fig. 25. Caeretan bronze mirror. Gerhard-Körte, *ES*, pl. XL.

97ff.

SPOUTED LEBES

Two vases of unusual type were first brought together by Sir John Beazley (*EVP* p. 148), to which he later added new examples (*Annuario*, p. 142). This particular shape, a spouted lebes, seems to be an admixture of the nuptial lebes and a situla, and such vases have been the object of a special investigation on my part which soon revealed that they were actually products of three different Etruscan centers.[39] Only the specimen which I have attributed to Caere is given here.

    1. Vatican, Museo Gregoriano Etrusco Z 109 (Pl. 87)
    Height, 27 cms.

    Two confronting female heads in profile; white bird (goose?) between the profile heads. The spout is plain and relatively long.

    Beazley, *EVP*, p. 148; Trendall, *VIE*, p. 237 and pl. LXI. i and l; *RömMitt* 76 (1969), p. 124 and pl. 44, figs. 3–4.

    There is no doubt that the spouted lebes is the work of a Torcop Group Painter, but the rendering of the hair in a curious, kinky fashion is unusual. Of the recognized artists who decorated oinochoai of the Torcop Group, the style of drawing on the Vatican lebes rests midway between that of the Villa Giulia Torcop Painter (see Pls. 68–69) and the Populonia Torcop Painter (see Pls. 70–71). There is something of each painter in the profile heads: the neck, mouth, eye (the large incised circle for an "eye" is, of course, modern), ear and part of the nose-line recall the Villa Giulia Torcop Painter; the chin and part of the nose-line are more characteristic of the Populonia Torcop Painter. Unfortunately, the useful clue for attribution—earring type—is not clear owing to the fugitive nature of the white paint employed as flesh color.

TERRACOTTA CISTA

To the best of my knowledge, the terracotta cylindrical receptacle with lid decorated in red-figured technique in the Castellani Collection of the Villa Giulia (Pl. 88) is unique. Despite the absence of feet, it is so like Etruscan bronze cistae in general form, particularly in the presence of perforated bosses placed at intervals along a horizontal encircling band, I prefer to call it "cista" rather than *pyxis*. The well-fitting lid, with central knob for lifting, is decorated with two pairs of profile heads, in each case a satyr confronting a woman. On the body, which is a simple cylindrical container, the painting is placed within two registers: an upper register with five profile heads of three satyrs and two

39. M. Del Chiaro, "One Vase-Shape, Three Etruscan Fabrics," *RömMitt* 76 (1969), pp. 122–127.

women, of which one woman and one satyr confront each other in two instances; and a lower register with a continuous pattern of palmettes alternating up and down. The strict silhouette style of this palmette motif calls special attention to a popular type of oinochoe (Shape VII) decorated exclusively with silhouette floral patterns which, in my estimation, belongs to the third century B.C.[40]

1. Rome, Villa Giulia 50576
   Castellani Collection
   Provenience, probably Caere
   Height with lid, 18.2 cms.; diam. 13 cms.

   ArchCl XIV (1962), p. 78f. and pls. XLVIII–XLIX; *Mingazzini*, no. 745 and pl. CXCVIII, figs. 1–2.

The style of drawing, particularly its sketchy character, directly recalls the Brooklyn Caeretan Painter who decorated vases with figured scenes (see Pls. 17–18), and the unusual Genucilia Group plate with satyr head in profile (Fig. 7).

"MESOMPHALIC PHIALE"

A vase in Munich is of singular interest for a shape which has not been encountered previously in the repertory of Caeretan pottery, namely, a *mesomphalic phiale*.[41] The decoration, however, follows a well-known theme in Caeretan red-figure—two sets of confronting heads (paired female and satyr) on the interior. The exterior, on the other hand, is painted with one of the more usual ornamental designs—the tongue pattern.

   Munich, Antikensammlungen 8654 (Pl. 89)
   Height, 4 cms.; diam. of rim, 17.5 cms.

   INTERIOR: omphallos or central boss decorated with long radiating tongue pattern bearing relief lines. At the rim, a narrow band with short tongues. Between the omphallos and rim there are two sets of confronting profile heads—a female with white flesh color at the left wearing a full-sakkos, and a bearded satyr at the right. The confronting heads are separated by a hanging floral / vegetal scroll.
   EXTERIOR: long tongues in vertical pattern round the bowl which is accented at the rim by a narrow horizontal band with short tongues.

40. E.g., Beazley, *EVP*, p. 183 and pl. XXXVIII, fig. 3. Beazley has observed that, "in the fourth century silhouette tends to usurp the place of red-figure in floral patterns" (*ibid.*, p. 143). See also *ArchCl* XIV (1962), p. 79, n. 3.
41. M. Del Chiaro, "A Caeretan Red-Figured Mesomphalic Phiale," forthcoming *AchCl* XXVI (1974).

The Munich *mesomphalic phiale* is one of the few Etruscan examples known to me with decoration other than ornamental, i.e., with patterns and floral work only.[42] Examination of the drawing style for the heads, particularly that of the women who wear full-sakkos, clearly points to the work of the Villa Giulia Torcop Painter.

FISH PLATE

The following product of a Caeretan potter and vase-painter is set apart because it differs so markedly not only in shape but also in decoration from any of the vases thus far presented in this study. Because the decoration is comprised of fish rather than figured scenes or profile heads,[43] it is impossible to assign the plate on stylistic grounds to any specific painter or Group for the vases listed in the foregoing chapters.

> Cerveteri, Museo Nazionale Cerite (Pl. 90)
> Provenience, Caere
> Height, 6 cms.; diam. of plate, 18 cms.; diam. of foot, 7.5 cms.
>
> INTERIOR: four sea creatures—a squid, two sea-perch, and a torpedo or ray—swim counter-clockwise round a circular eight-wave motif. The center of the plate is without groove or channel, or moulded ring. A reserved band with dot decoration runs round the edge of the plate. EXTERIOR: an overhanging rim or lip is decorated with a continuous wave pattern. There is no use of the relief-line. The foot is relatively high and elaborate.

Fish plates, appropriately named for the marine life represented on the interior, are especially common in South Italian red-figure, particularly Campanian and Apulian.[44] As mentioned above, the fish plate cannot be assigned to an individual Caeretan artist owing to the nature of its decoration; however, on

42. With birds: Beazley *EVP,* p. 158 and pl. XXXVI; with patterns and floral work; *ibid.,* p. 181f and pl. XXXI, figs. 3–4; see also, Trendall *VIE,* p. 272 and p. 271, fig. 36c.
43. M. Del Chiaro, "An Etruscan (Caeretan) Fish Plate," forthcoming *Festschrift* to A. D. Trendall.
44. For Campanian Fish plates, see *CVA* Capua, Museo Campano 1, IV Er, pls. 1–6; for Apulian fish plates, see *CVA* Lecce, Museo Provinciale Castromediano 2, pl. 59, figs. 1–6. See also, L. Lacroix, *La Faune Marine dans la Décoration des Plats à Poissons* (Verviers, 1937) and K. Zimmermann, "Unteritalische Fischteller" in *Wiss. Zeit. der Univ. Rostock* 16, 1967, Heft 7/8, pp. 561–570. In marked contrast, Attic red-figured fish plates show the fish represented on the interiors in an "upside-down" manner, i.e., with their bellies toward the rim; see D. Robinson, *Excavations at Olynthus* V (Baltimore, 1933) nos. 231–232 and pl. 113, and XIII (Baltimore, 1950), nos. 73–74, pls. 80 and 92.

the evidence of the general character of its clay and glaze paint, and my long experience with Caeretan red-figure, I am certain that the plate was fabricated at Caere.[45] Significantly, this Caeretan fish plate furnishes a unique example of this vase type in Etruscan vase-painting as a whole. It is interesting to speculate whether the fish represented on the Cerveteri fish plate are derived directly from South Italian fish plates or, as would prove likely, whether they document the existence of a similar edible fish from the immediate regions of the central Tyrrhenian Sea where Etruscan fishermen gained their daily catch for the local—Caere—fish market.[46]

45. Dr. J. Gy. Szilágyi had noted this same Caeretan fish plate in the Museo Nazionale Cerite and believed it to be of local manufacture; cf. *Acta Antiqua Academiae Scientiarum Hungaricae* XVIII (1970), p. 260, n. 60.
46. Cf. A. Palombi and M. Santarelli, *Gli animali commestibili dei mari d'Italia* (Milan, 1969).

III

〰〰〰〰〰

The Caeretan Environment

THE FIRST insight into the environment of Caeretan vase-painting during the second half of the fourth century B.C. was gained in the detailed investigation of the Genucilia Group.[1] The discovery of a red-figured fabric at Caere presented a great potential for the further recognition and study of the range and content of native Caeretan red-figure. As the present study has already disclosed, this potential has found confirmation.

For the moment, relatively little can be added to our knowledge of the contemporary sculptural activities at Caere than otherwise indicated during the detailed analysis of *earring* types which appeared on plates of the Caeretan Genucilia Group and their parallels in certain types of terracotta heads and figurines.[2] With the discovery of Caeretan red-figured vases and the revelation that they were created by potters and vase-painters centered at Caere, it may now be possible to detect a bronze mirror industry at Caere which was not clearly evident by examining profile heads alone.[3] But first, let us turn to the consideration of a statement originally presented in *Genucilia Group* (p. 314): "In the relationship of these vases to one another there is much that remains to be clarified, but in view of their generally larger forms and more imposing decoration it is scarcely possible to regard them as mere subsidiary products of the Genucilia artists."

1. *Genucilia Group*, Chapter X.
2. *Ibid.*, pp. 321ff.
3. *Caeretan Figured Group*, p. 36, n. 17. See also infra n. 16 (Chapter III).

INTERRELATIONSHIP OF CAERETAN RED-FIGURED PAINTERS

On the whole, the vases attributed to Caeretan vase-painters in the preceding chapters, regardless of their theme, whether decorated with figured scenes or with profile heads, represent the output of a closely interknit red-figured fabric. As noted periodically throughout the listing and discussion of these vases, a number of artists did not restrict themselves to the decoration of only one particular vase-shape, nor to a set subject—whether figured scene or profile head. Apart from the Genucilia Group, more than a dozen individual Caeretan vase-painters have been distinguished who were responsible for vases bearing figured scenes, the Torcop Group, and assorted shapes decorated with profile heads.

The first sound evidence that the newly recognized Caeretan vase-painters did not limit their activities to the decoration of Genucilia plates alone, was provided by vases identified as "Caeretan Genucilia Kylikes" (e.g., Pl. 75). In the medallions of these cups was painted a characteristic Genucilia female profile head—without the use of white for flesh color—which, to all intents and purposes, underwent no change but marked a simple transference of basic theme to another vase-shape. However, some large plates (e.g., the Vienna plate, Pl. 74), which are directly linked to the Genucilia Group in the style of drawing and the choice of wave pattern for the flattish rim, show a noteworthy change in sakkos type, i.e., a *full-sakkos* rather than the *sphendone* of the Genucilia Group. Likewise, there are kylikes with female head in profile wearing full-sakkos which, to judge by the profile style, are unquestionably products of Caeretan Genucilia Painters.

A closer association between the Genucilia Group and the Torcop Group than is illustrated by the full-sakkos on the large plates and kylikes, is found in the Tarquinia kylix which shows—in addition to the full-sakkos—the use of white paint for the female flesh color, thereby joining two features that characterize profile heads normally encountered on oinochoai of the Torcop Group. The two oinochoai are best placed within the orbit of the Torcop Group (although the sketchy style of drawing and lack of full-sakkos would at first argue against it), and reveal stylistic parallels with the Caeretan Genucilia Group, as discerned in the work of the Carthage Genucilia Painter (see Pl. 64).

Some individual painters, already distinguished in separate studies of the Torcop and Genucilia Groups, are identical. For example, the Villa Giulia Torcop Painter, whose style can be readily recognized on a number of Caeretan vases of varying shapes (listed below), may be responsible for the decoration on some Genucilia plates of the Caeretan branch of the Group (see Fig. 13).

The relationship between the Torcop Group and Caeretan Red-Figured Vases with figured scenes, needs no elaboration in the case of the Villa Giulia Torcop Painter who, judging from his replicas in Rome (e.g., Pl. 14), focused his attention on Caeretan vases with subjects other than profile heads. Unquestionably, the most conspicuous motif shared in common between the two groups is the *mesomphalic phiale* which frequently appears one or more times in the field as "filler" to the chief picture zones. Practically all of the painters of the Dotted-hem Group utilize the *mesomphalic phiale*, whereas the hanging wreath, so common to the Torcop Group, is known only on the vases by the Florence Caeretan Painter (see Pl. 23) and the Volterra Caeretan Painter (see Pl. 30), both of whom are artists of the Dotted-hem Group. In one instance, the hanging wreath with *mesomphalic phiale* directly below—the usual juxtapositioning on oinochoai of the Torcop Group—is found on the last-mentioned vase by the Volterra Caeretan Painter.

An additional "link" between the vases of the Torcop Group and Caeretan vases with figured scenes may be noted in the elaborate floral / vegetal-scrolls used as "filler" between the confronting heads represented by the Populonia Torcop Painter (e.g., Pl. 68) and the Villa Giulia Torcop Painter (e.g., Pl. 71). Special attention should be called to the sinuous upright floral / vegetal motif as it appears on the just cited oinochoe by the Populonia Torcop Painter which, I believe, has its counterpart on Etruscan bronze incense burners (*thymiateria*) in their ornamental vertical supports.[4] Varied versions of such floral / vegetal scrolls on the Torcop Group oinochoai are commonly found in the subsidiary ornamental decoration which frames the figured scenes on Caeretan Red-Figured Vases (contrast Pls. 6 and 25 with Pl. 68, and Pls. 26–29 and 32–33 with Pl. 71). The presence of an *altar* between confronting heads on a mug (Pl. 84), epichysis (Pl. 86), and lekythos has parallels on oinochoai of the Torcop Group.[5] *Earring types*, generally a most informative feature upon close analysis, have contributed little to what has already been learned in the study of Caeretan Genucilia plates.[6]

The Torcop Group artists, the Pennsylvania and the Brussels Torcop

---

4. See M. Del Chiaro, *Etruscan Art from West Coast Collections* (Santa Barbara, 1967), p. 46, no. 64 and colored plate; see also D. Mitten and S. Doeringer, *Master Bronzes from the Classical World* (Mainz, 1967), no. 221.
5. See the oinochoai by the Populonia Torcop Painter. *Torcop Group*, pl. XI, fig. 6 and vase no. 44 and p. 149.
6. Supra, n. 2 (Chapter III).

Painters, have shown interest in vases other than the oinochoe (Shape VII), as demonstrated by their lekythoi. However, two additional artists who decorated Torcop Group oinochoai, the Brooklyn Caeretan Painter and the Villa Giulia Torcop Painter, are equally at home in the Dotted-hem Group, that is, vases with figured scenes; they are also known to have decorated specimens classified here as "Assorted Vases" which exhibit female heads in profile. As indicated earlier in the discussion of oinochoai with figured scenes by the Brooklyn Caeretan Painter, his personal style is clearly evident on the unique Terracotta "Cista" in the Villa Giulia (Pl. 88) and the stemmed plate in Parma (Fig. 7). In sharp contrast to this latter artist, the Villa Giulia Torcop Painter deserves special consideration because he, above all of his colleagues, best exemplifies the interrelationship between the various Groups of red-figure attributed to Caere during the second half of the fourth century B.C.

As noted earlier, the works of the Villa Giulia Torcop Painter embrace a number of Groups (the Torcop Group and the Dotted-hem Group of Caeretan Red-Figured Vases), as well as a variety of "Assorted Vases." Since this painter is of considerable importance to our knowledge of Caeretan red-figured vase-painting, it will prove convenient to list here together the various vases attributed to his hand (or possibly by his hand), which have been discussed throughout this study.

Red-Figured Vases

Oinochoai

Rome, Villa Giulia 30
See no. 16, Chapter I (Pl. 14)

Rome, Villa Giulia 30
See no. 17, Chapter I

Cerveteri, Magazzino
See no. 18, Chapter I (Pls. 15–16)

Tarquinia, Museo Nazionale 1930
See no. 19, Chapter 1

Torcop Group

Rome, Villa Giulia
Torcop Group, p. 140, no. 1 and pl. X, fig. 1.

Rome, Villa Giulia
Ibid., p. 140, no. 2.

Rome, Villa Giulia 13 (Pl. 68)
Ibid., p. 141, no. 6 and pl. X, fig. 2.

Rome, Villa Giulia 14
Ibid., p. 141, no. 7

Rome, Villa Giulia 10837
Ibid., p. 142, no. 10.

Lille, Musée 46
Ibid., p. 141, no. 3.

Toulouse, Musée Saint-Raymond 26.609 (Pl. 69)
Ibid., p. 141, no. 4.

Newark, New Jersey, Museum 50.316
Ibid., p. 141, no. 5.

Assorted Vases

Skyphoi

Barcelona, Museo Arqueológico 608 (Pl. 76)
ArchEspArq XXXIX (1966), p. 93, figs. 5–6.

Orbetello, Antiquario Comunale 257 (Pl. 77)

Cerveteri, Museo Nazionale Cerite 6712 (?)

Long-Handled Cups

Kassel, Hessisches Landesmuseum T 545 (Pls. 78–79)
Genucilia Group, p. 317 and pl. 29, a and c; *AJA* 65 (1961),
p. 56f. and pl. 32, fig. 5.

Basel, Robert Hess Collection
AJA 65 (1961), p. 56f. and pl. 32, fig. 6.

Rome, Villa Giulia
Castellani Collection

Hydriae

Marseilles, Musée Archéologique Borély 7538 (Pl. 80)
AJA 65 (1961), p. 56 and pl. 31, fig. 1.

Toronto, Royal Ontario Museum C 698
Robinson and Harcum, Catalogue, pl. LXXIX, no. 426; *AJA*
65 (1961), p. 57, note 9.

Stamnoi

Cerveteri, Museo Nazionale Cerite 66625 (Pl. 81)

Cerveteri, Museo Nazionale Cerite 66626

Trefoil Oinochoe

Tarquinia, Museo Nazionale 908 (Pl. 82)
ArchEspArq XXXIX (1966), p. 93, fig. 7.

Oinochoai (Shape VIII)

Paris, Louvre K 487 (Pl. 83)
ArchEspArq XXXIX (1966), p. 93, fig. 8.

Rome, Villa Giulia (Pls. 84–85)
Castellani Collection
StEtr XXX (1962), p. 317f. and pl. XXVII

Epichyseis

Siena, Museo Archeologico (Pl. 86)
ArchCl XII (1960), p. 52 and pl. IX, figs. 1–2.

Tarquinia, Museo Nazionale 7478
ArchCl XII (1960), p. 52 and pl. XI, fig. 1.

Volterra, Museo Guarnacci (Fig. 12)
ArchCl XII (1960), p. 52 and pl. X, figs. 1–2.

Lekythos

Cerveteri, Magazzino

Spouted Lebes

Vatican, Museo Gregoriano Etrusco Z 109 (Pl. 87)
Trendall, *VIE* p. 237 and pl. LXI, k and l; *RömMitt* 76 (1969), p. 124 and pl. 44, figs. 3–4.

Mesomphalic Phiale

Munich, Antikensammlungen 8654 (Pl. 89)

Owing to the nature of the decoration found on Genucilia plates, I have been unable to associate with certainty any of the plates with known works of the Villa Giulia Torcop Painter. Although details given to the profile head, or rather *face*, may appear remarkably similar (see Fig. 13), the character of the head can easily assume a totally different aspect simply by a change of head cover (full-sakkos, sphendone, and the like). Nevertheless, the possibility that the Villa Giulia Torcop Painter may be equated with one of the already recognized Caeretan Genucilia Painters cannot be totally excluded.

CAERETAN VASES IN SUPERPOSED COLOR

As I have experienced with the investigation of the Genucilia Group and the subsequent discovery of the Caeretan branch for the Group, a number of vases of varying shapes tentatively presented as possible products of Caeretan vase-painters—oinochoai of the Torcop Group, a large plate, some kylikes, and a long-handled cup (see *Genucilia Group*, Chapter X)—were later confirmed as Caeretan in more detailed studies. Once again, through the investigation of a more extensive and diversified number of Caeretan red-figured vases as presented in this study, it is possible to detect strong resemblances to the now-established *Caeretan style* among vases of a hitherto unknown fabric created in a totally different technique that may very well designate them as Caeretan products.

In this section my presentation of vases decorated in *superposed color* as products of Caere is only tentative and it is hoped that future research will eventually corroborate my current supposition of their origin. In this technique the details of anatomy, drapery, etc. are not always incised, but may be indicated by additions in contrasting dark color. It is chiefly in the style of "drawing" that I cannot help but sense the reflection of a Caeretan "artistic climate" which I have attained over many years devoted to Caeretan red-figured vase-painting.

A relatively large number of Etruscan vases is known to have been decorated in superposed color, a technique of vase-painting discussed in detail for Etruscan pottery by Beazley,[7] for Campanian, where it is more common, by Anna Rocco,[8] and, of course, for Apulian. No vases executed in superposed color, as formerly with red-figure, were considered to be of Caeretan manufacture. On the strength of what has been learned about Caeretan red-figure, I believe it is now possible to place the three following vases within the framework of Caeretan vase-painting.

THE SACRIFICE PAINTER

The three vases listed below (nos. 1–3)—a volute-krater and two stamnoi—are of monumental proportions and have been attributed by A. D. Trendall to the "Sacrifice Painter" (*Pittore del Sacrificio*),[9] an artist named by him after a scene represented on Side A of the volute-krater (see Pl. 91). It should be pointed out that the volute-krater is rare in Etruscan pottery, especially in the elaborate form it assumes in the Vatican example.

Volute-Krater

1. Vatican, Museo Gregoriano Etrusco Z 64 (Pl. 91)
   Height with handles, 32.5 cms.; diam. of rim, 16 cms.

7. Beazley, *EVP*, Chapter XII. See also Trendall, *VIE*, pp. 258ff.
8. Anna Rocco, "Di una classe di vasi del Museo Nazionale di Napoli," *Memmorie della Accademia Archeologica di Napoli* VI (1942), pp. 1–13. See also, Trendall, *VIE*, pp. 258ff.
9. Trendall, *VIE*, p. 261.

A: NECK: naked youth between two *erotes*.

BODY: *sacrificial scene*; a woman, with mantle draped around lower portion of her body, kneels to the left between two youths. At the left, a completely naked youth places his left hand on the "victim's" head, a sword or dagger held blade-up in his right hand. His left leg is raised with foot resting on a "stand." At the right behind the kneeling woman, another youth, who is naked but for mantle over his left shoulder and wrapped tightly round his left arm, extends his right arm with beaded bracelet or wreath in hand. Above the woman is a bird (dove?); a small pillar with egg-shaped finial between the woman and the right-hand youth.

B: NECK: shaggy dog (Maltese?) between two bulls.

BODY: three standing youths engaged in conversation.

Trendall, *VIE*, p. 260 and pl. LXVII, a–b.

Stamnoi

The following stamnoi are near replicas of each other. Vase no. 2 is in a far better state of preservation than vase no. 3 which has large missing portions restored.

2. Vatican, Museo Gregoriano Etrusco Z 63 (Pl. 92)
Height, 25 cms.

A: a woman is seated on an altar between two youths, one of whom (right-hand figure) is very much like his counterpart on the volute-krater, vase no. 1 above. The left-hand youth, with his left leg raised and foot resting on a high stand, leans towards the seated woman. A small pillar with egg-shaped finial, as on vase no. 1 above, appears at the far left; and a similar egg-shaped object seems to be juggled in the outstretched fingers of the youth's left hand. The woman holds a beaded bracelet in her upraised left hand.

B: three standing youths in conversation arranged in pose and composition very much like those on Side B of the volute-krater, vase no. 1 above.

Trendall, *VIE*, p. 261f. and pl. LXVII, c–d.

3. Vatican, Museo Gregoriano Etrusco Z 65

A: near replica of above vase but for object in lowered hand of the right-hand youth and the addition of a second pillar at the far right.

B: near replica of above vase.

Trendall, *VIE*, p. 262, fig. 30.

Trendall cites no known parallels for the themes of drawing on any of the three above vases, but does note some analogies with the *Caivano Group* of Campanian red-figure.[10] Furthermore, he is puzzled by the shape of the vases—volute-krater and stamnoi—which are not proper to that fabric. Nevertheless, he does find in them some affinity to the "Campanizing Group,"[11] which we shall consider when discussing the interrelationship between Caeretan and South Italian red-figure (Chapter V).

The Caeretan elements which, to my mind, mark the Sacrifice Painter as an artist active at Caere during the third quarter of the fourth century B.C. (see Chronology, Chapter VI), are specifically found, apart from the general character of the profile heads and figures, in the details of the heads of the women on all three vases (see Pl. 91 and Fig. 14). Note the finely drawn, long, wavy tresses dangling before the ear in the characteristic Caeretan manner well known from Caeretan Genucilia plates and oinochoai of the Torcop Group.

RELATED VASES IN SUPERPOSED COLOR

In respect to the important similarities with Caeretan red-figure displayed by the details of the women's heads described for the vases by the Sacrifice Painter, four vases of far smaller proportions—two lekythoi and two kantharoi (vases nos. 4–7 below, Pls. 93–95)—are noteworthy for their technique and style. All four specimens are also decorated in superposed color by a single painter. Discovered at Populonia, they are presently in the Museo Archeologico, Florence.

Although the female profiles recall the style of the Torcop Group (see Pls. 71–72), the vases are best placed here because of their technique and proximity of style to the Sacrifice Painter. This may be observed clearly on the kantharoi in the delineation of profile, the outlining of the hair with white dots, and the diadem, all of which compare strongly with the woman on stamnos no. 2 (see Fig. 14).

Lekythoi (Type III)

The two lekythoi listed below are of Type III with flat base and bulbous body. They differ in shape from each other only in that vase no. 4 shows a slightly greater swell to the body. The subsidiary decoration on this last vase also differs in the choice of wave pattern at the shoulder below the tongue-pattern on the neck. Both vases show an *Eros* and a woman, but on vase no. 5 the woman has been abbreviated to head and right hand only. There are striking parallels in shape and subjects, perhaps even prototypes, in Attic red-figured lekythoi

10. Trendall, *PP*, pp. 84ff, and Trendall, *LCS*, pp. 305ff.
11. Beazley, *EVP*, pp. 63ff.

dating to the end of the fifth and the beginning of the fourth century B.C. (see *Langlotz*, pl. 208, figs. 595–597, and 599).

4. Florence, Museo Archeologico (Pl. 93)
   Provenience, Populonia

   BODY: at the right, a woman semireclines to the right with her head turned round to left toward an *Eros* who is posed in a very squat and hunched manner. Between the figures, a leafless tree or shrub with fruit.

   NSc 1905, p. 58, in fig. 6; *Minto*, pl. LX, in fig. 2.

5. Florence, Museo Archeologico (Pl. 94)
   Provenience, Populonia

   BODY: at the right, a profile head of a woman facing to the left. Her right hand appears near the chin. Directly in front of her and facing in her direction, *Eros* like that on vase no. 4 above.

   NSc 1905, p. 58 in fig. 6; *Minto*, pl. LX, in fig. 2.

Kantharoi

The two following kantharoi are replicas except for differences in the subsidiary decoration and different proportions of the confronting female profile heads on each side of the vases. Between the heads, a vertical rectangular panel carries a floral motif. For the decorative bands below the profile heads, the artist has chosen a modified checkerboard pattern for vase no. 6, and a wave pattern for no. 7. The association of these two kantharoi with Etruscan imitations of Attic kantharoi of the Saint-Valentin Group,[12] possibly via South Italian products, will be discussed later in this study (Chapter V).

6. Florence, Museo Archeologico 81910 (Pl. 95)
   Provenience, Populonia

   NSc 1905, p. 58, in fig. 5; *Minto*, pl. LX, in fig. 3.

7. Florence, Museo Archeologico 81911
   Provenience, Populonia

   NSc 1905, p. 58, in fig. 5; *Minto*, pl. LX, in fig. 3.

As mentioned earlier, all four vases were discovered at Populonia where, unfortunately, their archaeological context cannot be taken into consideration since they were brought to light through clandestine or fortuitous activities.[13]

12. *Ibid.*, p. 221f.
13. *NSc* 1905, pp. 57ff; *Minto*, pp. 203ff.

Nonetheless, it may be of some interest to note that an oinochoe by the American Academy Caeretan Painter of the Crescent-hem Group (vase no. 89 and Pl. 55) is included with the "context" of the above kantharoi (nos. 6 and 7).[14]

Vases decorated in superposed color, as those presented here, should open new vistas in the study of Etruscan vase-painting. Although I have labeled relatively few vases in superposed color as Caeretan, they may readily serve to attract an even larger number of vases painted in a similar technique. Many have already been grouped and classified by Sir John Beazley (*EVP*, Chapter XII); for example, his "Phantom Group" (ibid., p. 205f.), a part of which may have been produced at Caere; or such specimens as the two oinochoai (Shape VII) found together with our two lekythoi, nos. 4 and 5 (Pls. 93–94).[15]

CAERETAN BRONZE MIRROR-ENGRAVING

It has been my suspicion in the past that the recognition of a Caeretan red-figured fabric with its distinctive stylistic traits would one day lead to the discovery of a bronze mirror industry at the important Etruscan center of Caere.[16] Even though I had entertained the hope for the presence of a "school" or workshop of mirror-engravers at Caere early in my investigations of Caeretan vase-painting —during researches into the Caeretan branch of the Genucilia Group—I did not then wish to base such an hypothesis on the stylistic evidence provided by profile heads alone.[17] However, since the discovery of the much larger and more important series of Caeretan red-figured vases decorated with figured scenes, I

14. *NSc* 1905, p. 58, in fig. 5; *Minto*, pl. LX, in fig. 3.
15. See *NSc* 1905, p. 58, in fig. 6; Minto, pl. LX, in fig. 2.
16. See M. Del Chiaro, "An Etruscan Mirror Produced at Caere," *AJA* 75 (1971), p. 85f. That the celebrated life-size Etruscan bronze "Arringatore" was produced in a major bronze-casting establishment at Caere, see T. Dohrn, *Der Arringatore*, Monumenta Artis Romanae VIII (Berlin, 1968), p. 17f. In addition to the bronze *thymiateria*, dating to the second half of the fourth century B.C., with elaborate floral / vegetal-scroll supports which recall decorative motifs on Caeretan red-figured vases (supra, n. 4, Chapter III), there are Archaic bronze specimens with repoussée decoration believed to have been manufactured at Caere; see H. Scullard, *The Etruscan Cities and Rome* (London, 1967), p. 163f.
17. C. van Essen, *Bibliotheca Orientalis* XVII (1960), p. 97f, in which there is given an impressive list of parallels between the profile heads on the Genucilia Group plates— both Caeretan and Faliscan—and mirrors published in all volumes of Gerhard-Körte, *ES*.

believe a sounder base now exists to search for parallels in the engraved scenes on Etruscan mirrors and cistae.[18]

A striking example which may illustrate the presence of bronze mirror-engravers at Caere is provided by a mirror published by E. Gerhard (Fig. 25).[19] The chief clue for consideration of the bronze mirror as a product of Caere is found in the fleur de lis at each shoulder of the light garment worn by the one figure of a *Lasa* incised on the mirror's disc.[20] As stressed in the early portion of this study, the fleur de lis, which must be the tied bow of the garment, is especially characteristic of Caeretan vases assigned to the Dotted-hem Group (see Pls. 1, 14 and 34) and those by the Castellani Caeretan Painter of the Crescent-hem Group (see Pls. 40 and 46). Even though there is a conspicuous absence in the mirror engraving of the broad band down the center of the garment, and the expected decoration of the hem that normally indicates the particular Group of the "Workshop" responsible for the vases with figured scenes, there remains an indelible "Caeretan" cast to the *Lasa* on the mirror. The manner in which the *Lasa*'s hair is combed back from the forehead, tied at the back of the head with a fillet, and then allowed to fall freely, should be noted for its similarity to the coiffure of the women normally found on Caeretan Red-Figured Vases. In addition, the "flurry" of the folds at the lower edge of the garment between the feet of the *Lasa* strongly suggests the *crescents* of the Crescent-hem Group (see Pls. 49, 51 and 55).

Although a *Lasa* bearing a situla—as represented on the mirror—is unknown on Caeretan red-figured vases, such an object is often carried by a woman or *Eros,* e.g., on vases by the Sambon Caeretan Painter (Pls. 26 and 28) and the Castellani Caeretan Painter (Pl. 44). These last two painters, and a few of their colleagues—the Villa Giulia Torcop Painter and the American Academy Caeretan Painter—are fond of bracelets which they indicate by three parallel lines engraved on the bronze mirror (see Pls. 16, 25, 26 and 52).

A detail of particular significance for the correlation of Caeretan red-figured vases and the bronze mirror—here proposed as Caeretan—is seen in the *vegetal motif* (wild-flower or weed?) that grows near the feet of the *Lasa* on

18. An opinion I expressed in *Studi L. Banti*, p. 137 and *Caeretan Figured Group*, p. 36, n. 17.

19. E. Gerhard, *ES*, I, p. 24, pl. XL. The mirror once formed part of the collection of the *Collegio Romano* which no longer exists. I have been unable to trace the present whereabouts of this important Etruscan mirror.

20. *Ibid.* Gerhard identifies the female figure with situla as "Nike" or "Iris mit Eimer."

the mirror and various figures on vases by the Campana and Castellani Caeretan Painters (see Pls. 20–22 and 46–47). At times, the motif may be rendered horizontally or pendant in the field of the figured scenes (see Pls. 53–55).

Hence, on the stylistic evidence derived from the study of Caeretan red-figured vases with figured scenes, my early inclination that one day some Etruscan engraved mirrors would prove to have been manufactured at Caere has found reliable support in the mirror here cited and which, hopefully, may mark the beginning of an important and useful list of Caeretan mirrors that future research will readily augment.[21] Although it can be argued that the mirror was engraved at a site other than Caere where Caeretan red-figured vases are known to have been imported (see Distribution, Chapter IV), I am convinced that the general character of the engraved figure and the details associated with it reflect a "Caeretan" character that would not be natural to an Etruscan center other than Caere.

CAERETAN SCULPTURE

As mentioned earlier, the typological analysis of the earrings worn by the women of the Genucilia Group brought into consideration a number of terracotta votive heads, all significantly from Caere,[22] but unfortunately limited to details associated solely with profile heads. Together with the subjects represented on Caeretan red-figured vases with figured scenes, a terracotta torso (Fig. 15) discovered by Raniero Mengarelli in his excavation of the "Tempio di HRA" at Caere[23] provides a fine analogy with most women represented on Caeretan vases with figured scenes. The terracotta fragment shows a bare-armed female, "Menade" according to Mengarelli, with knots or bows at the shoulder of the garment and traces of beaded necklace. In every sense, the lady is *Caeretan* and calls to mind the women of the Castellani Caeretan Painter (see Pl. 51) or the *Lasa* engraved on the Caeretan mirror (Fig. 25).

Providentially, the consideration of this terracotta sculpture in a discussion

---

21. The major portion of *published* Etruscan bronze mirrors, in my opinion, date to the third and second centuries B.C. (e.g., Gerhard-Körte *ES* and G. Matthies, *Die Praenestinischen Spiegel*, Strassburg, 1912).
22. *Genucilia Group*, p. 323, figs. 8 and 9; p. 324, fig. 10.
23. R. Mengarelli, "Il luogo e i materiali del tempio di *HRA* a Caere" *StEtr* X (1936), pp. 27–86; see p. 81f and pl. XXVI, 4.

of Caeretan red-figured vase-painting has brought me full circle to the Genucilia Group, for a Caeretan Star plate—with the dipinto HRA on its rim—was included in my original study of the Group,[24] and was discovered in the very same archaeological context as the female torso by Mengarelli in 1936.[25]

24. *Genucilia Group*, p. 295.
25. *StEtr* X (1936), p. 85, fig. 7; see also Beazley, *EVP*, p. 176.

IV

꒰꒱꒰꒱꒰

Distribution

DURING the initial investigation of the Genucilia Group, an interesting pattern of distribution (see *frontispiece*) was discovered which corroborated the stylistic division for the two distinct red-figured centers responsible for the Genucilia plates, *Falerii Veteres* (Cività Castellana) and *Caere*.[1] In the light of red-figured vases with figured scenes recognized here as Caeretan, and the discovery of additional examples of Caeretan vases decorated with female heads in profile, a reconsideration of the distribution of Caeretan Red-Figured Vases is definitely required.[2]

The proveniences already known for Caeretan red-figure based on the study of the Genucilia and Torcop Groups have been notably augmented. To the sites previously recorded, there may now be added: Alalia, Ampurias, Castiglioncello, Orbetello, Pyrgi, Roselle, San Giuliano, Santa Marinella, and one or two others (see Table of Proveniences). With the exception of Ampurias and Alalia, the new proveniences in the districts of ancient Etruria and Latium are not surprising, since they could be anticipated by the pattern of distribution revealed by the Caeretan Genucilia plates and oinochoai of the Torcop Group. As would be expected, *Caere* remains the most prolific center for Caeretan red-figured vases with recorded proveniences.

For the Caeretan finds in Latium in the environs of Rome, Ostia, Satricum,

---

1. *Genucilia Group*, Chapter VIII.
2. A tentative reconsideration of distribution for products of Caeretan red-figured workshops has been made since publication of *Genucilia Group*; see M. Del Chiaro, "Distribution of Caeretan Red-Figured Pottery," *ArchCl* XVIII (1966), pp. 115–118.

Praeneste, and Grottaferrata, I can add very little to what has already been said in *Genucilia Group* and *Torcop Group*, with the exception of the Genucilia plates discovered at the *Regia* in the Roman Forum (see Index of Collections) and the two lekythoi with profile heads from Satricum, as well as the "kylix" fragment from the Palatine (now better regarded as a large plate). Since no Caeretan vases with figured scenes have thus far been discovered in these environs, it seems that the Romans preferred Caeretan red-figure of relatively "minor" scale. Nonetheless, an important discovery, based on the detailed investigation of Caeretan red-figure in respect to the Roman "environment," is that a goodly portion of vases earlier believed to be "Faliscan" should now be considered *Caeretan*,[3] a change in concept of paramount importance for the better understanding of the relationships between Caere and Rome during the late fourth and early third centuries B.C.

Evidence for the export of Caeretan red-figure beyond Etruria and Rome— first realized during the study of the Genucilia Group and then limited to the sites of ancient Carthage, Genoa, and possibly Malta and Cumae[4]—have been reconfirmed in the case of Carthage. A revisit to this latter site has brought to my attention a Caeretan star plate (see Index of Collections: Carthage, *Musée de Carthage*, inv. no. 05.24) which I had overlooked during my original investigation of the Genucilia Group that included only the head plates by the Carthage Genucilia Painter.[5] Since publication of *Genucilia Group*, two exceedingly interesting proveniences beyond Italy have been encountered for products of Caeretan vase-painters: *Ampurias* on the northeastern coast of Spain, and *Alalia* (modern Aléria) on the east coast of Corsica.

Although most of the Caeretan finds are concentrated in Etruria and northern Latium, the examples discovered at Carthage, Ampurias, and Alalia reveal the important commercial relationships between these cities and the Etruscan center of Caere during the second half of the fourth century B.C. That Carthage and Caere were on exceptionally good terms during the fourth century B.C. has been clearly demonstrated by Massimo Pallottino in his discussion of the now celebrated gold tablets unearthed at Pyrgi in 1964.[6]

3. See I. S. Ryberg, *An Archaeological Record of Rome* (Philadelphia, 1940).
4. *Genucilia Group*, p. 299.
5. *Ibid.*, p. 255f. At the time, the plates formed part of the collection of the *Musée Lavigerie*, now incorporated into the new *Musée de Carthage* in the same monastic building.
6. M. Pallottino, "Scavi nel Santuario Etrusco di Pyrgi," *ArchCl* XVI (1964), pp. 49–117, and "Nuova Luce sulla Storia di Roma Arcaica dalle Lamine d'Oro di Pyrgi," *Studi Romani* XIII, no. 1 (January–March, 1965), pp. 3–15. My visit to Carthage in search of Caeretan red-figure and subsequent viewing of the Etruscan pottery exhibited

TABLE OF PROVENIENCES

The following table includes the proveniences given in *Genucilia Group* and *Torcop Group*. For reasons explained previously, "Caere" will be regarded as the provenience for vases of the Campana and Castellani Collections.

CFV signifies Caeretan Figured Vases, i.e., red-figured vases assigned to the Dotted-hem, Crescent-hem, or Unidentified Group; *GG* the Caeretan Branch of the Genucilia Group; *TG* the Torcop Group; and *AV* (Assorted Vases) for those examples here listed as Vases with Female Heads in Profile.

In order to attain a better concept of the proportionate number of vases with known proveniences and their relative distribution, the approximate total number of vases assigned to each individual Group will be denoted by the number in the parenthesis below the abbreviation for the group.

Provenience	CFV (107)	GG (ca. 475)	TG (ca. 85)	AV (31)
Alalia	6	92	2	–
Alba Fucens	–	4	–	–
Ampurias	–	–	–	I
Arezzo	–	–	I	–
Caere	55	130	15	II
Carthage	–	3	–	–
Carsoli	–	I	–	–
Castiglioncello	–	–	I	–
Castronovani	–	–	I	–
Cortona	–	6	I	–
Cosa	–	I	–	–

in the new Musée de Carthage has pointed out an interesting facet of the relationship between Caere and Carthage. Exhibited in some showcases was a goodly number of bucchero *sottile*, chiefly small amphorae, which I take to be Caeretan in origin, dating to the sixth century B.C. and derived from the seventh century "spiral" or "Lazian" amphorae (see T. Dohrn, "Die Etruskische Bandhenkelamphorae des 7. Jh. v. Chr.," *Studi L. Banti*, pp. 143–152). The presence at Carthage of both sixth-century Caeretan bucchero *and* fourth-century Caeretan red-figure—as represented by the Genucilia plates—attests to the good commercial contacts enjoyed by the two cities during these periods. A contact, however, seemingly interrupted during the fifth century B.C., to judge by the conspicuous absence of recognizable Caeretan material at Carthage for this period. For the close ties between Carthage and Etruria, with a consideration of bucchero sottile and Caeretan Genucilia plates, see E. Colozier, "Les Étrusques et Carthage," *MélRome* 65 (1953), pp. 63–98 and J. Ferron, "Les relations de Carthage avec l'Étrurie," *Latomus* XXV (1966), pp. 689–709.

Provenience	CFV (107)	GG (ca. 475)	TG (ca. 85)	AV (31)
Cumae	–	I	–	–
Genoa	–	I	–	–
Grottaferrata	–	9	–	–
Orbetello	–	–	I	I
Ostia	–	II	–	–
Populonia	IO	17	24	–
Praeneste	–	I	–	–
Pyrgi	–	3	–	–
Rome	–	29	I	–
Roselle	–	2	–	–
San Giuliano	–	6	–	–
Santa Marinella	–	I	–	–
Satricum (Conca)	–	3	2	–
Siena	–	–	I	–
Talamone	–	I	–	–
Tarquinii	5	31	I	5
Todi	–	I	–	–
Veii	–	7	–	–
Volterra	2	5	5	I

Surprisingly, a special "overseas" or "provincial" fondness for Caeretan red-figure is acknowledged by the Caeretan skyphos discovered at Ampurias and now in Barcelona (Museo Arqueológico, inv. no. 608, Pl. 76), which, though of no special aesthetic merit, appears to have been a prized possession, to judge by the evidence of ancient mending; note the matching drill holes along the breakages for insertion of small lead clamps. Further evidence for the importation of Etruscan products at Ampurias is provided by a bronze mirror engraved with the "Judgment of Paris" and which possibly dates to the end of the fourth century B.C.[7]

Alalia, as the Table of Proveniences discloses, is particularly important to better comprehend the flow of Caeretan exports, as well as other Etruscan fabrics, throughout the western Mediterranean during the second half of the fourth century B.C.[8] Its favorable position on the Tyrrhenian Sea, at a point

7. M. Almagro, *Ampurias* (Barcelona, 1951), fig. 99. I find the words of Professor Almagro regarding this mirror of particular interest, "y una de las pocas importaciones etruscas halladas en Ampurias, ya que la rivalidad entre focenses y etruscos fué siempre manifesta" (*ibid.*, p. 224).

8. M. Del Chiaro, "Etruscan Red-Figured Pottery at Ancient Alalia," *Corse Historique* IX (1969), pp. 43–58.

where well-frequented sailing routes were governed by prevailing winds,[9] unquestionably served to develop Alalia into an important "hub" or *emporium*
for quantities of Etruscan and South Italian pottery.[10] It may very well be that
from Alalia, as well as the Etruscan ports of Pyrgi and Populonia, Caeretan red-
figure found its way farther west to such centers as Ampurias and its "mother-
city," Massalia.

As yet no examples of Caeretan pottery have been discovered at this latter
site, but the new excavations in Marseilles (ancient *Massalia*), those projected
for Sardinia, as well as those which—it is hoped—may one day be undertaken
on the Balearic Islands, and along additional stretches of the Spanish, French,
and Ligurian coasts,[11] may bring various specimens to light. Such evidence will
offer new insight into a flourishing commerce that must have existed in the
western Mediterranean during the second half of the fourth and the early part
of the third century B.C.

9. J. Jehasse, *Aléria, Grecque et Romaine* (Excavation Guidebook), p. 10 and maps
   opposite p. 6 and p. 14.
10. *Ibid.*, p. 12; J. and L. Jehasse, "La Céramique Campanienne d'Aléria (I)," *Etudes
    Corses*, nos. 27–28 (1960); "La Céramique Campanienne d'Aléria (II)," *Revue
    d'Etudes Corses*, Oct.–Dec., 1961.
11. N. Lamboglia, "I limiti dell'espansione Etrusca nel territorio dei Liguri," *StEtr* X
    (1936), pp. 137–152.

V

Interrelationship Between
Caeretan and Other Red-figured Fabrics

TRUE RED-FIGURE executed with relief-line in Etruscan vase-painting, as Beazley has pointed out, does not begin much earlier than the middle of the fifth century B.C., when it was mainly derived from Attic models, some of which are still preserved.[1] It is now clear that during the second half of the fourth century B.C., the period with which I am most concerned in the present study, a number of fairly active centers of red-figured vase-painting, each with its own characteristic style, was widely dispersed throughout ancient Etruria. Of these centers, *Falerii* became the most prolific once a red-figured industry was established at the beginning of the fourth century B.C.[2]

About a generation later, and very probably stimulated by an influx of some migrant Faliscan potters and vase-painters, a reputable red-figured fabric developed at *Caere* and soon competed successfully with Faliscan products, as is shown by the common appearance of the two fabrics at Rome, Populonia, San Giuliano, Alalia, and elsewhere. Although Faliscan red-figured vases have been found at Caere, I am totally unaware of any Caeretan specimens discovered in the *Ager Faliscus*,[3] for which Giovanni Colonna has rightly observed that there was no need for such rival products where an extensive local Faliscan red-figure already flourished.[4]

1. Beazley, *EVP*, pp. 3 and 25.
2. *Ibid.*, p. 6f, Chapters IV and VIII.
3. See frontispiece map in *Genucilia Group*.
4. *ArchCl* XI (1959), p. 135.

In this chapter, I propose to investigate the interrelationship between Caeretan and Faliscan red-figure, with special attention to the latter's influence on the early development of the former, and a return to the consideration of the "Falisco-Caeretan" classification posed for plates of the Genucilia Group.[5] It will be important also to trace the simultaneous influence of both Caeretan and Faliscan on the newly discovered red-figured fabric produced contemporaneously at Tarquinii, a center with a long artistic tradition best reflected in its celebrated tomb paintings. More significantly, particular attention will be paid to the strong and constant influence of South Italian red-figure on Caeretan and Faliscan potters and vase-painters which, together with the earlier stimuli from Attic pottery, continued to play an influential role on these Etruscan fabrics.

Since it is beyond the scope of this study to include red-figured vases attributed to Vulci,[6] Chiusi or Volterra,[7] I am limiting my consideration of the interrelationships between the Etruscan fabrics to *Caeretan, Faliscan* and *Tarquinian* vases. Fairly convincing evidence for the close correspondence between these three red-figured fabrics may be seen in three examples of an unusual vase-shape, namely, the spouted lebes (see Pl. 87) decorated with profile heads; each lebes is attributable to Caeretan, Faliscan or Tarquinian vase-painters.[8]

RELATIONSHIP WITH FALISCAN RED-FIGURE

The similarity of vase-shapes, theme of decoration, and stylistic affinities in painting between contemporary Caeretan and Faliscan red-figured vases had, *before* publication of the *Genucilia Group* and the subsequent studies emanating

5. *Genucilia Group*, Chapter II.
6. See Beezley, *EVP*, Chapter VII, "Later Red-Figured I" which he believes are products of Vulci on the evidence of proveniences (p. 133). Despite the proveniences, I have been compelled to consider one of Beazley's groups, the "Funnel Group" within this category (pp. 141ff) as Tarquinian; see M. Del Chiaro, *The Etruscan Funnel Group: A Tarquinian Red-Figured Fabric* (Florence, 1974).
7. Beazley, *EVP*, Chapters V and VI; E, Fiumi, Intorno alle ceramiche del IV Sec. a. C. di fabbrica erroneamente chiamata Chiusini," *StEtr* XXVI (1958), pp. 243ff; Trendall, *VIE*, p. 223; G. Maetzke, "Tazza di Fabbrica Chiusina nel Museo di Cortona," *StEtr* XXI (1950–51), pp. 379ff.; A. Wotschitzky, "Zwei etruskische Vasen in Innsbruck," *StEtr* XXVI (1958), pp. 229 ff; A. Stenico, "Nuove Pitture Vascolari del Gruppo Clusium," *Studi L. Banti*, pp. 293ff. See also, M. Pasquinucci, *Le Kelebai Volterrane* (Florence, 1968).
8. M. Del Chiaro, "One Vase-Shape, Three Etruscan Fabrics," *RömMitt* 76 (1969), pp. 121ff and pls. 44–47.

from it,[9] consistently led to mistaking the two distinct fabrics as solely Faliscan.

In the past, I have devoted a number of studies to the differentiation of Caeretan and Faliscan vases of similar shape and decoration comprised of female heads in profile. This stylistic distinction was first illustrated in my investigation of the Genucilia Group. However, it was the detailed study of the Torcop Group oinochoai and vases of corresponding shape but with heads stylistically different, which led to the analysis of two distinct *full-sakkos* types (see Fig. B) and the subsequent discovery that each type was indicative of two red-figured fabrics, the *Caeretan* Torcop Group and the *Faliscan* Barbarano Group.[10] In sharp contrast to the Caeretan full-sakkos (Fig. B1), the Faliscan counterpart (Fig. B2) carries decoration ("embroidery") which divides the sakkos longitudinally into registers embellished with circles, dots, dashes, wavy lines, and the like.

Hence, a very special detail as the full-sakkos type on oinochoai (Shape VII), which helps to identify a particular Etruscan red-figured fabric, can now be conveniently extended to distinguish between Caeretan and Faliscan products among vases other than oinochoai, as has already been done for hydriae[11] and kylikes.[12] Furthermore, it has been possible to bring together, on the evidence of the full-sakkos type, a number of vases exclusively Faliscan, and to designate them as the "Full-Sakkos Group."[13]

The association of the Faliscan Barbarano Group with the Caeretan Torcop Group in regard to vase-shape and, in part, to the theme of decoration emphasizes the close relationship between these two different red-figured fabrics. Two Caeretan vases in particular illustrate this association well: the Warsaw oinochoe with confronting satyr and female profiles, which has a Faliscan counterpart;[14] and the Limoges oinochoe with confronting profiles on the body but palmette at the neck (Pl. 73) which recalls Faliscan examples with a single female profile on the body and palmette at the neck (see Fig. 16).[15]

Although rendered in slightly varying form, certain "filler" motifs (already

9. See supra, notes to Introduction.

10. In *Torcop Group*, pp. 159ff.

11. M. Del Chiaro, "Caeretan vs. Faliscan: Two Etruscan Red-Figured Hydriae," *AJA* 65 (1961), p. 56f.

12. M. Del Chiaro, "Caeretan vs. Faliscan: Some Etruscan Red-Figured Kylikes," *MAAR* XXVII (1962), pp. 203ff.

13. M. Del Chiaro, "The Full-Sakkos Group: Faliscan Red-Figured Skyphoi and Bell-Kraters," *StEtr* XXXII (1964), pp. 73ff.

14. *Torcop Group*, pl. XVII, fig. 12a.

15. *Ibid.*, pl. XVII, figs. 14–15 and pl. XVIII, fig. 16.

noted on Caeretan vases decorated with figured scenes, the Torcop Group, and various Caeretan vases with profile heads) were commonly shared by contemporary Faliscan vase-painters. The hanging wreath, for example, is normally more simple and of generally smaller scale on Faliscan than on Caeretan vases (e.g., Fig. 16).[16] Whereas the Faliscan *mesomphalic phiale* may undergo a more varied treatment, it nevertheless continues to function as a "filler" in very much the same manner as the Caeretan. In the hands of Faliscan artists, this latter motif may sometimes receive inner markings—chevrons or a series of radiating lines—around a smaller central circle, with a border of white dots encircling the outer perimeter[17] or three white dots arranged in triangular groups at the quarter points of the circle (e.g., Fig. 17).[18] As with Caeretan examples, the white dots may not often be visible owing to the fugitive nature of the white paint.[19] Later in this chapter, it will be demonstrated that such "filler" ornamentation present on Caeretan *and* Faliscan vases is also common in the repertory of South Italian red-figured vase-painters.

MIGRATION OF FALISCAN VASE-PAINTERS TO CAERE

A parallel—similar to the "Falisco-Caeretan" classification given to a number of the earliest plates of the Genucilia Group—is discernible for Caeretan Red-Figured Vases and a handful of Faliscan red-figured vases known to me. The name "Falisco-Caeretan" was created during the investigation of the Genucilia Group in recognition of the *Faliscan* provenience (in the *Ager Faliscus*) and the continuity of style evident on Genucilia plates attributed to *Caeretan* workmanship.[20]

Vases by the Villa Giulia Caeretan Painter, vases considered to be the earliest examples of Caeretan red-figured vases with figured scenes, when compared with certain red-figured Faliscan vases of comparable size—distinct from Genucilia plates—may add credence to my theory presented in *Genucilia Group* (Chapter IX), that some Faliscan potters and painters migrated to Caere where they soon became an integral part of red-figured activities. To a great extent,

16. Beazley, *EVP*, pl. XXXVI, figs. 2 and 4; *MonAnt* XLII (1954), c. 392, fig. 89, 2; *AJA* 65 (1961), pl. 126, figs. 2 and 3; *StEtr* XXXII (1964), pl. XII, B, pl. XV, F and pl. XVII.
17. *Bildertafeln des Etruskischen Museums, Ny Carlsberg Glyptothek* (Copenhagen, 1928), pl. 52; Beazley, *EVP*, pl. XXXV, figs. 2 and 7; Trendall, *VIE*, pl. LXV, f.
18. Beazley, *EVP*, pl. XXXV, fig. 1 and pl. XXXVI, figs. 1–4 and 6; *AJA* 65 (1961) pl. 31, figs. 4.
19. *Torcop Group*, pl. XVII, fig. 13 and pl. XVIII, fig. 17; Trendall, *VIE*, pl. LXI.
20. *Genucilia Group*, Chapter II.

this theory may explain the strong Attic *and* South Italian features—general themes, stock poses and gestures, special details, etc.—paralleled on Caeretan Red-Figured Vases. As Beazley observed (*EVP*, p. 70), *Falerii Veteres* marked an important center where local red-figured vase-painting of the mid-fourth century B.C. stood in such a close relationship to Attic red-figure that it suggested the presence of migrant Attic vase-painters; and, I might add, strong stimuli were continuously received from South Italian red-figure throughout the remainder of that century.

The five vases listed below—three of which were discovered in the *Ager Faliscus* (Falerii Veteres and Fabbrica di Roma), the fourth at Tarquinii, and the fifth at Caere—will readily illustrate Caeretan features on vases of doubtless Faliscan origin. Admittedly, while few specimens are given here, they can be augmented.[21] Even though the general poses of striding or seated women, and male with foot resting on high stone are known on Caeretan red-figured vases was figured scenes, the subject, need not detain us here for I am more concerned at the moment with special details.

The detail of greatest significance, seen in the major areas of decoration on these Faliscan vases, is a profuse use of relief-line, with the exception of vase no. 5. On vases nos. 1–3, and 5 (Pls. 96–98 and Fig. 21), the fleur de lis at the shoulders of the woman is particularly analogous to Caeretan vases with figured scenes. This feature par excellence for women of the Dotted-hem Group appears on four of the five Faliscan specimens in white; on stamnoi nos. 1 and 2 it is finely outlined in black. Although the calyx-krater, vase no. (Pl. 99), does not show the fleur de lis, it may have been present originally, judging by traces of white paint at the maenad's left shoulder. Nevertheless, this last vase does offer a close parallel to the Villa Giulia Caeretan Painter in the pose of the maenad and the treatment of her garment—primarily in the sweep of the folds and the diagonal direction of the broad band below the waist of the striding women (see Pl. 5).

This analogy is not made to argue that such Faliscan vases are the work of the Villa Giulia Caeretan Painter, but to reemphasize the possibility that he and some colleagues who decorated the earliest Caeretan red-figured vases may have been migrant Faliscan vase-painters who settled in Caere. The decorative bands below the picture field of the five Faliscan vases listed below show a modified meander pattern with diagonal- or checkered-box which, at times in varied form, have their counterparts on vases of the Dotted-hem Group (see Pls. 1–8). The particularly ornate character of the double-register decorative bands above

21. Museo di Villa Giulia, *CVA* fasc. I, IV Br., pl. 2, figs. 1–2.

the picture field on the Aleria oinochoe by the Villa Giulia Caeretan Painter (Pls. 3–4) is common to Faliscan red-figure (see Fig. 21).[22]

Stamnoi

Of the two following stamnoi, Beazley follows Giglioli in attributing vase no. 1 to the same hand as that of the Stamnos, Villa Giulia 26017 from Vignanello.[23] On the evidence of style, I believe that the second stamnos, vase no. 2, may also be ascribed to his hand.

1. Rome, Villa Giulia 2349 (Pl. 96)
   Provenience, Falerii Veteres
   Preserved height, 34 cms. The mouth and neck are missing.
   Beazley, *EVP*, p. 102; *NSc* 1916, p. 58f.

2. Rome, Villa Giulia 8238 (Pl. 97)
   Provenience, Fabbrica di Roma
   Height, 31 cms.

Oinochoe (Shape VII)

3. Tarquinia, Museo Nazionale RC 5340 (Pl. 98)
   Provenience, Tarquinii
   Height, 36.5 cms.

Calyx-Krater

4. Rome, Villa Giulia 8236 (Pl. 99)
   Provenience, Fabbrica di Roma
   Height, 38 cms.; diam. of rim, 38 cms.

Stamnos

The following stamnos (Fig. 21) has been reserved for discussion at this point because it was discovered at *Caere* and does not show the use of relief-lines in the major decoration, yet they are retained in the subsidiary decorative bands above the picture field. Such a vase may serve to bridge the gap between Caeretan and Faliscan vases with figured scenes.

5. Rome, Villa Giulia (Fig. 21)
   Provenience, Caere
   Height, 22 cms.

   A: at the center, a woman is seated on a cut block (altar?) with body
      to right and head turned round to left facing *Eros* who approaches

22. *Giglioli*, pl. CCLXXIV; Museo di Villa Giulia, *CVA* fasc. I, IV Br., pl. 1, figs. 1–2, pl. 4, figs. 1, 3, 5 and 6; *CVA* fasc. II, IV Br., pl. 11.
23. Beazley, *EVP*, p. 101f; see also G. Giglioli in *NSc* 1916, p. 58f.

from the left with small chest in his upraised left hand. At the right, a woman stands with her right leg raised and object (bowl or linens) in her upraised right hand.

B: an old satyr pursues a maenad to the right. The maenad looks round toward the satyr, her thyrsos held diagonally across her body.

Although a label indicates the stamnos to be from "Tomb 161, Necropoli della Banditaccia," it is *not* listed by Ricci in *MontAnt* XLII (1954); see c. 613f.

Consideration of the Faliscan vases listed above has once again brought into focus a "Falisco-Caeretan" artist of the Genucilia Group, the Berkeley Genucilia Painter, who has been credited with the origin of the Caeretan branch of the group and who may well have been an emigrant vase-painter from Falerii.[24] An extremely interesting stylistic comparison may be made between the female profile on one of his characteristic Genucilia plates (Fig. 20) and the female profiles on stamnoi nos. 1 and 2 above (Pls. 96–97) on which the "spiked-diadem" of the sphendone is worthy of note. At the same time, I must draw special attention to the facial details of these female profiles which are carefully indicated in extremely fine relief-line, for they recall the female head at side A of the volute-krater decorated in *superposed color* by the Sacrifice Painter (Pl. 91) whom I have already regarded as a vase-painter working within a purely *Caeretan* environment.

RELATIONSHIP WITH TARQUINIAN RED-FIGURE

As the investigation of oinochoai comprising the *Caeretan* Torcop Group focused attention on vases which comprise the *Faliscan* Barbarano Group, an avenue has also opened to the important discovery of a previously unrecognized red-figured fabric produced at Tarquinii during the second half of the fourth century B.C. During the analysis of Torcop Group vases, two oinochoai (Shape VII), replicas of each other (one of these, Fig. 18), stood considerably apart from the Caeretan and Faliscan oinochoai due to their style of drawing, vase-shape and clay color. At that time, the two unusual vases were tentatively attributed (with query) to Tarquinian red-figure vase-painters;[25] this marked the first instance that a red-figure industry was claimed for the ancient and important Etruscan city of Tarquinii. It has always seemed to me rather strange that such a center, already

24. *Genucilia Group*, p. 251f.
25. *Torcop Group*, pp. 156ff and pl. XIV.

renowned for its artistic tradition in sculpture and tomb-painting, would not have inspired a suitable local red-figured fabric.[26]

This tenative attribution to Tarquinii eventually found confirmation in a later study which reconsidered the two Tarquinian oinochoai, together with two skyphoi—an example at Tarquinia (Fig. 19) and another in Geneva—all of which were subsequently recognized as the work of a single artist, the Painter of Geneva MF 142.[27] Cognizance of a Tarquinian red-figured fabric is in large part due to knowledge of contemporary Caeretan and Faliscan vases, of which numerous examples were imported by Tarquinii.[28] Through the work of the Painter of Geneva MF 142, I attempted to demonstrate that Tarquinian red-figure was highly eclectic in character, for it derived elements from both Caeretan and Faliscan sources. Some of these eclectic or "borrowed" features are easily traced. The composition of *confronting profile heads* on the bodies of the Tarquinian oinochoai and on one of the skyphoi points directly to the Caeretan Torcop Group; however, the *palmette* at the necks of the oinochoai strongly suggests vases of the Faliscan Barbarano Group (see Fig. 16) more than the sole Caeretan example with palmette presented earlier in this study (Pl. 73). Although the "spiked diadem" of the Tarquinian women recalls a similar type of diadem on plates of the Caeretan Genucilia Group, the *sphendone* is decorated with motifs from both Caeretan (net) and Faliscan (palmette) half-sakkoi. A *mesomphalic phiale* is used as "filler" between confronting heads on one of the Tarquinian skyphoi, and a *hanging wreath*, though not present on any of the four aforementioned Tarquinian vases, is known to me in the work of the "Tarquinian Epaulets Painter," an artist whom I have named after epaulet-like forms on the shoulders of his women.[29]

Additions have been made to the above "first members of Tarquinian red-figure,"[30] of which one study devoted to Tarquinian skyphoi has disclosed a

26. L. Banti in *Il Mondo degli Etruschi* (Rome, 1960), p. 60, has also expressed surprise that no red-figured fabric had been proposed for Tarquinii.

27. M. Del Chiaro, "An Etruscan (Tarquinian?) Vase in Geneva," *RömMitt* 67 (1960), pp. 29ff.

28. For *Caeretan* red-figure discovered at Tarquinii, see Table of Proveniences, Chapter IV. At least one *Faliscan* Genucilia plate was found at Tarquinii (*CVA*, Tarquinia IV B, pl. 4, fig. 3), and some thirteen *Faliscan* red-figured oinochoai (Shape VII) of the Barbarano Group are known for that site; see *Torcop Group*, p. 160f, nos. 12–24.

29. In M. Del Chiaro, "The 'Orbetello Group,' Two Etruscan Red-Figured Fabrics," *StEtr* XXVIII (1970), pp. 91ff; in particular pp. 97ff and pls. VIII–IX.

30. M. Del Chiaro, "A Tarquinian Oinochoe and Skyphos," *RömMitt* 73–74 (1966–67), pp. 256ff; "Additional Tarquinian Red-Figure," *RömMitt* 80 (1973), pp. 199ff.

particularly strong influence from the Faliscan Full-Sakkos Group.[31] More recently, I have completed a detailed investigation of Beazley's "Funnel Group" (*EVP*, pp. 141ff.) which I believe represents a major Tarquinian red-figured production dating to the last quarter of the fourth century B.C.[32]

RELATIONSHIP WITH SOUTH ITALIAN RED-FIGURE

In a few earlier studies devoted to specific Caeretan vases, I attempted to demonstrate—with particular attention to vase-shape—strong influences directly derived from South Italian red-figured pottery. For example, the "mug" or *oinochoe*, *Shape VIII B*, with knotted handle (see Pls. 83–85)[33] and the *epichysis* (see Pl. 86)[34] seem to have their immediate prototypes in Apulian red-figure where the distinctive shapes are especially popular during the fourth century B.C. (for the "mug", see Fig. 22).[35] A shape par excellence for South Italian red-figure, Campanian and Apulian in particular, is the fish plate which finds its Caeretan counterpart in the specimen at Cerveteri (Pl. 90). As is well known, column-kraters, bell-kraters, and calyx-kraters are much more common in South Italian than in Etruscan red-figure, where the *stamnos* replaces them in popularity. In Caeretan red-figure, on the other hand, the krater is represented only by the calyx-krater and in that case by a sole example, vase no. 11 by the Villa Giulia Caeretan Painter (Louvre K 403 and Pl. 11).

In regards to vase-shape, the "mug" and epichysis noted in Caeretan red-figure point specifically to Apulian, while the fish plate is also common to Paestan and Campanian red-figure. In matters of decoration, however, the influences on Caeretan vase-painting may be traced in varying degrees to all known South Italian productions: Lucanian, Apulian, Campanian, Paestan, and Sicilian. As will soon be seen, this is especially true for general themes, certain stock poses, minor features of the garments of the women and other relative details, and similarities of "filler" motifs, etc. The citing of these significant parallels between Caeretan and South Italian red-figure has been greatly facilitated by Professor

31. M. Del Chiaro, "Tarquinian Red-Figured Skyphoi," *RömMitt* 70 (1963), pp. 63ff.
32. M. Del Chiaro, *The Etruscan Funnel Group: A Tarquinian Red-Figured Fabric* (Florence, 1974).
33. M. Del Chiaro, "A Caeretan Red-Figured Mug," *StEtr* XXX (1962), pp. 317ff.
34. M. Del Chiaro, "Caeretan Epichyseis," *ArchCl* XII (1960), pp. 15ff.
35. For Apulian epichyseis, see Lecce, Museo Provinciale, inv. nos. 797 and 819, *CVA* fasc. II, pl. 51; Naples, Museo Nazionale, *CVA* fasc. III, pls. 71 and 72; London, British Museum, *CVA* fasc. I, IV Dc., pl. 6.

A. D. Trendall's extensive contributions over the years; more timely in his recent publication, *The Red-Figured Vases of Lucania, Campania, and Sicily* (Oxford, 1967). For reasons of simplification and convenience, these analogies are best distinguished according to the classifications given below.

FIGURED SCENES

Themes

Apart from a relatively few rare exceptions (musical contest between Aplu and Marsyas, Pl. 40; stag- and horse-drawn chariots, Pls. 41, 43 and 52; and Skylla, Pl. 50)—all products of the Crescent-hem Group—the subjects on Caeretan vases with figured scenes are chiefly concerned with satyrs, maenads, *lasas*, ordinary women, erotes, or youths. Although Dionysos (*Fufluns*) is not present, a *Dionysiac* character generally pervades the themes as a whole.[36] This correspondence with subjects frequently found on late South Italian red-figured vases strongly suggests that Caeretan themes are in some way based on South Italian models which, in themselves, must originally descend from Attic prototypes.[37]

In brief, some parallels in South Italian red-figure can be cited for an unusual theme or figure encountered on Caeretan vases with figured scenes. Although the animals harnessed to the chariot are *stags* rather than *does*, an analogy may be drawn between the oinochoai of the Castellani and American Academy Caeretan Painters (Pl. 41 and Pl. 52) and a Lucanian vase by the Primato Painter who, according to Trendall, may have intended the charioteer to be "Artemis."[38] The theme of *Skylla* on a stamnos by the Castellani Caeretan Painter (Pl. 50) has numerous parallels in Apulian and Campanian, as I have demonstrated at some length in a special study of this Caeretan vase.[39] On the fragmentary stamnos by the Volterra Caeretan Painter (Pl. 34), the nearly frontal female figure holding a long torch in each hand recalls representations of *Hecate*, with a torch in either hand, who is often portrayed on South Italian vases.[40]

---

36. For Dionysos and the Underworld or Cult of the Dead in Etruria, cf. Beazley, *EVP*, p. 152; see also M. R. Turcan, "Dionysos Ancien et le Sommeil Infernal," *MélRome* LXXI (1959), pp. 187ff as the god pertains to funerary art of the second and third centuries A.D.

37. For the close stylistic relationships which suggest that some of the first South Italian vase-painters were probably of Greek origin trained in Athens, see Trendall, *LCS*, p. 3ff.

38. Trendall, *VIE*, p. 15 and pl. III, b.

39. M. Del Chiaro, "Skylla on a Caeretan Red-Figured Vase," *ArchCl* XXI (1969), pp. 210–215.

40. E.g., Trendall, *LCS*, p. 589 and pl. 228, fig. 1.

A number of stock poses, not to be counted as indicative of specific influence, are shared in common by Caeretan red-figure and all South Italian fabrics. A few of these are worthy of brief mention before considering more concrete instances of unusual features and motifs derived by Etruscan vase-painters from one or other of the South Italian fabrics. These "stock poses" may be assumed by either male or female figures, and may undergo considerable variations through the mere interchange of gesture, placement of arms and legs and, of course, by the choice of objects borne by the individuals. Two frequent and conspicuous stock poses for the female figures depicted on Caeretan vases with figured scenes are the *seated* and *striding* women, each of whom may face or move to right or left, or may look straight ahead or turn their head around.

The *seated woman* normally sits on a rock[41]—sometimes a "cut" block or even an altar[42]—with her body more in three-quarter view than in profile. One arm is held straight down at the back to brace the body which leans gently backwards, the hand placed palm down with fingers usually gripping the edge of the rock. The "free" arm may simply rest on the thigh or is bent and upraised to accept a gift from an approaching figure, or may hold or support any one of an infinite number of objects: mirror, small fan, small vase, offering tray, chest, beaded necklace or bracelet, wreath, etc. In the positioning of the feet, the foot of the far leg is crossed in behind the foot of the near leg and the seated figure displays a remarkably close resemblance to a Nike seated on an altar which appears on late fifth century coins of *Terina* (Fig. 23), a Lucanian city on the west coast of Italy.

The *striding woman*,[43] at times a maenad, may move to the right or left

41. For *seated women* in South Italian red-figure, see (Apulian) the Bendis Painter, Cambitoglou-Trendall, *APS*, pl. XXXV, fig. 173; (Campanian) the Laghetto Painter and the Whiteface Painter, Trendall, *LCS*, pl. 120, fig. 5 and pl. 146, fig. 5; (Paestan) the Dirce Painter and the Asteas Group, Trendall, *PP*, figs. 4, 28, and 38, pl. XIII, a; (Sicilian) the Lentini Painter, Trendall, *LCS*, pl. 226, fig. 1 and pl. 227, figs. 5 and 7.

42. In a discussion of South Italian Phlyax vases, H. R. W. Smith draws attention to "altar-sitting" figures; see *AJA* 66 (1962), p. 329.

43. For *striding women* in South Italian red-figure, see (Lucanian) the Painter of Naples 1959 and the Primato Painter, Trendall, *LCS*, pl. 68, figs. 1, 3–6, pl. 75, fig. 6, pl. 76, fig. 7; (Apulian) the Tarpoley Painter and the Painter of Karlsruhe B 9, Cambitoglou-Trendall, *APS*, pl. XII, figs. 54 and 55, pl. XIV, fig. 61, pl. XVII, fig. 80; (Campanian) the Painter of Vienna 687 and the Capua Painter, Trendall, *LCS*, pl. 83, fig. 5, pl. 140, figs. 5, 7, and 8; (Paestan) the Dirce Painter and the Boston Orestes Painter, Trendall, *PP*, fig. 5 and pl. XXIX, pl. XXXII, c; (Sicilian) the Lentini-Manfria Group, Trendall, *LCS*, pl. 238, fig. 2.

with her body in nearly frontal view, and normally shows the leading foot in profile and the trailing foot in frontal foreshortened view with heel raised and toes seemingly touching the ground. One arm is usually down, the other bent at the elbow and upraised with an object in hand. The variety of objects which may be held in the hands are by now well known. However, if a *situla* is carried, it is normally held in the trailing, lowered hand.

A third and fourth "stock pose" is generally assumed by a satyr, *Eros*, or youth. Although the posture of the striding woman may be considered as stationary, I have regularly been interpreting it as a moving or "approaching" figure.[44] Normally, such a figure bears a "gift"—more often than not a beaded necklace, bracelet, or wreath—between the outstretched hands, one up and one down. The fourth stock pose is popular to South Italian and Etruscan red-figure, and may find its ultimate source in a Lysippic prototype,[45] i.e., a male figure who stands with one knee upraised and foot resting on a high stone or the like. On

44. For the "approaching" *male figure* in South Italian red-figure, see (Lucanian) the Sydney Painter, Trendall, *LCS*, pl. 63, fig. 2 (young warrior); (Apulian) the Eton-Nika Painter or near his work, Cambitoglou-Trendall, *APS*, pl. XX, fig. 97 (youth), pl. XXII, fig. 104 (satyr); (Campanian) the Painter of B.M. F 63 and the Ixion Group, Trendall, *LCS*, pl. 125, fig. 3 (Eros), pl. 134, fig. 8 (youth); (Paestan) Asteas, the Asteas Group, and Python, Trendall, *PP*, fig. 20 (Eros), figs. 25 and 27 (youths), fig. 46 (satyr). In the general attitude of the body and position of the legs, the "approaching" figure in red-figured vase-painting strongly recalls its sculptural counterpart on the mid-fourth century B.C. column-drum from Ephesos on which the figure of Hermes assumes this basic stock pose; M. Bieber, *The Sculpture of the Hellenistic Age* (New York, 1961), figs. 66 and 67. To the same period, and perhaps a more appropriate analogy in view of its provenience—Taranto—is the young warrior on a relief in the Metropolitan Museum of Art: G. Richter, *Handbook of the Greek Collection* (Cambridge, 1953), p. 108 and pl. 87, c.

45. For the *male figure with one foot resting on an elevation* in South Italian red-figure, see (Lucanian) the Amykos Painter, Trendall, *LCS*, pl. 10, fig. 1 (satyr), pl. 13, fig. 6 (youth); (Apulian), Trendall, *VIE*, pl. XXX, f (satyr), pl. XLVIII, g (Eros), pl. LIII, d (youth); (Campanian) the Painter of Naples 2074 and the Three Dot Group, Trendall, *LCS*, pl. 81, fig. 6 (Eros), pl. 113, fig. 8 (satyr); (Paestan) Asteas, Asteas Group, and Python, Trendall, *PP*, fig. 22 (satyr), pl. XII, c and d (youths), fig. 45 (Eros); (Sicilian) related to the Lentini Painter, Trendall, *LCS*, pl. 228, fig. 2 (youth), pl. 229, fig. 2 (Eros), figs. 5 and 7, satyrs). For the pose of the male figure with one foot set on an elevation in sculpture. see M. Bieber, *Sculpture of the Hellenistic Age*, p. 74 and figs. 148 and 149. See also, Beazley, *EVP*, p. 60f. A quite accidental yet convenient juxtaposition of the Lyssipic sculptural type—the "Sandalbinder" or the "Jason" —with its varied counterpart in red-figured *Faliscan* vase-painting may be seen in *AJA* 68 (1964), pl. 36, fig. 20 and pl. 37, figs. 1 and 2.

vases, this figure—occasionally a woman[46]—may have both arms extended, one up and one down or, on more rare occasions, one forearm resting across the thigh of the upraised leg in closer analogy to its sculptural male counterpart. As frequently mentioned throughout this study, the gestures of arms and hands for this stock pose may often appear meaningless owing to the fugitive nature of the white paint added to indicate beads and the like which are retained between the hands.

Details of Garments: the "Broad Band"

The presence of the *broad band* which runs down the length of the women's garment—whether peplos or chiton—from the neckline to the hem, has been shown to be a relatively consistent feature on Caeretan vases decorated with figured scenes. This broad band may be rendered by two parallel lines, the more usual practice in the Dotted-hem Group, or by a broad black band over which a narrower band is painted in white, characteristic for vases of the Crescent-hem Group. In South Italian red-figure the broad band is normally rendered with two parallel lines and appears occasionally in Lucanian,[47] is not uncommon in Apulian and Campanian,[48] and is extremely rare in Sicilian; a broad black band with painted white stripe is frequently encountered in Paestan pottery, especially on vases of the Asteas Group.[49] On Lucanian, Apulian, and Campanian vases, the broad band, which is frequently set off to the side of the garment, may appear only from the waist down or, more rarely, from the waist up.

On some Caeretan red-figured vases (e.g., Pl. 35) and on Etruscan vases of the "Campanizing Group" to be discussed in this chapter, the broad band may be embellished with a series of blacked-out squares ("embattled border")[50] or dots ("dot-stripe") along the outer sides. Although analogies can be found

46. On Caeretan red-figured vases with figured scenes, see vases nos. 6 and 8, pl. 7 and pl. 8. In South Italian red-figure, see (Apulian), Cambitoglou-Trendall, *APS*, pl. XXI, fig. 101 and Trendall, *VIE*, pl. XXIX, i; (Campanian) the Libation Painter and the CA Painter, Trendall, *LCS*, pl. 164, fig. 6, pl. 175, fig. 5; (Paestan) Asteas Group and Python, Trendall, *PP*, pl. XIV, d, pl. XXV, a.
47. The Amykos Painter, the Intermediate Group, and the Creusa Painter, Trendall, *LCS*, pl. 16, fig. 4, pl. 25, fig. 2, pl. 30, fig. 4, pl. 31, fig. 2, pl. 32, fig. 7, pl. 41, figs. 5 and 6.
48. (Apulian) The Painter of Bari 1364, the Truro Painter, and the Berkeley Painter, Cambitoglou-Trendall, *APS*, pl. XXV, fig. 115, pl. XXXVII, fig. 186, pl. XLI, fig. 209; (Campanian) the Painter of Vienna 687, the Pilos Head Group, and the Rhomboid Group, Trendall, *LCS*, pl. 83, figs. 4 and 5, pl. 108, fig. 2, pl. 211, figs. 2 and 6.
49. Trendall, *PP*, Chaper III, pp. 46ff, pp. 117ff and pl. XI, f.; see also, pl. XXVI, c.
50. *Ibid.*, p. 8, n. 7.

for both the embattled and / or dot-stripe borders in Apulian and Campanian red-figure,[51] they are especially prevalent on Paestan vases.[52] In all probability, the earlier embattled border degenerates into the dot-stripe border. In Paestan red-figure, the more cursory dot-stripe border along the broad band or the hem becomes the most common drapery decoration.

There are several instances on Caeretan vases with figured scenes—an oinochoe by the Villa Giulia Caeretan Painter and an example by the Frontal Satyr Caeretan Painter, vases no. 4 and 107 (Pls. 3 and 62)—in which the hem of the female garment is decorated with elongated rays pointing upward from the hem. This distinctive motif not only recalls a similar motif on South Italian vases,[53] but also fourth century wall paintings from Etruscan tombs: the *Tomba Golini I* near Orvieto and the celebrated *Tomba dell'Orco* at Tarquinia.[54]

"Filler" and Other Relevant Detailing

The *mesomphalic phiale*, in various forms, provides the most common "filler" in the field of Caeretan vases decorated with figured scenes. Parallel in form and frequency of appearance on South Italian red-figured vases, the *hanging wreath*—noted on some specimens of Caeretan figured vases and oinochoai of the Torcop Group—has no exact counterpart in South Italian.[55] A closer analogy for the Caeretan hanging wreath is found on Faliscan red-figured vases.[56]

The floral / vegetal motif which appears in the lower field on Torcop Group oinochoai (see Pl. 68 and Pl. 71) and which gives evidence to the possible presence of bronze workers at Caere (see Chapter III, note 4) has its counter-

---

51. (Apulian) Cambitoglou-Trendall, *APS*, pl. XI, fig. 51, pl. XVIII, fig. 89. The dot-stripe is rare in Apulian; (Campanian) the Painter of Vienna 687, the Fienga Painter and the Scoglitti Group, Trendall, *LCS*, pl. 8, figs. 2–3, pl. 85, figs. 1–6.

52. Trendall, *PP*, pl. I, b, pl. III, pl. VIII, pl. XII, etc.

53. (Apulian) *CVA*, Lecce, Museo Provinciale Castromediano, 2 pl. 9, figs. 1 and 3; (Paestan) Trendall, *PP*, pl. II, b and pl. XI, a.

54. See P. Ducati, *Pittura Etrusca-Italo-Greca e Romana* (Novara, 1942), pl. 19 on the garment worn by *Phersipnai* (Greek Persephone) and pl. 23 on the *chitoniskos* worn by the Etruscan death-demon, *Charon*. For *Phersipnai*, see also, Giglioli, pl. CCXLV.

55. As a rule, the *hanging wreath* or (better) *sash* in South Italian red-figure is represented as hanging in an "M" configuration on two pegs or simply draped over a single peg with one end suspended considerably longer than the other; see (Lucanian), Trendall, *LCS*, pl. 32, fig. 2, pl. 35, fig. 1, pl. 39, fig. 3; (Campanian) pl. 76, figs. 4 and 7, pl. 78, fig. 4, pl. 158, fig. 1, pl. 181, fig. 6; (Paestan) Trendall, *PP*, figs. 21, 27, 32 and pl. I, a, pl. IX, a, pl. XXX, b; (Sicilian) Trendall, *LCS*, pl. 236, fig. 6, pl. 248, figs. 3–5.

56. See supra, n. 16 (Chapter V).

part—in approximately the same form or somewhat modified—on South Italian red-figured vases.[57]

On the neck of an oinochoe, Shape VII, assigned as "miscellaneous" within the Dotted-hem Group (Pl. 37), a young satyr is seated on a rock which receives unusual treatment by the Caeretan painter who decorated the vase. The reserved form of the rock is cursorily outlined in white with white dots or dashes added to a scattering of black dots. This peculiar rendering of the rock calls attention to the *Campanian* Spotted Rock Group.[58]

Satyrs, erotes, and youths represented on vases of the Caeretan Figured Group more often than not wear a beaded "bandolier," which is sometimes worn in "corps diplomatique" fashion over one shoulder and across the chest in a single diagonal strand. However, in many cases, the "bandolier" is comprised of two strands of beads which cross the chest diagonally in "Mexican-bandit" fashion. In South Italian red-figure, the beaded "bandolier" does not appear on Lucanian vases. It can be traced, however, on Apulian, Campanian, Paestan, and Sicilian specimens, where it is normally the single strand variety. The "Mexican-bandit" beaded bandolier is, as far as known, characteristically Etruscan; most common in Caeretan red-figure, it is paralleled, to a degree, in Tarquinian red-figure.[59]

The numerous objects carried by the figures represented on Caeretan vases —whether youths, erotes, satyrs, women, maenads, lasas, etc.—can, of course, be found readily on vases of all South Italian fabrics, for which cited parallels would prove far too burdensome.[60]

Before turning our attention to the relationship between Caeretan red-

57. See in particular a bell-krater by the Apulian Eumenides Painter (Cambitoglou-Trendall, *APS*, pl. V, fig. 21) and a hydria by the Campanian Astarita Painter (Trendall, *LCS*, pl. 155, fig. 3). See also, (Lucanian) the Roccanova Painter who is particularly fond of a floral/vegetal motif as filler, Trendall, *LCS*, pl. 64, figs. 1 and 3, pl. 65, figs. 1–5; (Campanian) the Painter of Vienna 687, the Fienga Painter and the Scoglitti Group, *ibid.*, pl. 8, figs. 2–3, pl. 85, figs. 1–6.

58. Trendall, *LCS*, pp. 234ff; see in particular pl. 181, fig. 3.

59. In my investigation of the Etruscan Funnel Group (*op. cit.*), which I take to be Tarquinian, both the single strand and crossed variety are known. Because of the broad band and central boss-like feature at the crossing of the bands, I have designated the bandolier as "parachute harness." In Faliscan red-figure, the *beaded bandolier* is, as a rule, of the single strand variety; see Beazley, *EVP*, pl. XXXV, figs. 3 and 7; *NSc* 1914, p. 271, fig. 7; *MonAnt* XLII (1954), col. 961, fig. 229.

60. Perusal of Cambitoglou-Trendall, *APS* and Trendall, *PP*, *VIE*, and *LCS* should adequately reveal the correspondence for such details between Caeretan red-figure and all South Italian fabrics.

figured vases decorated with female heads in profile and their South Italian counterparts, there remains one more feature of detailing that may have significance in our study of the associations between the Etruscan fabric and those of South Italy and Sicily. In the representations of altars on the neck of his oinochoai, the Castellani Caeretan Painter has made a conscientious effort to render three-quarter perspective (e.g., Pl. 46). This is accomplished not simply by a vertical line indicating the turn of the altar (see Pl. 45), but by a sharp contrast of colors: white for the frontal and reserved side plane, clearly set off by a black background.

In South Italian red-figure, pillars, stelai, altars, and the like, are rendered in most cases in three-quarter perspective with a vertical line for the turning edge and a diagonal line for the corresponding "diminishing" view.[61] On some Campanian and Sicilian vases, however, the perspective is attained in very much the same manner as that noted on vases by the Castellani Caeretan Painter of the Crescent-hem Group (e.g., Pl. 46): i.e., the contrast of frontal and side planes by added white paint and a reserved, unpainted area.

FEMALE HEADS IN PROFILE

Vases decorated with female heads in profile are well represented in South Italian red-figure vase-painting. Apulian alone accounts for well over a thousand such vases, but not with the flesh painted in white, which is a particular attribute of Campanian red-figure.[62] In Trendall's words, "Female heads are regularly used, from about the middle of the fourth century onwards, as the sole figure decoration on vases in all the five generally accepted red-figure fabrics of South Italy. For the most part they have clearly defined characteristics which enable the fabrics to be readily distinguished one from another."[63]

In Chapter II of this study, attention was drawn to Caeretan red-figured vases bearing female heads in profile, either single or confronting. A correspondence with South Italian red-figure, confirmed by Trendall's statement above,

---

61. (Lucanian) Trendall, *LCS*, pl. 30, figs. 1, pl. 42, figs. 3, 4 and 6; (Apulian) Cambitoglou-Trendall, *APS*, pl. XIV, fig. 64, pl. XXX, figs. 140–141; (Campanian) Trendall, LCS, pl. 88, fig. 2, pl. 98, fig. 5; (Paestan) Trendall, *PP*, pl. XXXIV, b; (Sicilian) Trendall, *LCS*, pl. 230, fig. 1. See also G. Richter, *Perspective in Greek and Roman Art* (London, 1970), Chapter V, pp. 39ff.

62. (Campanian) The Pilos Head Group and the CA Painter, Trendall, *LCS*, pl. 108, fig. 6, pl. 176, figs. 1–3, pl. 177, fig. 3, pl. 180, fig. 1; (Sicilian) the Biancavilla Painter and the Painter of Catania 4229, *ibid.*, pl. 246, fig. 1, pl. 250, fig. 8.

63. A. D. Trendall, "Head Vases in Padula," *Apollo II* (1962), see p. 28f and p. 29, n. 4.

is clearly evident, especially for a single female head in profile which, as a rule, faces to the left.[64]

In relationship to the Caeretan Genucilia Group, a Campanian stemless cup in Valencia from Ampurias is of special interest for the tight wave pattern that encircles the medallion. As would be expected, the profile head shows the distinctive Campanian full-sakkos.[65] Such a configuration of female head in profile surrounded by a wave pattern is remarkably akin to the normal formula encountered on Genucilia head plates. Another association, perhaps of greater significance, between Campanian and Caeretan red-figured vases related to the Genucilia plates, i.e., the Caeretan Genucilia kylikes (e.g., Pl. 75), may be found in the products of the *Campanian* Rhomboid Group, where the kylikes with their medallions are decorated with a female profile head wearing a *net sphendone*.[66] As shown already, the net sphendone is an especially characteristic feature of the Caeretan Genucilia Group. That it makes so rare an appearance in Campanian must be attributed to influences emanating from Etruscan (i.e., Caeretan) to South Italian (i.e., Campanian) red-figure, an occurrence already acknowledged by Trendall.[67]

Apart from epichyseis, oinochoai (Shape VIII B), skyphoi, and the like, which are decorated with single profile heads by Caeretan vase-painters and readily find their parallels in South Italian red-figure, there is the long-handled cup that bears *three* female heads in profile, one in the interior, and one on each side (see Pls. 78–79). Again, we must turn to Campanian red-figure for the closest analogy to the Caeretan specimens, i.e., those by the APZ Painter of the Campanian Apulianizing Group.[68]

CONFRONTING HEADS

Our acquaintance with *confronting* female profile heads in Caeretan vase-painting is based primarily on the oinochoai of the Torcop Group. Not surprisingly, analogies can be found in South Italian red-figure, specifically in Campanian

64. (Lucanian) The Primato Painter and the Primato Group, Trendall, *LCS*, pl. 76, figs. 6 and 8, pl. 77, fig. 7; (Apulian) A. Cambitoglou, "Group of Apulian Red-Figure Vases Decorated with Heads of Women or of Nike," *Journal of Hellenic Studies* 74 (1954), pp. 111ff; (Campanian) numerous, peruse Trendall, *LCS*; (Paestan) the Caivano Group and the Painter of Naples 1778, Trendall, *PP*, pl. XXXIII, a and d, pl. XXXIV, d; (Sicilian) the Etna Group, Trendall, *LCS*, pl. 251, figs. 1–7, pl. 252.

65. Trendall, *LCS*, pl. 134, fig. 6.

66. *Ibid.*, Chapter XIX, see pl. 214, fig. 2.

67. *Ibid.*, p. 538f.

68. *Ibid.*, Chapter CVII.

but even more commonly in Sicilian.[69] Trendall has already noted the need to compare the heads of his Ixion Group of Campanian (*LCS*, Chapter VIII) with the Caeretan Group (*ibid.*, p. 344); but the Sicilian red-figured fabric truly offers the closer relationship, at least in regards to the composition of confronting female heads. However, even such major artists as the ZA Painter and those of the Etna Group do not employ added white for the flesh color of the women portrayed on their vases (*ibid.*, p. 643). Nor do the "fillers" placed between the confronting profiles on the Sicilian vases share anything in common with that normally found on oinochoai of the Torcop Group. Nonetheless, as noted by the presence of the *net sphendone* on kylikes of the Campanian Rhomboid Group, an equally strong influence may have been exerted on Sicilian red-figure from Etruscan (i.e., Caeretan) sources, to judge by the theme of *confronting heads* which, with the exception of the Sicilian fabric, is not common in South Italian vase-painting.

Before leaving the discussion of Caeretan profile heads and their relationship with South Italian red-figure, attention should be called once again to the small profile heads *outlined* on the curious Genucilia star plate (Fig. 6). In this instance, there seems to be a certain broad connection between the *outlined* rendering of the profile heads which is unusual to Caeretan red-figure, and that found on one of the Campanian *kemai*.[70]

THE ETRUSCAN "CAMPANIZING GROUP"

Although parallels and analogies have been pointed out between Caeretan red-figured products and *all* South Italian fabrics, the strongest links seem to be found in Campanian and Paestan red-figure. Of these two fabrics, Beazley has listed a number of vases within his "Earlier Red-figure" of Etruscan vase-painting (*EVP*, Chapter III) which, owing to their especially strong Campanian features, he was persuaded to name the "Campanizing Group" (*ibid.*, pp. 63ff). Of the three vases given below, which I believe to be produced at *Caere* for reasons to be discussed shortly, vase no. 1 is from Beazley's Campanizing Group and another, vase no. 3, he has placed close to his "Group of Toronto 495" (*ibid.*, p. 182). Vase no. 2 has been associated with the Campanizing Group by Trendall

69. (Campanian) Related to the Capua Painter and the CA Painter, Trendall, *LCS*, pl. 142, fig. 3, pl. 183, fig. 10; (Sicilian) the ZA Painter and the Etna Group, pl. 244, pl. 251, figs. 8–12.
70. Trendall, *LCS*, Appendix II, pp. 674ff; see in particular the Campanian *kemai* now in Sydney, Nicholson Museum, inv. no. 67.164, formerly Norcera, Fienga Collection, p. 674, no. 3 and *Fasti Archaeologici* XXII (1971), pl. I, fig. 3.

in his study of the Vatican vases. All three specimens are *calyx-kraters*. In addition, I would like to venture that vase no. 2 may be a rather hasty example by the painter of the Bonn krater; if not, it is certainly closely allied, perhaps a direct imitation by an artist of lesser competence.

1. Bonn, inv. no. 83 (Pl. 100 and Fig. 24)
   Akademisches Kunstmuseum, University
   Height, 38 cms.; diam. of rim, 33 cms.

   A: Dionysos and Ariadne with frolicking satyrs and female flutist.
   B: Obese reveler between two mantled youths.

   Beazley, *EVP.*, p. 63.

2. Vatican, inv. no. Z 91 (Pls. 101–102)
   Museo Gregoriano Etrusco
   Height, 38 cms.; diam. of rim, 30 cms.

   A: Figures of Perseus, deer-headed female, and Nike or Lasa.
   B: Bearded man, woman, maenad, and satyr.

   Trendall, *VIE*, p. 231f. and pl. LX.

   Related (?) to the Campanizing Group:

3. Vatican, inv. no. Z 110
   Museo Gregoriano Etrusco
   Height, 35 cms.; diam. of rim, 27.3 cms.

   A: at the center, a warrior wearing cuirass and crested helmet with upturned cheek-piece faces to the left. A *phiale* is held in his right hand in preparation for a libation. Two *nikai* or *lasas* appear one on each side; the one on the left is about to pour from an oinochoe into the *phiale* extended by the warrior. A lamb-like quadruped (probably a dog) stands near the legs of the warrior. Wreath and cornucopia in the field.
   B: a young satyr pursues a woman who carries a cushion or tambourine. Feline in the field between the legs of the satyr.

   Beazley, *EVP*, p. 182; Trendall, *VIE*, p. 238f., pl. LXII, a and b.

The subject depicted on side A of vase no. 2 above (Pl. 101) is intriguing to say the least, but at this time I have nothing to add to Trendall's interpretation that the scene represents a particularly Etruscan variation of the *Medusa* theme (see Trendall, *VIE*, p. 232). Irrespective of the enigmatic subject on this last vase and those of more usual character found on others, I believe there is good reason to regard the above three vases as products of potters and vase-painters active at Caere. There is something strikingly "Caeretan" on these special vases in the general character of the female heads and, more specifically, in the presence of the *wavy tress* which dangles in front of the ear. This can be noted on the Bonn krater (see Fig. 24) and the Vatican vase no. 2 (Pl. 102), and directly recalls a detail which is by now well known in Caeretan red-figure. The female heads on the Vatican krater, vase no. 3, are markedly similar to the heads painted on oinochoai of the Caeretan Torcop Group.

A feature shared by all three of the above listed vases and a Caeretan oinochoe decorated with figured scenes, vase no. 51 (Pl. 35), is the *embattled* or, in its degenerate stage, *dot-stripe* border on the broad band normally found on the female garment which was shown earlier in this study to be characteristic of Paestan and, to a lesser extent, Campanian red-figure.[71] Beazley believes the vases of his Campanizing Group most resemble the work of the Campanian Errera Painter (*EVP*, p. 66), whose work is closely related to the Caivano Painter.[72] On the evidence of the Vatican vase no. 2 above, Trendall, on the other hand, sees a closer stylistic analogy with another prolific Campanian artist whom he believes must have collaborated with the Caivano Painter, namely, the Painter of B.M.F. 63.[73]

Trendall's association of the Campanizing Group vases with the Caivano Group once again brings into focus the vases decorated in *superposed color* by the Sacrifice Painter (see Pls. 91–92) whom Trendall suspects of having some affinities with the Campanizing Group (*VIE*, p. 262), and whose vases I proposed earlier (Chapter III) as likely products of *Caere.* There are striking similarities between the vases of the Sacrifice Painter and those cited here for the Campanizing Group. Compare, for example, the female heads and fleshy portions (arms, hands, feet, etc.) represented by the Sacrifice Painter with their counterparts on the Vatican krater no. 2, and more specifically, with "Ariadne" on the Bonn vase (compare Fig. 14 with Fig. 24). Although I do not claim that these works—painted in two such markedly contrasting techniques—are by one and the same artist, I do wish to draw special attention to a characteristic detail—the *wavy tress* before the ear—which is shared in common and does not fail to reflect the artistic climate of *Caere* which may very well be the center of manufacture.

71. See supra, nn. 50, 51, 52 (Chapter V).
72. For the Campanian Caivano Painter, see Trendall, *LCS*, pp. 305ff, whom Trendall now prefers to regard as a *Campanian* rather than Paestan artist as once suspected (cf. Trendall, *PP*, pp. 84ff and 126 and *PP Supplement,* i.e., "Paestan Pottery—A Revision and a Supplement," *Papers of the British School at Rome* 20 [1952], pp. 1–53; see in particular pp. 17–18 and 38–40); for the Errera Painter, see Trendall, *LCS*, pp. 321ff.
73. *Ibid.,* pp. 314ff.

Although it may be argued that I have limited myself to only a few vases of Beazley's Campanizing Group to illustrate the association with Caere, I have done so for two primary reasons. First, I do not believe that *all* of Beazley's "Campanizing" vases are attributable to Caere, since I have noted some examples that are better assigned to other Etruscan red-figured fabrics;[74] and secondly time does not permit here the very special and detailed investigation that the "Campanizing Group" deserves, particularly in regards to the possible presence in Etruria of immigrant South Italian vase-painters and their subsequent influence on various Etruscan red-figured fabrics. That such a movement of potters and vase-painters from South Italy to Etruria was indeed possible has been duly considered by scholars other than Beazley who readily acknowledge "Campanizing" and "Paestanizing" Groups of Etruscan red-figure.[75]

MIGRATION OF SOUTH ITALIAN VASE-PAINTERS TO ETRURIA

I cannot wholly conceive that the influences from South Italian red-figure on Caeretan vases, as pointed out and discussed thus far, were due entirely to mere exposure to or acquaintance with South Italian vases imported into Etruria. On the contrary, very few South Italian vases have actually been discovered in Etruria. If influences were truly derived from South Italian red-figure, they must have come directly from the presence of South Italian vase-painters (and potters) who had settled into one or more productive centers of Etruscan red-figure. In the context of the present study, I believe this to be the case with Caere, but I also suspect that South Italian artisans—Paestan and Campanian in particular— may have moved during the course of the latter half of fourth century B.C., from one Etruscan center to another—Falerii Veteres,[76] Volterra, Chiusi, Vulci, and Tarquinii.

74. There are several vases of Beazley's "Campanizing Group"—a stamnos in Baltimore, Walters Art Gallery, inv. no. 48.62 and a stamnos in Toronto, Royal Ontario Museum, inv. no. 427 (*EVP* p. 64f and p. 65, pl. XIII, figs. 1–2) which I believe were possibly produced at Tarquinii; see supra n. 32, Chapter V.

75. R. Zahn in *Berliner Museem* (1934), p. 208; see "Pocola" by P. Moreno in *Enciclopedia dell' Arte Antica* VI (Rome, 1965), pp. 254ff; L. Forti, "Una Officina di Vasi Tarantini a Vulci," *Rendiconti della R. Accademia di Archeologia ed Arti, Napoli* XLV (1970), pp. 233–265; "Campanizing" and "Paestanizing" in Beazley, *EVP*, pp. 63ff and pp. 226ff.

76. The *wave pattern* commonly found as a decorative element to the female garment on Paestan and Campanian red-figured vases is rare in Caeretan (cf. the Bonn krater of the Campanizing Group, pl. 100) but especially popular in Faliscan red-figure (e.g., 109). See also Beazley, *EVP*, pl. XV, figs. 1 and 4, pl. XVIII, figs. 3, 9 and 10, pl. XIX, fig. 1,

If it were possible to trace the hand of a South Italian painter on a red-figured vase attributable to Etruscan manufacture, a discovery which, I believe, can be accomplished by a thorough study of Etruscan vases rich in South Italian details, our present knowledge of the interrelationships of South Italy and Etruria would be greatly enhanced. Such a project, however, which need not be limited to vase-painting alone but broadened to include sculpture, metal-work, etc., must be reserved for the future.

SUMMARY

An extremely close relationship between Caeretan and Faliscan red-figured vase-painting, as first detected for the plates of the Genucilia Group through the "Falisco-Caeretan" specimens, has also been noted between the earliest Caeretan vases with figured scenes and certain examples of Faliscan red-figure. Such a correspondence once again suggests the strong possibility of a migration of some Faliscan vase-painters to Caere during the second half of the fourth century B.C. An equally close association is discernible between Caeretan and South Italian red-figure through special types of vases (epichyseis, oinochoe, Shape VIII, and fish plate) and general themes of decoration. On the evidence of the rarity of South Italian red-figured vases from Etruscan context, it can be safely assumed that the conspicuous influence from South Italian vase-painting is more likely derived from the presence of Paestan and / or Campanian artists in Caeretan workshops. The preponderance of evidence for South Italian influence places a strong emphasis on Paestan and Campanian vase-painting, and indicates that the migrant artists who settled into Caeretan pottery establishments may have originated in the broad Campanian "circle" of Trendall's Laghetto, Caivano, and Errera Painters (see Trendall, *LCS*, Chapter VII, pp. 296ff.). Trendall believes the former two—the Laghetto and Caivano Painters—worked briefly at Paestum where they left a considerable influence on the painters of that city's fabric (Trendall, *LCS*, p. 305).

The arrival of "'southern" immigrants may not have been restricted to Caere, for there is good evidence to suggest that some individuals may have

---

pl. XX, fig. 3, pl. XXI, pl. XXII, fig. 1, pl. XXIII, pl. XXIV, fig. 4, pl. XXVI, fig. 1. That this decorative motif for the female garment is common in Faliscan and not known on Caeretan red-figured vases with figured scenes, suggests to me that an immigrant South Italian artist who introduced it to Faliscan pottery may have abandoned it at Caere in deference to local tastes.

found their way to other centers of Eruscan red-figured production. It may also be true that a number of these migrant vase-painters settled in one community for a brief period of time, after which they may have journeyed on to another Etruscan center not far distant. Such a phenomenon would explain the South Italian features—Paestan and Campanian in particular—which various Etruscan red-figured fabrics seem to share in common.

Recognition of the influences exerted by South Italian on Etruscan red-figure, in addition to those discerned between various Etruscan fabrics—whether due to imported vases or migration of painters—is of paramount importance for the better understanding of the relationships between certain groups of Etruscan pottery which continue to puzzle students of Etruscan vase-painting. Perhaps some insight into the production of Caeretan red-figure may eventually help resolve some of the perplexing problems such as the relationship between the "Campanizing Group" and the "'Settecamini Painter" (Beazley, *EVP*, p. 64 and pp. 52ff), or the relationship between the "Group of Toronto 495" and the "Turmuca Group" (Beazley, *EVP*, p. 182 and pp. 135ff).

VI

⧉⧉⧉⧉⧉

Chronology

THE CHRONOLOGY first proposed for the Caeretan branch of the Genucilia Group,[1] has since required serious revision as a result of later studies.[2] Although the beginning date for the group, as initiated by the Berkeley Genucilia Painter,[3] has been considerably lowered to the last three decades of the fourth century B.C., there is no change implied for the relative position already set forth for the painters of the Group. The chronological range now more acceptable for the Caeretan Genucilia Group does not seem to extend beyond a single generation, nor do I believe that the plates—whether head or star variety—were produced much later than the first decade of the third century B.C., a date which I take to be a satisfactory *terminus ante quem*.

TOMB GROUPS

Of more than one hundred vases which comprise the Caeretan vases with figured scenes, a goodly number have a recorded or assumed provenience (see Table of Proveniences, p. 103f.). Regrettably, however, relatively few have been published as parts of tomb groups. The paucity of information regarding such conditions is well illustrated by the limited number of sites—those known to have yielded Caeretan red-figured vases—which offer published examples, name-

1. *Genucilia Group*, Chapter IX.
2. *Caeretan Figured Group*, p. 36.
3. *Genucilia Group*, pp. 251ff.

ly, *Caere* and *Populonia*. For *Alalia*, especially rich in Caeretan red-figure, we must anxiously await publication of its finds and tomb groups which, I believe, may hold the key to the relative, if not absolute, chronology for Caeretan red-figured vase-painting. For the sake of convenience and completeness, I shall list anew general references to Caeretan vases other than those with figured scenes.

CAERE

For this important Etruscan city and center of production of the red-figured vases which comprise the subject of the present study, the desired tomb contexts are conveniently recorded in *MonAnt* XLII (1954), cols. 201–1048, a work of inestimable value by Goffredo Ricci who undertook the herculean task of compiling the mainly unpublished material from excavations in the *Necropoli della Banditaccia, Zona A "del Recinto"* dating back to the earliest excavations of Raniero Mengarelli during the first decades of this century.

Caeretan-Red-Figured Vases

At least seven vases which I have brought together as Caeretan Red-Figured Vases (i.e., vases with figured scenes) have been published or mentioned in Ricci's text.

Tomb no. 236

1. Stamnos, vase no. 56
   Dotted-hem Group; miscellaneous
   MonAnt XLII (1954), c. 720, no. 208, fig. 161A.

2. Stamnos, vase no. 50 (Pl. 34)
   Dotted-hem Group
   Close to the Volterra Caeretan Painter
   Ibid., c. 721, no. 209, fig. 162A.

3. Stamnos, vase no. 111
   Unidentified Group; miscellaneous
   Ibid., c. 722, no. 211, fig. 163A.

   Tomb no. 291

4. Oinochoe, vase no. 69 (Pl. 45)
   Crescent-hem Group
   Castellani Caeretan Painter
   Ibid., c. 778, no. 1, fig. 173.

   Tomb no. 407

5. Oinochoe, vase no. 110
   Unidentified Group; miscellaneous
   Ibid., c. 928, no. 30, fig. 218.

6. Stamnos, vase no. 49 (Pls. 32–33)
   Dotted-hem Group
   Volterra Caeretan Painter
   Ibid., c. 932, no. 31, figs. 219A and B.

7. Stamnos, vase no. 48
   Dotted-hem Group
   Volterra Caeretan Painter
   Ibid., c. 932, no. 32; *AJA* 70 (1966), p. 34, no. 1 and pl. 12, figs. 9–10.

Kylix with Profile Head

Tomb no. 407

Fragmentary kylix (Rome, Museo di Villa Giulia)
Caeretan Kylix Painter
MonAnt XLII (1954), c. 923, no. 35, fig. 220; *MAAR* XXVII (1962), pl. I, fig. 3.

Genucilia Group

As would be expected, Caeretan Genucilia plates of both head and star variety appear with great frequency amongst the tomb groups reported by Ricci and others.[4] Since they are so common as tomb offerings, I shall single out only one tomb for which Ricci has published three examples of head plates.

Tomb no. 428

Of the two-hundred-and-twenty-four items listed for this tomb, twenty-one are Caeretan Genucilia plates: fifteen star plates and six head plates, of which three examples of the latter are illustrated (*MonAnt* XLII, 1954, figs. 250–252).

Torcop Group

Tomb no. 24

Only the neck with profile head has survived for this oinochoe of the Torcop Group from Caere (*Ibid.*, c. 383, no. 15 and fig. 87, 2) where at least fifteen examples of the Group have been discovered.

4. R. Mengarelli in *StEtr* X (1936), p. 85 and M. Pallottino in *NSc* 1955, p. 102.

On the whole, the contents of the above tombs excavated at Caere do not offer wholly reliable evidence for dating our Caeretan red-figured products. About two hundred and fifteen items have been listed for *Tomb no. 236*, which include the three stamnoi with figured scenes (nos. 1–3 above, vases nos. 50, 56 and 111), together with thirty-five Caeretan star plates. Other specimens of pottery are represented by bucchero, Protocorinthian aryballoi and pyxis lid, a dove-askos of East-Greek ("greco-orientale") type, some "impasto", Italo-Corinthian aryballoi, a Laconian column-krater, and numerous black-glazed vases (chiefly oinochoai, Shape VII) with decoration in added white, which I take to mean examples of Beazley's "Vases with Decoration in Superposed Color" (*EVP*, Chapter XII).

Thirty-nine objects, including one oinochoe (Shape VII) and two stamnoi with figured scenes (nos. 5–7 above, nos. 48, 49, and 110), a kylix by the Caeretan Kylix Painter, and seven Caeretan star plates have been listed by Ricci for Tomb no. 407. This same tomb also contained an extremely large Arretine plate, black-glazed vases with impressed designs reminiscent of *Calenian Vases* and, of course, black-glazed vases with decoration in added white. Both *Tombs nos. 236 and 407* seem to have undergone multiple burials, especially the former for which the contents extend from the sixth through the third century B.C., whereas the latter strongly suggests a period from the fourth through the first century B.C.

For the two above mentioned tombs and *Tombs nos. 291, 428 and 24*, there is an abundance of "ciotole," "ciotolettine," and "pocula"—types not so easily dated. The Caeretan oinochoe (Shape VII) with figured scene (no. 4 above, vase no. 69) is numbered among seventy-three items of usual variety, which include thirty-four Caeretan star plates. *Tomb no. 428*, also disclosed bucchero, an Attic red-figured kylix (*MonAnt* XLII, 1954, fig. 253) and black-glazed hydria, and black-glazed Etruscan vases with decoration in added white. Together with the Torcop Group fragment in *Tomb no. 24* were found 141 items: some Caeretan star plates, black-glazed vases with added white decoration, and much plain black-glazed ware. This later tomb seems to be more representative of the third century B.C., with the Torcop Group specimens possibly representing the earliest objects.

POPULONIA

The important Etruscan seaport city of Populonia which is known to have imported Caeretan red-figured vases of various types (see Table of Proveniences, Chapter IV), may have also served as a center for "overseas" export of Caeretan products. Of the ten Caeretan vases with figured scenes discovered at this site, four have been published together with their tomb context in periodic reports in *Notizie degli Scavi.*

Caeretan Red-Figured Vases

1. Trefoil Oinochoe, vase no. 109 (Pl. 63)
   Unidentified Group
   Frontal Satyr Caeretan Painter
   NSc 1905, p. 58, fig. 5; *Minto*, pl. LX, fig. 3.

2. Oinochoe, vase no. 14
   Dotted-hem Group
   Painter of Würzburg 817 (Villa Giulia Caeretan Painter)
   NSc. 1934, p. 45, fig. 69; *Minto*, pl. LXI, fig. 6.

3. Oinochoe, vase no. 86
   Crescent-hem Group
   American Academy Caeretan Painter
   NSc 1957, p. 39, fig. 62, right.

4. Oinochoe, vase no. 92
   Crescent-hem Group
   American Academy Caeretan Painter
   NSc 1957, p. 39, fig. 62, left.

Genucilia Group

For Populonia, seventeen plates of the Caeretan branch of the Genucilia Group are known (see Table of Proveniences), some of which have been published or mentioned in various excavation reports.[5]

Torcop Group

As the Table of Proveniences will disclose, twenty-four oinochoai attributed to the Torcop Group have been discovered at Populonia. Of these, only about one-third have been mentioned or illustrated in archaeological reports.[6]

Superposed Color

Two Lekythoi (Pls. 93–94)
NSc 1905, p. 58, fig. 6; *Minto*, pl. LX, fig. 2.

Two Kantharoi (e.g., Pl. 95)
NSc 1905, p. 58, fig. 5; *Minto*, pl. LX, fig. 3.

5. *NSc 1905*, p. 56 and fig. 2; *NSc* 1923, pp. 128, 132, and 147; *NSc* 1934, p. 416 and fig. 71; see also *Minto*, p. 128, pl. LXV, figs. 1 and 2.
6. *NSc.* 1924, p. 22; *NSc* 1925, p. 366 and *Minto*, p. 213 pl. LXII, fig. 2; *NSc* 1934, pp. 414, 416 and fig. 70 and *Minto*, p. 217, pl. LXIV, figs. 3 and 4.

The trefoil oinochoe attributed to the Caeretan Figured Group (no. 1 above, vase no. 109) and the four vases—two lekythoi and two kantharoi—in superposed color have been found at Populonia under unusual circumstances: "suppellettili riferibili ad una o più tombe," according to Minto's report of Milani's offering in *NSc* 1905. As illustrated in the published photographs by Milani (whence *Minto*, pl. LX), the finds could easily be mistaken for tomb groups, which they are not, for they are the result of haphazard mining operations or clandestine activities at Populonia early in the century.

The Caeretan oinochoe (Shape VII) with figured scene (no. 2 above, vase no. 14) as well as oinochoe of the Torcop Group and a Caeretan Genucilia star plate, as reported in *NSc* 1934, are the results of confiscations arising from clandestine activities and thereby provide unreliable data regarding tomb context. However, the circumstances of the more recently discovered oinochoai (Shape VII) by the American Academy Caeretan Painter (nos. 3 and 4 above, vases nos. 86 and 92) are fully recorded by Alfredo de Agostino who excavated them from the "Tomba a sarcofago" in the "Campo del Debbio." The contents consisted of a "sarcofago" of Hellenistic type (*NSc* 1957, p. 48, fig. 73) and sixty objects represented by pottery, lead, and bronze articles. The red-figured vases include our two oinochoai with figured scenes and two kylikes of Faliscan fabrication (*ibid.*, p. 40, fig. 63). In addition, as would be expected, by now there were examples of black-glazed vases with decoration in added white, as well as plain black-glazed and unglazed vases of assorted shapes. I am in accord with de Agostino's dating for this context, that is, the fourth through the third century B.C.

Caeretan Genucilia plates and oinochoai of the Torcop Group have been discovered in relatively the same contexts. Three Torcop Group vases shared a tomb in the "Podere di S. Cerbone" with a large bronze mirror of late date, black-glazed oinochoai and skyphoi decorated in added white, and innumerable "ciotole" and "poculi."[7] Such a context, according to Minto, belongs wholly to the third century B.C.

In addition to the tomb contexts mentioned in the past for the Caeretan branch of the Genucilia Group,[8] a number of new sites have disclosed examples of Caeretan Genucilia plates (see Index of Collections). The three star plates from *Pyrgi* were unearthed together with specimens of far ranging chronological periods: bucchero, Italo-geometric, impasto, Attic and Etruscan black-figure,

7. *NSc* 1925, p. 366 and *Minto*, pp. 213ff and pl. LXII.
8. *Genucilia Group*, p. 297, n. 1; Chapters VIII and IX.

and terra sigillata.[9] Subsequently, the sixth to first century date for the Pyrgi material does not offer conclusive evidence for dating the Caeretan Genucilia plates. Likewise, both *Roselle*[10] and *San Giuliano*[11] provide equally unreliable evidence to help establish an absolute chronology based on the presence of Caeretan Genucilia plates which are associated with material ranging from the seventh to the end of the third century B.C. For the Caeretan Genucilia plates discovered in the archaeological context related to the investigations of the Forum and environs in *Rome* by E. Gjerstad[12] and the fortified Roman colony (*castrum*) at Ostia by R. Meiggs,[13] a fourth century B.C. date has been found acceptable by these two scholars.

In his review of *Genucilia Group*, Giovanni Colonna argued strongly for a date far later than that proposed in my revised chronology; this he has based on the presence of Caeretan Genucilia plates at the Roman colonies of *Alba Fucens* and *Cosa*, founded respectively in 303 and 273 B.C.[14] The few examples from these two sites—four very fragmentary star plates at *Alba Fucens* and an infinitesimal fragment of rim with traces of a wave at *Cosa* (see Index of Collections)—are admittedly in a later context than I would have desired; yet there may be a plausible reason for not associating the foundation dates for these Roman colonies with the chronology proposed for the Genucilia plates. It is indeed difficult to regard Genucilia plates as "heirlooms"—which might explain their presence at *Alba Fucens*—but in regards to *Cosa*—where my participation in the American Academy in Rome excavations of Spring, 1965, has familiarized me with its environs—I can at least suggest that some Caeretan specimens could have belatedly reached Latin owners directly from pilfered Etruscan tombs which abound to the north and east of that coastal city.[15]

9. *NSc* 1959, pp. 224ff.
10. *StEtr* XXXIII (1965), pp. 109ff.
11. *NSc* 1963, pp. 1ff.
12. Scattered references in E. Gjerstad, *Early Rome*, vols. II and III (Lund, 1960–1966); see indices, "Genucilia fabrics" or "plates." For Rome, see also P. Romanelli in *MonAnt* XLVI (1963), p. 295 and fig. 69, a–c.
13. R. Meiggs, *Roman Ostia* (Oxford, 1960), pp. 20ff.
14. *ArchCl* XI (1959), pp. 134ff. However, see *MonAnt* XLVI (1963), p. 376.
15. Apart from the once vast Etruscan necropolis of Orbetello directly to the north of Cosa, there are considerable clusters of Etruscan tombs in the regions across the *Via Appia* to the east of Cosa. In view of the centuration of this territory by the colony of Cosa (see F. Castagnoli, "La centurazione di Cosa," *MAAR* XXIV, 1956, pp. 149–156), it is not wholly improbable that some of the Roman colonists chanced upon any number of these tombs and simply helped themselves to their contents.

Although at first glance it may be argued that the source of inspiration for the composition of the medallion decoration on the Regia Caeretan plate (Fig. 5) is the *aes grave*, generally dated from the third century B.C. of the Roman Republic,[16] I believe that coin types other than Roman may provide a chronological framework more consistent with the Regia plate. For example, there is a silver issue of Zancle-Messana dating from as early as the fifth century B.C. that is based on a Samian type which shows the prow of a ship on its reverse.[17] However, like the *aes grave*, the foremost part of the galley's prow fills the circular field of the coin and thereby contrasts noticeably with the greater section of prow to be seen in the medallion of the Regia plate. In this case, a better analogy is found between the composition in the Regia medallion and certain late fourth century B.C. silver coins of Aradus and Sidon in Phoenicia.[18] Although a complete galley rather than prow appears on the reverse of the Phoenician coins, they at least display round shields along the ship's railing.

I have not cited the above coin types as actual sources for the general composition of the Regia Genucilia plate, but wish to dispel any suspicion that the Roman *aes grave* provides the *only* source for the ship's prow composition on the Regia plate and, subsequently, that the date for the plate must be based on the *aes grave*. On the contrary, I find that the ship's prow theme on the Caeretan Regia plate differs considerably from that represented on the *aes grave*. In addition, I believe the Regia plate to be earlier in date, i.e., the last decade of the fourth century B.C.

Although I have attempted to reconcile the circular composition on the Regia plate with a numismatic prototype, it may be explained more simply as the original and individual creation of a Caeretan artist who did not necessarily rely on any special compositional source. Nonetheless, this unusual Caeretan

16. G. Belloni, *Le Monete Romane dell'Età Repubblicana* (Milano, 1960), pls. 3 and 4, and various publications into Roman numismatics by A. Alföldi, E. Haeberlin, H. Mattingly, and H. Sydenham.

17. See J. Barron, *The Silver Coins of Samos* (London, 1955).

18. The reverse for silver issues of the Phoenician cities of Aradus and Sidon, dating to the last decades of the fourth century B.C., show a war-galley with round shields at the outer railing; C. Seltman, *Greek Coins* (London, 1955), pl. XLI, figs. 14 and 16; B. Head, *A Guide to the Principal Gold and Silver Coins of the Ancients* (Chicago, 1968), p. 61, no. 35 and pl. 29, no. 35. It is interesting to note in the exergue of this last coin that the wavy or zig-zag bands which signify the sea are reminiscent of the dot-wave on the Regia Genucilia plate. A coin of *Demetrios Poliorketes*, dating to the late decade of the fourth century B.C., shows on its reverse, a ship's prow with *eye* (*ibid.*, p. 63, no. 17 and pl. 31, no. 17).

Genucilia plate, together with the seven additional Caeretan examples discovered with it (see Index of Collections) may provide a vital source for coping with the dating of the Regia and its environs.

ABANDONMENT OF RELIEF-LINE

The gradual disappearance of *relief-lines* as noted for the *Caeretan* branch of the Genucilia Group, but more importantly for Etruscan red-figure as a whole, has found confirmation in the study of the Caeretan vases with figured scenes. This significant change in vase-painting technique, first discerned in the work of a single artist of the Genucilia Group—the Berkeley Genucilia Painter and his "Falisco-Caeretan" plates[19]—is paralleled in the Caeretan Red-Figured Vases by the Villa Giulia Caeretan Painter who tends to give up relief-line between his early and later works (compare Pl. 19 with Pls. 20–22). This is also true for the Villa Giulia Torcop Painter and a few other artists of the Dotted-hem Group which I believe begins slightly earlier and overlaps the products of the Crescent-hem Group.

The gradual disappearance of the technique can be traced from its prolific use in the main picture field, to its relegation to the subsidiary decoration, and its eventual total absence of any part of the Caeretan vases with figured scenes. Hence, Beazley's observation (*EVP*, p. 25) that the relief-line technique was dominant in Etruscan vase-painting from the middle of the fifth century and continued for a good part of the fourth century B.C., is once again corroborated by red-figured vases produced at Caere: originally through the plates of the Genucilia Group, and now by means of the larger and more significant Caeretan Red-Figured Vases.

Likewise, the tendency of *silhouette* to "usurp" red-figured floral patterns during the fourth century B.C., as noted by Beazley (*EVP*, p. 143), may also be found in Caeretan red-figure, and is best illustrated on the terracotta "cista" by the Brooklyn Caeretan Painter (see Pl. 88). The change from red-figure to silhouette for the floral motifs on this last vase may provide an exceptional clue for the future attribution to *Caere* of a large proportion of vases, chiefly oinochoai (Shape VII), with silhouetted palmettes and the like running around their bodies. Such vases, I believe, are best dated to the third century B.C.[20]

19. *Genucilia Group*, p. 251 and p. 310f.
20. E.g., Beazley, *EVP*, p. XXXVIII, fig. 3. One may compare the same phenomenon on the very late fourth and early third century B.C. Campanian *kemais* on which silhouette palmettes frequently appear; see Trendall, *LCS*, Appendix II, pp. 674ff.

SUMMARY

With the possible exception of the finds from *Alalia*, publication of which is forthcoming, the evidence yielded by archaeological excavations at scattered sites where Caeretan red-figured vases have been discovered (see Table of Proveniences, Chapter IV) has offered little or no conclusive evidence for the establishment of an absolute chronology applicable to the activities of the vase-painters at Caere. Apart from the vases decorated in superposed color (see the Sacrifice Painter and the vases associated technically with him, Chapter III and Pls. 91–95) and examples of the *"Campanizing Group"* (Chapter V and Pls. 100–102), which I have tentatively attributed to Caere, specimens of the different groups of Caeretan red-figure presented in this study have actually been discovered together in the same tomb context.[21] Unfortunately, the broad chronological range represented by the varied context of such tombs has all but negated their value as a means for dating Caeretan red-figured products.

The earliest vases of the Villa Giulia Caeretan Painter—their seeming connection or continuity with vases of obvious Faliscan origin as discussed and illustrated in Chapter V (see Pls. 96–99)—clearly show by the quality of their execution and profuse use of *relief-line*, that they stand at the head of the series of vases comprising the Caeretan Figured Group. This corroborates a similar observation made years earlier for the superior drawing on the "Falisco-Caeretan" Genucilia plates by the Berkeley Genucilia Painter (e.g., Fig. 20) who also employed the relief-line technique and who also stood at the head of the especially long series of plates attributed to the Caeretan branch of the Genucilia Group. In each instance, it has been pointed out that these two Caeretan vase-painters gradually gave up relief-lines between their earliest and latest works.

As indicated earlier in this study, the abandonment of the relief-line technique was discernible between the products of the two Groups of Caeretan vases decorated with figured scenes; that it was slowly relinquished by the artists of the Dotted-hem Group, first in the main and then in the subsidiary decoration, and abandoned altogether by the painters of the Crescent-hem Group. It may be argued on this evidence that there is a relative chronological progression from the vases of the former to the latter Group. However, I believe it more likely that an overlapping existed between these two Groups of Caeretan red-figure, as demonstrated by the conspicuous contemporaneous influence exerted by the Campana Caeretan Painter (Dotted-hem Group) on the Castellani Caeretan Painter (Crescent-hem Group).

21. E.g., Tomb no. 407 at Caere; *MonAnt* XLII (1954), cc. 929ff.

Hence, the presence of relief-lines and the particularly fine quality of drawing on the earliest Caeretan vases decorated with figured scenes argue strongly and, I believe, quite convincingly for a *terminus post quem*, that is, an upper date about a decade after the beginning of the middle of the fourth century B.C. (ca. 340 B.C.) at the earliest, or 330 B.C. at the latest.

For the *terminus ante quem*, I cannot in all good conscience extend the date much later than the end of the fourth century B.C., with the possible concession that the most barbarized products of *Caeretan* red-figure may fall into the first decade or decades of the third century B.C. As this chronology may be applied to Caeretan Genucilia star plates in the minds of some readers, I must repeat my views expressed in *Genucilia Group* (p. 283) that the Caeretan star plates (e.g., Pl. 67) are contemporaneous with the Caeretan Genucilia head plates which show the sphendone "embroidered" with *star-pattern* (e.g., Pl. 66), but may have continued for a period after the head plates were no longer produced.

This chronology marks a more emphatic revision of the original dating for Caeretan red-figure as first recognized for plates of the Genucilia Group,[22] and was later altered in favor of a lower date during preliminary investigation of the "Caeretan Figured Group" (i.e., Caeretan vases with figured scenes).[23] On the whole, I do not believe that the total production of Caeretan Red-Figured Vases—this must also be true for the Genucilia and Torcop Groups and related vases with profile heads—was due to the efforts of more than a single generation of Caeretan vase-painters.

I must place those vases which are decorated in superposed color or form part of Beazley's "Campanizing Group,"—attributed here to Caere—earlier in date than the Caeretan red-figured vases presented in this study. The close stylistic kinship of these vases with the early specimens of the Dotted-hem Group, the plates by the Berkeley Genucilia Painter and, by extension, with the red-figured vases of Faliscan origin which are closely related to the latter specimens (e.g., Pls. 96–99), suggests that they may be products produced at Caere slightly later in date than the middle of the fourth century B.C. preceding the vases of the Dotted-hem Group by at least a decade. Such a chronology accords well with Trendall's consideration of the "Campanizing Group."[24]

In closing, it should be mentioned that the date proposed here for Caeretan red-figure, the late fourth century B.C. (340–300 B.C.), may find confirmation

22. *Genucilia Group*, Chapter IX.
23. *Caeretan Figured Group*, p. 36.
24. Trendall, *VIE*, p. 262.

in the subsidiary palmette decoration on the terracotta "cista" (Pl. 88) by the Brooklyn Caeretan Painter, a bonafide member of the Dotted-hem Group. This follows Beazley's observation that floral silhouette in Etruscan red-figure, during the course of the fourth century B.C., tends to replace similar decorative motifs formerly executed in the red-figured technique.

VII

⌐⌐⌐⌐⌐⌐

Conclusion

IN VIEW OF the *summaries* set forth in some of the preceding chapters of this study, the conclusions to be drawn at this point may be relatively brief. The distinctive details which have led to the recognition of a Caeretan branch for the Genucilia Group, or permitted attribution to Caere for a goodly number of red-figured vases decorated with female heads in profile, have now been augmented by new features that serve to characterize Caeretan vases with figured scenes. An awareness of details which disclose the origin of fabric and the chronological data associated with it can prove of some value to the field-archaeologist who may encounter even the most fragmentary specimens of Caeretan red-figure (see Figs. 1–4).

Equally significant, an acceptance of special details as exclusive features of Caeretan vase-painting should greatly aid the attribution to Caere of various works of art executed in different disciplines—e.g., sculpture and engraving on bronze mirrors—which may be associated stylistically with Caeretan red-figured vases. This has been the case in the engraving on an Etruscan bronze mirror (Fig. 25) which, on the evidence of its stylistic similarities with Caeretan vases bearing figured scenes, may be credited to a craftsman working in Caere during the latter decades of the fourth century B.C.

The vases with *figured scenes* which are relatively larger vary considerably from those smaller vases which carry *female heads in profile* in the choice of vase-shape and their decoration; nevertheless they disclose a fairly homogeneous character which attests to the close relationship that must have existed between the vase-painters of Caere. I have attributed the origin of the Caeretan branch of the Genucilia Group to a vase-painter (the Berkeley Genucilia Painter) who revealed particularly strong ties with Faliscan red-figure; similarly, the *Villa Giulia Caeretan Painter* of the Dotted-hem Group provides a parallel link between Faliscan and Caeretan red-figured vases of more major size and complexity of decoration.

This close association between the styles of Caeretan and Faliscan red-figured products for the closing decades of the fourth century B.C.—now noted independently in two separate detailed studies some ten years apart—has drawn special attention to the possible *migration* of potters and vase-painters from *Falerii Veteres* to *Caere.* The conspicuous influence from South Italian red-figure, Paestan and, to a lesser extent, Campanian, has also suggested that vase-painters migrated from Southern Italy and settled into various Etruscan centers which possessed established ceramic industries. Such a movement of artisans and craftsmen may help to explain certain similarities in style, subjects, and details commonly shared by South Italian, Caeretan and other Etruscan red-figured fabrics.

In this respect, special significance is given to Beazley's "Campanizing Group" in Etruscan red-figure; he acknowledged conspicuous Campanian features in the decoration of vases which are assuredly Etruscan. A detailed investigation of the Campanizing Group and its special position in Etruscan red-figure vase-painting would extend far beyond the scope of the present study. I have attempted to illustrate three examples of Campanizing vases (Pls. 100–102), and others decorated in *superposed color* (Pls. 91–95), which strongly suggest their origin at *Caere* on the evidence of the Caeretan artistic environment reflected in certain details of their decoration. Hence, there is good reason to believe that some Paestan and / or Campanian vase-painters settled at Caere where they continued their craft, and that some of these very same South Italian immigrants may have worked at other Etruscan centers—Falerii Veteres, Volterra, Tarquinii, Vulci and the like—before their arrival in Caere.

The distribution and frequency of finds for Caeretan red-figured vases have confirmed the patterns of distribution already visualized for the Genucilia and Torcop Groups, and shed further light on the overseas "desirability" of Caeretan vases as disclosed by the obvious exports discovered at Alalia, Ampurias, and Carthage, in the western Mediterranean and along its seaboard. For Etruria, the Caeretan vases imported at ancient Tarquinia have seemingly inspired, together with contemporary Faliscan examples, a somewhat eclectic local fabric.

Although it may be argued that the presence or absence of *relief-line* is not in itself a valid criterion for dating, the actual abandonment of this important vase-painting technique in Etruscan red-figure can readily be observed in the

Caeretan examples presented in this study. The disappearance of relief-line first traced in Caeretan vase-painting on plates of the Genucilia Group, has a parallel development discernible on later Caeretan vases decorated with figured scenes where relief-lines are initially abandoned in the main field of decoration, retained for a time in the subsidiary decoration (e.g., tongue- or egg-patterns) and eventually discarded altogether. Chronologically, this abandonment of the relief-line technique in Caeretan red-figured vase-painting seems to take place during the last third of the fourth century B.C.

On the evidence offered by the archaeological data surrounding Caeretan red-figured vase-painting and other fabrics associated with it, it is indeed a difficult task to interweave the contemporary historical events which took place in the relevant regions of southern Etruria and northern Latium.[1] From the early decades of the fourth century B.C., the political picture was turbulent to say the least, especially as it applied to the impending and eventual open conflict between Veii and Rome. For the second half of the fourth century B.C., the period with which we have been primarily concerned, very little correspondence can be made between archaeological and historical findings (based primarily on the writings of Livy) other than to acknowledge the well known fact that Caere and Rome enjoyed a particularly good relationship,[2] and that a goodly amount of commerce existed between Etruria and centers abroad, as indicated by the discovery of Caeretan products beyond Etruria and Latium along the western Mediterranean seaboard. This sign of prosperity may have been due in large measure to the relatively long period of peace, some forty years, initiated about the middle of the fourth century with a truce between Falerii and Rome (Livy VII, 22), which was unfortunately broken in the last decades of that century by a Faliscan revolt (Livy IX, 32–37).[3]

Even though a true insight into the relationship between red-figure vase-painting and its historical-political setting is not presently obtainable—signs of profitable commercial contacts disclose patterns of distribution—much has been learned to gain a better understanding of the interrelationships between the

1. For the historical events of the strife-ridden early fourth century B.C. in southern Etruria and northern Latium, see R. Fell, *Etruria and Rome* (Cambridge, 1924); *Genucilia Group*, pp. 306ff; A. Alföldi, *Early Rome and the Latins* (Ann Arbor, 1963), Chapter VIII; and G. Baffioni, "Sappinates o Capenates?" *StEtr* XXXV (1967), pp. 127ff.

2. See M. Sordi, *I Rapporti Romano-Ceriti e l'Origine della 'Civitas Sine Suffragio'* (Rome, 1960); R. Meiggs, *op. cit.*, p. 24; A. Alföldi, *op. cit.*, p. 341.

3. In 293 B.C. (Livy X, 45), the Faliscans revolted against Rome and were eventually crushed and their city destroyed in 241 B.C. (Polybius I, 65).

Etruscan red-figured fabrics of southern Etruria. This has been clearly demonstrated for the contemporaneous productions of Caere, Falerii, and Tarquinii.
With an expanded knowledge of these important Etruscan fabrics, future studies
should clarify the connections between them and various red-figured wares of
northern Etruria (e.g., Volterran and Chiusine), not to mention a number of
specimens hitherto unattributed to specific centers, as may be the case for Orvieto.

There can now be no question that the place of Caeretan red-figure has
been firmly established, and that these products of potters and vase-painters,
active in this once great Etruscan center during the years 340–300 B.C., must be
fully considered in any future discussion of Etruscan art and history.

Index of Collections

Page references are indicated only for vases which possess inventory numbers or for which there can be no confusion. The vases for which the present whereabouts are unknown, are given at the end of their respective sections.

CAERETAN RED-FIGURED VASES
(Vases with Figured Scenes)

Unless otherwise indicated, all of the vases listed in this section are oinochoai, Shape VII.

GENUCILIA GROUP

The list of Caeretan plates given below must be considered solely as an addenda to the Index of Collections *set forth in* Genucilia Group *(pp. 330–340). Attributions have been made to recognize Genucilia Group painters only in cases when photographs or reproductions were available.*

    The specimens belonging to the various French museums were originally in the Campana Collection from which they were distributed among the provincial museums. Hence, it may be assumed that they were discovered in Caere and its environs.

Aléria, *Musée Archéologique*
      head plates: twenty-five examples
      star plates: sixty-seven examples

Avignon, *Musée*
    36 head plate

Brno, *Moravian Museum*
    328 Near the Carthage Cenucilia Painter
      Listy Filogicke VII (LXXXII), 1959, pl. IV, fig. 1; *RömMitt* 67 (1960), pl. 11, fig. 6.

    329 star plate
      Listy Filogicke VII (LXXXII), 1959, pl. IV, fig. 2.

Carthage, *Musée de Carthage* (expanded Musée Lavigerie)
    05.24 star plate
      Latomus XXV (1966), pl. XXV.

Cerveteri, *Magazzino*
> Near the Carthage Genucilia Painter
> *NSc* 1955, p. 102, fig. 66.

Christchurch (New Zealand), *Logie Collection, University of Canterbury*
> CML 11 (AR 555.0) c 1969.4—Star plate
> A.D. Trendall, *Greek Vases in the Logie Collection*
> (Christchurch, 1971), p. 78 and pl. XLa.

Dijon, *Musée*
> two head plates

Florence, *Museo Archeologico*
> By the Torcello Genucilia Painter. *Catalogue, Mostra dell'Etruria Padana e delle*
> *Citta di Spina* (Bologna, 1960) No. 855, pl. LVII, lower right.

Grenoble, *Musée*
> 34 (511) head plate
> 35 (512) head plate

Limoges, *Musée*
> 80–44 By the Sydney Genucilia Painter
> with star pattern in half-sakkos.
> 80–46 By the Louvre Genucilia Painter

Narbonne, *Musée*
> head plate

Parma, *Museo Nazionale di Antichità*
> C. 109 head plate
> *CVA* 2, IV B, pl. 9, figs. 1 and 5.
> C. 110 head plate
> *Ibid.*, IV B, pl. 9, fig. 2.
> C. 246 star plate
> *Ibid.*, IV B, pl. 9, figs. 3–4.

Populonia, *Antiquario*
> By the Ostia Genucilia Painter
> six star plates

Pyrgi, *Magazzino* (Santa Severa)
> three star plates
> *NSc* 1959, pp. 231 and 234.

Rennes, *Musée*
> 386 By the Louvre Genucilia Painter
> Heavily repainted
> 387 Near the Torcello Genucilia Painter
> Rare example with profile facing to right instead of left.
> 388a By the Sydney Genucilia Painter
> 388b By the Ostia Genucilia Painter
> 390 Near the Florence Genucilia Painter

Rome, *Museo di Villa Giulia*
    10874 three star plates with the same inv. number
        Provenience, Satricum

Roselle, *Magazzino*
        two star plates
        StEtr XXXIII (1965), pl. XLIX, no. 1761 and pl. LII, no. 2006.

Excavations, Alba Fucens
        four star plates
        AntCl XXIII (1954), p. 100, fig. 15, 2 and p. 373, fig. 23, 1–3.

Excavations, Regia, Roman Forum
        four star plates
        By the Ostia Genucilia Painter
        By the Zurich Genucilia Painter
        By the same hand as Palazzo dei Conservatori, inv. no. 12107 (see, *Genucilia*
        Group, p. 266).

Excavations, San Giuliano
        six star plates
        NSc 1963, p. 31, fig. 31, 4; p. 46, fig. 47.

TORCOP GROUP

The following list of oinochoai (Shape VII) should be considered an addenda to those given in Torcop Group *and subsequent articles (see note 17, Chapter II). Attributions have been made in cases when adequate photographs or reproductions were available. Like the Genucilia Group plates, the Torcop Group oinochoai in the French museums were formerly in the Campana Collection and presumably from Caere.*

Aléria, *Musée Archéologique*
    396a By the Populonia Torcop Painter
        Height, 22.8 cms.
    586c By the Populonia Torcop Painter
        Height, 29 cms.

Besançon, *Musée*
        one example

Bordeaux, *Musée*
    1086 (116) By the Populonia Torcop Painter
    1233 (111) By the Populonia Torcop Painter

Florence, *Museo Archeologico*
        By the Populonia Torcop Painter
        Provenience, Populonia
        Catalogue, Mostra dell'Etruria Pandana e della Citta di Spina (Bologna, 1960),
        no. 853, pl. LVII, top right.

150 INDEX OF COLLECTIONS

Milano, *Collezione "H.A."*
> By the Villa Giulia Torcop Painter
> Height, 27 in.
> *CVA*, 2, IV B, pl. 4, lis. 1.

Parma, *Museo Nazionale di Antichità*
> C. 116 By the Populonia Torcop Painter
> Height, 30 cms.
> *CVA* 2, IV B, pl. 11, figs. 3–4.

Prague, published in *Zprávy*
> By the Populonia Torcop Painter
> *Zprávy* VII, 2 (1965), pl. III, fig. 2.
> By the Populonia Torcop Painter
> *Ibid.*, pl. III, fig. 3.

Rennes, *Musée*
> 530 By the Populonia Torcop Painter
> Height, 28 cms.
> 533 By the Populonia Torcop Painter
> With floral motif between confronting heads on the body very similar to pl. 71.
> Height, 31 cms.

Torino, Private Collection
> By the Populonia Torcop Painter
> Height, 36 cms.
> F. Porten Palange, "Materiale Archeologico
> Conservato in Collezioni Privati a Torino," Acme XXII (1969), pp. 357ff. and pls. VIII–IX.

RELATED TO THE TORCOP GROUP

Florence, *Museo Archeologico*
4043 72
Limoges, *Musée*
78.93 69
Orbetello, *Antiquario Comunale*
256 71

Paris, *Musée du Louvre*
K 471 70
Warsaw, *National Museum*
140471 69

ASSORTED CAERETAN VASES
WITH FEMALE HEADS IN PROFILE

LARGE PLATES

Tarquinia, *Museo Nazionale*
RC 2839 73
Vienna, *Kunsthistorisches Museum*
4035 73

Rome, Palatine, *Antiquario*
fragment 74

KYLIKES

SKYPHOI

LONG-HANDLED CUPS

HYDRIAE

STAMNOI

TREFOIL OINOCHOE

OINOCHOAI (SHAPE VIII B); "MUG"

EPICHYSEIS

LEKYTHOI

Large

Small

SPOUTED LEBES

TERRACOTTA "CISTA"

MESOMPHALIC PHIALE

VASES IN SUPERPOSED COLOR

FISH PLATE

STEMMED PLATE WITH SATYR HEAD

Illustrations

FIGURES

PLATES

Plates

PL. 1. Oinochoe by the Villa Giulia
Caeretan Painter. Paris, Louvre K 445.
Photo: M. Chuzeville, Paris.

PL. 2. Oinochoe by the Villa Giulia
Caeretan Painter. Rome, Villa Giulia,
Castellani Collection 50608.
Photo: Soprintendenza Antichità, Rome.

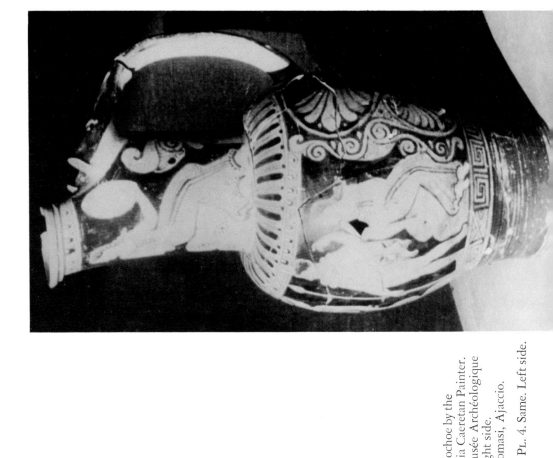

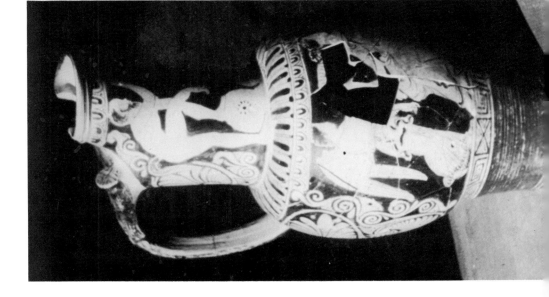

Pl. 3. Oinochoe by the
Villa Giulia Caeretan Painter.
Aléria, Musée Archéologique
1075a. Right side.
Photos: Tomasi, Ajaccio.

Pl. 4. Same. Left side.

Pl. 5. Oinochoe by the Villa Giulia
Caeretan Painter. Aléria, Musée
Archéologique N 696a. Front view.
Photos: Tomasi, Ajaccio.

Pl. 6. Same. Back view.

PL. 7. Oinochoe by the Villa Giulia
Caeretan Painter. Vienna,
Kunsthistorisches Museum IV. 4009.
Photo: Kunsthistorisches Museum.

PL. 8. Oinochoe by the Villa Giulia
Caeretan Painter. Florence, Museo
Archeologico 4086.
Photo: Soprintendenze Antichità, Florence.

Pl. 9. Oinochoe by the Villa Giulia Caeretan Painter. Aléria, Musée Archéologique 724b. *Photo:* Tomasi, Ajaccio.

Pl. 10. Oinochoe by the Villa Giulia Caeretan Painter. Madrid, Museo Arqueológico 11483. *Photo:* Museo Arqueológico.

PL. 11. Calyx-krater by the Villa Giulia
Caeretan Painter. Paris, Louvre K 403.
Side A. *Photo:* M. Chuzeville, Paris.

Pl. 12. Stamnos by the Villa Giulia Caeretan Painter (*Painter of Würzburg 817*). Philadelphia, Pennsylvania University Museum MS 400. Side A. *Photos:* Courtesy Pennsylvania University Museum.

Pl. 13. Same. Side B.

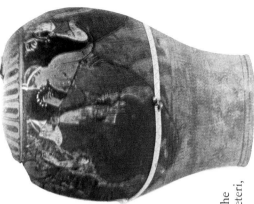

PL. 14. Oinochoe by the Villa Giulia
Torcop Painter. Rome, Villa Giulia 30.
Photo: Soprintendenza Antichità, Rome.

PL. 15. Fragmentary oinochoe by the
Villa Giulia Torcop Painter. Cerveteri,
Magazzino. Left side.

PL. 16. Same. Right side.

PL. 17. Oinochoe by the Brooklyn Caeretan Painter. Paris, Louvre K 470. *Photo:* M. Chuzeville, Paris.

PL. 18. Oinochoe by the Brooklyn Caeretan Painter. Würzburg, Martin von Wagner Museum, University 814. *Photo:* Martin v. Wagner—Museum der Universität.

PL. 19. Oinochoe by the Campana Caeretan Painter. Paris, Louvre K 439. *Photo:* M. Chuzeville, Paris.

PL. 20. Oinochoe by the Campana Caeretan Painter. Paris, Louvre K 469. *Photo:* M. Chuzeville, Paris.

Pl. 21. Oinochoe by the Campana Caeretan Painter. Paris, Louvre K 441. *Photo*: M. Chuzeville, Paris.

Pl. 22. Oinochoe by the Campana Caeretan Painter. Rome, Villa Giulia. *Photo*: Soprintendenza Antichità, Rome.

PL. 23. Oinochoe by the Florence Caeretan
Painter. Rome, Palazzo dei Conservatori 26.
Photo: Palazzo dei Conservatori.

PL. 24. Oinochoe by the Florence Caeretan
Painter. Tarquinia, Museo Nazionale 5436.
Photo: Valeristi, Tarquinia.

PL. 25. Oinochoe by the Sambon Caeretan Painter. Paris,
Sambon Collection. *Photo:* German Institute of Archaeology,
Rome, Neg. no. 60.428.

PL. 27. Same. Side B.

PL. 26. Stamnos by the Sambon Caeretan Painter.
Rome, Villa Giulia. Side A. Photos: Soprintendenza Antichità, Rome.

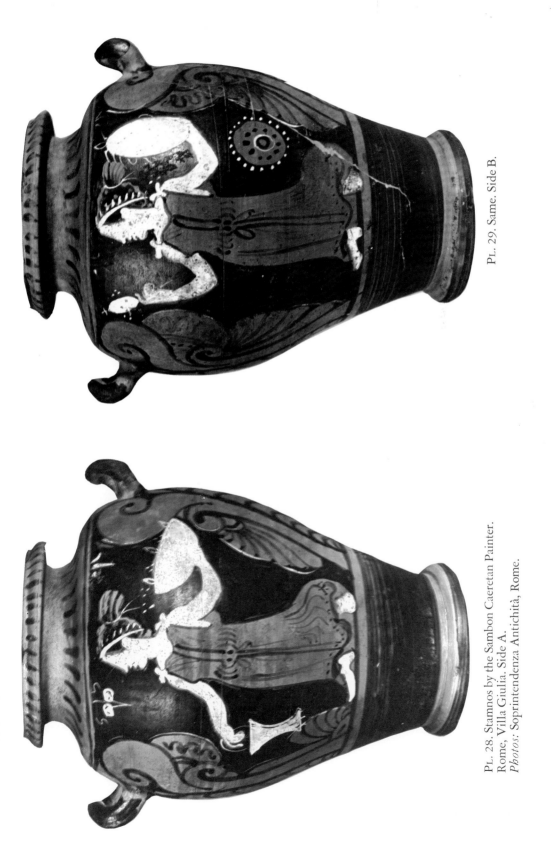

PL. 28. Stamnos by the Sambon Cæretan Painter.
Rome, Villa Giulia. Side A.
Photos: Soprintendenza Antichità, Rome.

PL. 29. Same. Side B.

PL. 30. Oinochoe by the Volterra Caeretan Painter. Milano, formerly Market. *Photo:* A. Stenico.

PL. 31. Oinochoe by the Volterra Caeretan Painter. Aléria, Musée Archéologique 616c. *Photo:* Tomasi, Ajaccio.

PL. 32. Stannos by the Volterra Caeretan Painter. Rome, Villa Giulia. Side A. *Photos*: Soprintendenza Antichità, Rome.

PL. 33. Same. Side B.

PL. 34. Fragmentary stamnos possibly by the
Volterra Caeretan Painter. Cerveteri, Magazzino. Side A.

PL. 35. Oinochoe; Dotted-hem Group.
Rome, Villa Giulia. *Photo:* Soprintendenza Antichità, Rome.

PL. 36. Oinochoe; Dotted-hem Group.
Rome, Villa Giulia. *Photo:* Soprintendenza Antichità, Rome.

PL. 38. *Top,* Skyphos; Dotted-hem Group.
Cerveteri, Magazzino 49800. Side A.

PL. 39. *Above,* Same. Side B.

PL. 37. Oinochoe; Dotted-hem Group.
Rome, Villa Giulia. *Photo:* Soprintendenza
Antichità, Rome.

PL. 40. Oinochoe by the Castellani Caeretan Painter.
Rome, Villa Giulia, Castellani Collection 50668.
Photo: Soprintendenza Antichità, Rome.

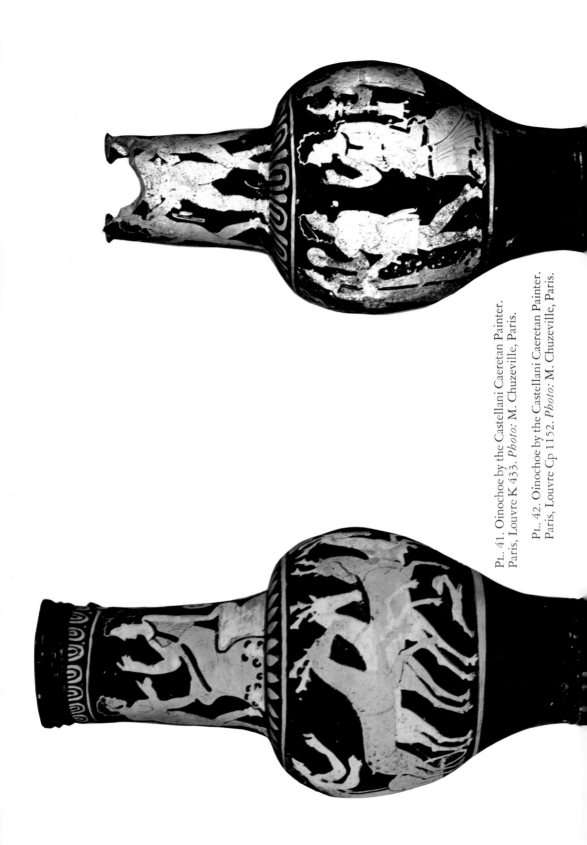

PL. 41. Oinochoe by the Castellani Caeretan Painter. Paris, Louvre K 433. *Photo:* M. Chuzeville, Paris.

PL. 42. Oinochoe by the Castellani Caeretan Painter. Paris, Louvre Cp 1152. *Photo:* M. Chuzeville, Paris.

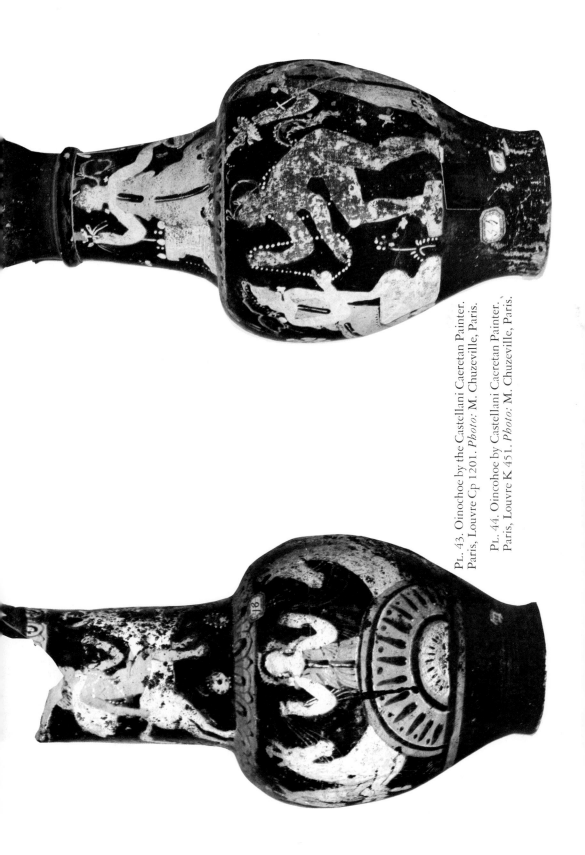

PL. 43. Oinochoe by the Castellani Caeretan Painter. Paris, Louvre Cp 1201. *Photo:* M. Chuzeville, Paris.

PL. 44. Oinocohoe by Castellani Caeretan Painter. Paris, Louvre K 451. *Photo:* M. Chuzeville, Paris.

PL. 45. Oinochoe by the Castellani Caeretan Painter. Cerveteri, Magazzino.

PL. 46. Oinochoe by the Castellani Caeretan Painter. Florence, Museo Archeologico 4135. *Photo:* Soprintendenza Antichità, Florence.

PL. 47. Stamnos by the Castellani
Caeretan Painter. Rome, Villa Giulia.
Side A. *Photos:* Soprintendenza Antichità, Rome.

PL. 48. Same. Side B.

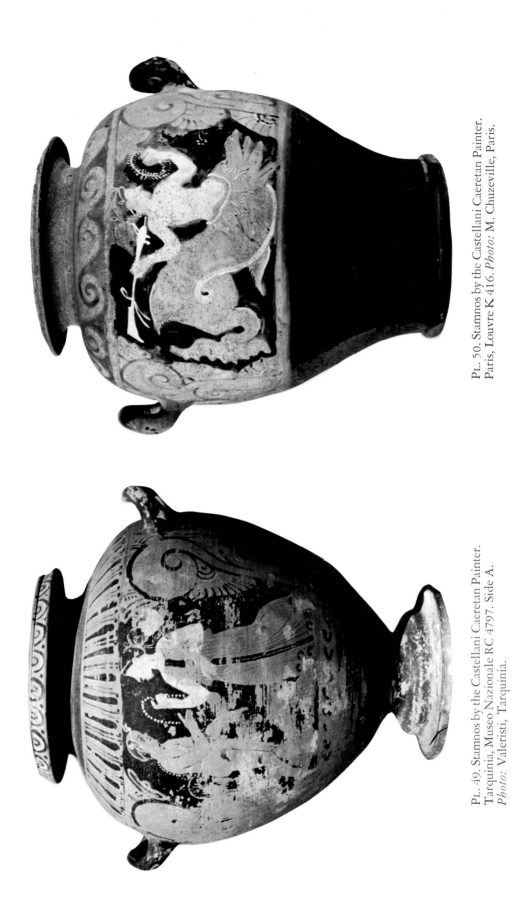

PL. 50. Stamnos by the Castellani Caeretan Painter.
Paris, Louvre K 416. *Photo:* M. Chuzeville, Paris.

PL. 49. Stamnos by the Castellani Caeretan Painter.
Tarquinia, Museo Nazionale RC 4797. Side A.
Photo: Valeristi, Tarquinia.

PL. 51. Kylix by the Castellani Caeretan Painter.
Formerly Munich, Adolf Preyss Collection. *Photo:*
German Institute of Archaeology, Rome, neg. no. 60.432.

PL. 52. Oinochoe by the American Academy
Caeretan Painter. Rome, Villa Giulia.
Photo: Soprintendenza Antichità, Rome.

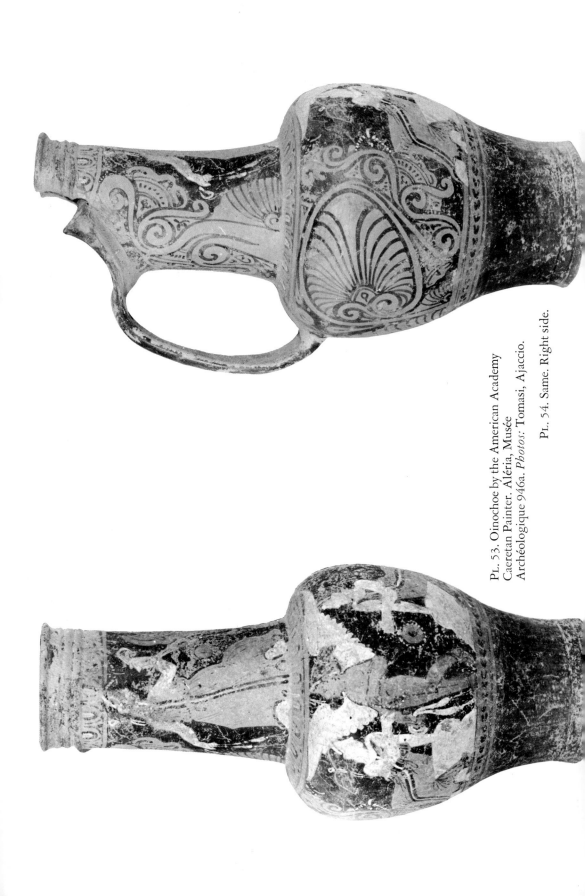

PL. 53. Oinochoe by the American Academy Caeretan Painter. Aléria, Musée Archéologique 946a. *Photos*: Tomasi, Ajaccio.

PL. 54. Same. Right side.

PL. 55. Oinochoe by the American Academy Caeretan Painter. Florence, Museo Archeologico 81915. *Photo*: Soprintendenza Antichità, Florence.

PL. 56. Oinochoe by the American Academy Caeretan Painter. Rome, American Academy in Rome 1839. *Photo*: Felbermeyer, Rome.

PL. 57. Oinochoe by the Painter of
Brussels R 273. Brussels, Musées Royaux
d'Art et d'Histoire R 274.
Photos: Musées d'Art et d'Histoire.

PL. 58. Same. Right side.

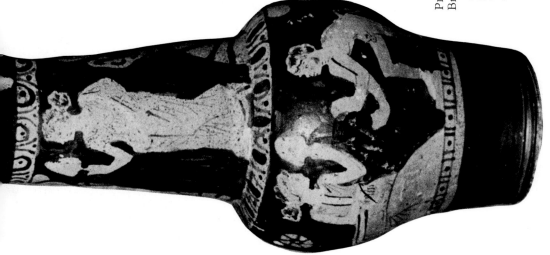

PL. 59. Oinochoe by the Painter of
Brussels R 273. Viterbo, Museo Civico 336/33.

PL. 60. Oinochoe by the Painter of Brussels R 273.
Rome, Palazzo dei Conservatori 115.
Photo: Palazzo dei Conservatori.

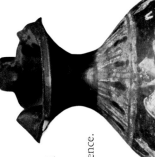

PL. 61. Kylix; Crescent-hem Group.
Rome, Palazzo dei Conservatori 547.
Photo: Palazzo dei Conservatori.

PL. 62. Oinochoe by the Frontal Satyr
Caeretan Painter. Paris, Louvre K 447.
Photo: M. Chuzeville, Paris.

PL. 63. Trefoil oinochoe by the Frontal
Satyr Caeretan Painter. Florence,
Museo Archeologico 81909.
Photo: Soprintendenza Antichità, Florence.

PL. 64. Caeretan Genucilia plate by the
Carthage Genucilia Painter. Carthage,
Musée de Carthage.

PL. 65. Caeretan Genucilia plate by the
Louvre Genucilia Painter. Limoges,
Musée 80–44. *Photo:* Courtesy Madame
Touchefeu-Meynier.

PL. 66. Caeretan Genucilia plate by the
Copenhagen Genucilia Painter. Copenhagen
National Museum 5344. *Photo:* National Museum.

PL. 67. Caeretan Genucilia star plate.
Brno, Moravian Museum 329.
Photo: courtesy Jiri Frel.

PL. 68. Torcop Group oinochoe by the
Villa Giulia Torcop Painter. Rome, Villa Giulia 13.
Photo: Soprintendenza Antichità, Rome.

PL. 69. Torcop Group oinochoe by the
Villa Giulia Torcop Painter. Toulouse,
Musée Saint-Raymond 26.609.
Photo: Musée Saint-Raymond.

PL. 70. Torcop Group oinochoe by the
Populonia Torcop Painter.
Toronto, Royal
Ontario Museum C.732.
Photo: Royal Ontario Museum, Toronto.

PL. 71. Torcop Group oinochoe by the
Populonia Torcop Painter. Madrid, Museo
Arqueológico 11481.
Photo: Museo Arquelológico.

PL. 72. Torcop Group oinochoe by the
Brussels Torcop Painter. Brussels, Museés
Royaux d'Art et d'Histoire A 3419.
Photo: Musées d'Art et d'Histoire.

PL. 73. Torcop Group oinochoe by the
Pennsylvania Torcop Painter. Limoges,
Musée 78.93. *Photo:* Courtesy
Madame Touchefeu-Meynier.

PL. 74. Large Caeretan plate. Vienna,
Kunsthistorisches Museum 4035. Interior
and exterior. *Photos:* Kunsthistorisches Museum.

PL. 75. Caeretan Genucilia kylix.
Hollywood, Dr. Norman Neuerburg Collection.
Interior and exterior. *Photos:* Courtesy owner.

PL. 76. Caeretan skyphos. Barcelona,
Museo Arqueológico 608. Side A.
Photo: Museo Arqueológico.

PL. 77. Caeretan skyphos by the Villa Giulia Torcop
Painter. Orbetello, Antiquario Comunale 257. Side A.
Photo: Anna Marguerite McCann.

PL. 78. Caeretan long-handled cup by the Villa
Giulia Torcop Painter. Kassel, Hessisches
Landesmuseum T 545. Exterior.
Photos: Hessisches Landesmuseum, Kassel.

PL. 79. *Right,* Interior.

PL. 80. *Left,* Hydria by the
Villa Giulia Torcop Painter.
Marseilles, Musée
Archéologique Borély 7538.
Photo: Musée Archéologique
Borély.

PL. 81. *Right,* Stamnos by the
Villa Giulia Torcop Painter.
Cerveteri, Museo Nazionale
Cerite 66625.

PL. 82. *Left,* Trefoil oinochoe
by the Villa Giulia Torcop
Painter. Tarquinia, Museo
Nazionale 908. *Photo:*
Valeristi, Tarquinia.

PL. 83. *Right,* Oinochoe by the
Villa Giulia Torcop Painter.
Paris, Louvre K 487.
Photo: M. Chuzeville, Paris.

PL. 84. *Left,* Oinochoe by the
Villa Giulia Torcop Painter.
Rome, Museo di Villa Giulia,
Castellani Collection 50605.
Front. *Photos:* Soprintendenza
Antichità, Rome.

PL. 85. *Right,* Same. Right side.

PL. 86. *Left,* Epichysis by the Villa Giulia Torcop Painter. Siena. Museo Archeologico. *Photo:* Grassi, Siena./PL. 87. *Middle,* Caeretan spouted lebes. Vatican, Museo Gregoriano Etrusco Z 109. *Photo:* Archivo Fotografico Vaticano./PL. 88. *Right,* Terracotta cista by the Brooklyn Caeretan Painter. Rome, Museo di Villa Giulia, Castellani Collection 50576. *Photo:* Soprintendenza Antichità, Rome.

PL. 89. Mesomphalic phiale by the Villa Giulia Torcop Painter. Munich, Antikensammlungen 8654. *Photos:* Courtesy Antikensammlungen.

PL. 90. Caeretan red-figured fish plate. Cerveteri, Museo Nazionale Cerite.

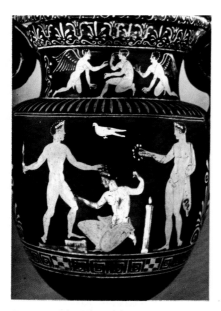

PL. 91. Volute-krater by the
Sacrifice Painter. Vatican, Museo
Gregoriano Etrusco Z 64. Side A.
Photo: Archivo Fotografico Vaticano.

PL. 93. *Left,* Caeretan lekythos in superposed
color. Florence, Museo Archeologico. *Photo:*
Soprintendenza Antichità, Florence.

PL. 94. *Right,* Caeretan lekythos in superposed
color. Florence, Museo Archeologico. *Photo:*
Soprintendenza Antichità, Florence.

PL. 92. Stamnos by the
Sacrifice Painter. Vatican,
Museo Gregoriano Etrusco Z 63.
Side A. *Photo:* Archivo
Fotografico Vaticano.

PL. 95. Caeretan kantharos
in superposed color. Florence,
Museo Archeologico 81910.
Photo: Soprintendenza
Antichità, Florence.

PL. 96. Fragmentary Faliscan stamnos.
Rome, Villa Giulia 2349.
Photo: Soprintendenza Antichità, Rome.

PL. 97. Faliscan stamnos.
Rome, Villa Giulia 8238.
Photo: Soprintendenza Antichità, Rome.

PL. 98. Faliscan oinochoe.
Tarquinia Museo Nazionale RC 5340.
Photo: Valeristi, Tarquinia.

PL. 99. Faliscan calyx-krater.
Rome, Villa Giulia 8236.
Photo: Soprintendenza Antichità, Rome.

PL. 101. Calyx-krater of the Campanizing Group. Vatican, Museo Gregoriano Etrusco Z 91. Side A. *Photo*: Archivio Fotografico Vaticano.

PL. 102. Same. Detail, side B.

PL. 100. Calyx-krater of the Campanizing Group. Bonn, Akademisches Kunstmuseum, University 83. Side A. *Photo*: Akademische Kunstmuseum.